A History of Modern Mercenary Warfare

This book is dedicated with much affection to:

Lee Massingham

Who's support, friendship, strength and compassion helped the author through one of the most difficult periods of his life. He is without doubt the best solicitor, best friend and best man I know.

A History of Modern Mercenary Warfare

Harry McCallion

Pen & Sword
MILITARY
AN IMPRINT OF PEN & SWORD BOOKS LTD.
YORKSHIRE – PHILADELPHIA

First published in Great Britain in 2023 by
Pen and Sword Transport
An imprint of
Pen & Sword Books Ltd.
Yorkshire - Philadelphia

ISBN 9781399050098

A CIP catalogue record for this book is available from the British Library.

Typeset in INDIA by IMPEC eSolutions
Printed and bound in England by CPI Group (UK) Ltd, Croydon CR0 4YY.

Pen & Sword Books Ltd incorporates the imprints of Pen & Sword Books Archaeology, Atlas, Aviation, Battleground, Discovery, Family History, History, Maritime, Military, Naval, Politics, Railways, Select, Transport, True Crime, Fiction, Frontline Books, Leo Cooper, Praetorian Press, Seaforth Publishing, Wharncliffe and White Owl.

For a complete list of Pen & Sword titles please contact

PEN & SWORD BOOKS LIMITED
47 Church Street, Barnsley, South Yorkshire, S70 2AS, England
E-mail: enquiries@pen-and-sword.co.uk
Website: www.pen-and-sword.co.uk

or

PEN AND SWORD BOOKS
1950 Lawrence Rd, Havertown, PA 19083, USA
E-mail: Uspen-and-sword@casematepublishers.com
Website: www.penandswordbooks.com

MIX
Paper | Supporting responsible forestry
FSC® C013604

Contents

Introduction

Before considering what a mercenary is, it is perhaps best to pause and reflect what a soldier is and does. In the film *Donnie Brasco,* Al Pacino characterised a soldier as someone you don't know sending you out to "whack" someone else you don't know. If even a shred of this somewhat brutal and simplistic definition is true, it must be doubly true of mercenary soldiers of fortune.

So what is a mercenary? The dictionary definition describes *a professional soldier who is hired to serve in a foreign army*. On the other hand, Niccolò Machiavelli (1469 - 1527), the author of *The Prince* had a very critical view of mercenaries describing them as, among other things, "disunited," lacking discipline, "unfaithful," "ambitious," gallant amongst friends, vile amongst enemies, not God-fearing, and without faith in men.

I have been described as a mercenary, although I never considered myself to be one. I served for over two years with the elite Reconnaissance Commando Special Forces of the South African Defence Force from 1977 - 1980. By the same definition, the Gurkha battalions of the British Army—not to mention the Swiss Guards who protect the Pope—are mercenaries. However, as the reader will find on reading his books, foreign volunteers in a regular army are not legally considered mercenaries.

Mercenaries are drawn to war, and wars—as has been seen all too clearly in Iraq, Afghanistan, and now in Ukraine—are brutal affairs, costly in both treasure and lives. The first casualty of any soldier in a war, mercenary or not, is not the truth, but his own humanity. It takes a rare type of man to voluntarily go into a combat zone, to kill and risk his life daily. Most mercenaries, but not all, are former professional soldiers, fighting—and often dying in—other peoples' wars.

What motivates a former professional soldier to become a mercenary? For the majority, it is simply the only trade they know. Soldiering is a profession, and governments around the world invest millions in the training and development of professional armies. Traditionally, British soldiers have been—and probably still are—the best trained and most professional soldiers in the world. After all, what do you do with all that professional training once your service is up?

For example, if a former soldier goes to a job centre and is asked what skills he has, they might include shooting a man from 400 yards, firing mortars, knocking out tanks, and bringing in an air strike. What reply is he going to get? "Sorry, no wars today?" So if you're a former soldier who still wants to ply your trade, you go where those skills are needed.

For others it may be a desire to see combat. As Hemingway famously noted, the hunting of man is like no other, and men who have hunted other armed men never care to hunt anything else. Put another way, as a training sergeant in the Parachute Regiment famously told me, "I know hundreds of men who can put their elbows on a bar and talk soldiering, but when the air is filled with little buzzing bees that really sting, that's when you find out who can really soldier."

For a very few—like the mercenaries who flocked to fight for the Republican cause in the civil war in Spain and formed the famed "International Brigade" or the foreign volunteers who have chosen to join the fight against Russian aggression in the war in Ukraine—it is a noble cause that is worth fighting and dying for.

At the other end of the spectrum, some mercenaries are little more than psychopathic killers whose lust for inflicting death—often on innocents—is their main motivation. This book explores the sometimes heroic, sometimes tragic and comical, but often brutal history of modern mercenaries, or, as they currently prefer to be called, "private military contractors."

The author has attempted where possible to tell the story of modern mercenary warfare in chronological date order. Within its chapters are numerous stories of individual modern mercenaries, and hopefully in those individual stories, the reader might find some answers as to the motivations that drove these men to fight, kill, and often die in conflicts around the world.

As readers progress through this book, they'll learn that mercenaries have been a part of warfare for time immemorial and in the modern world, especially in the United States, Britain and Russia, far from receding into history, the use of mercenaries has expanded to become big business on a global scale.

One of the reasons that present day governments have expanded the use of mercenaries is precisely because *they* are mercenaries, fighting for money and not love of country, their deaths are not seen as a patriotic sacrifice, and they often go unreported, which helps to conceal the true tragic human cost of waging a war. As one former private military contractor recently stated, "If you want to conquer in the 21st century…you use mercenaries, special forces, things to keep war secret; and nobody's better at secret wars than mercenaries."

Chapter One

The Historical Perspective

As long as one man had what another man wanted, men have fought other men. Men who couldn't fight, hired mercenaries. They have been described in many ways in historical texts, from "sell swords," and "freebooters" to "adventurers." The most modern term is "private military contractors" or "PMCs," but they have been around since the first time man swung out of the trees and walked upright on two legs.

It is probably the second oldest profession in history, selling sex being the first, of course. Before recorded history began, it was easy to imagine that those who were bigger, stronger, more aggressive, more violent (and eventually better armed) would be provided food and shelter to protect the weaker from those who would threaten them, steal their food, or hunting grounds, their woman, children or even their very lives.

As civilisation developed, man moved from being a hunter/gatherer to cultivate the land and eventually to congregate into villages, towns and cities, so the need for armed protection grew. At first, this would have been drawn from the community itself, but as citizens became more organized—first into primitive militias and later into armies—those armies fought each other, so the need for greater manpower grew. A quick troll through recorded history reveals the almost constant use of mercenaries by every state, king, and conqueror.

In 1887, over three hundred and fifty tablets were discovered in the ancient Egyptian city of Akhetaten. They dated back to 2500 BC and became known as the Amarna Letters. The tablets were political and military correspondence between the rulers of Egypt, Babylon, Hatti, Mitanni, and Assyria, and contained the first reference in history of the use of mercenary forces described in the tablets as "Nomads" from the Far East.

History is unclear as who exactly these Nomads were, but the arrival of fierce organised groups of "barbarian" warriors on the borders of "civilised" societies must have caused fear and apprehension amongst both the population and their rulers, some of whom, instead of sending troops to fight them, *hired* them.

Probably out of fear of starting a civil war, in 2350 BC, King Sargon of Akkad, in the first documented account of the using these Nomad mercenaries, engaged five thousand to put down an uprising in his own kingdom. Egyptian pharaohs frequently hired Medjay Numidians to do exactly the same, and by the time of the New Kingdom—from the fifteenth to eleventh centuries BC—the Medjay had become Egypt's official police force.

As armies became more organised, the use of mercenary forces grew. Philip II of Macedonia was one of the world's first great military conquerors, and a large part of his army were mercenaries, Thessalon cavalry and foot soldiers from the Aegean and Balkans, served under their charismatic leader for plunder and glory. Philip II trained his mercenary forces and Macedonian troops in the very latest innovations in weapons and tactics and created an army that was fixable, able to change formation in very quick time, disciplined, and lethal.

By the time of Philip II's invasion of Achaemenid Empire of Persia in 338 BC, he led probably the finest fighting military machine of the ancient world, even though more than a half of his army came from outside Macedonia. After Philip's death, his successor, Alexander the Great, used the army that Philip II created to conquer most of the then-known world.

In northern Africa, a city state that history was to call "Carthage" rose to prominence in the late ninth century BC, and fought almost continual wars with its neighbour states. The largest part of the Carthaginian army were mercenaries. After a disastrous campaign against the Roman Republic in during which Carthage was forced to pay reparations to Rome, the city state could not pay its mercenary force, which led to a rebellion by the mercenaries, which was eventually suppressed with great brutality.

Carthage's most famous general, Hannibal, famously crossed the Alps and laid waste to much of Italy, almost completely destroying a Roman army of more than 80,000 men at the Battle of Cannae. Ultimately, the Roman citizen army they faced prevailed, Hannibal retreated back to Carthage, and the Romans pursued them and laid waste to the city.

The original Roman army—like the one that defeated Hannibal—was a volunteer citizens army, with highly disciplined troops, loyal generals, and honourable traditions. By the first century AD, the republic had gone and Rome became an empire. The Roman army, in turn, became a professional force of regular soldiers who served twenty-five years, with the last five spent as veterans with reduced duties. Upon retirement, legionaries were granted land and a bounty. Auxiliaries, mercenary troops, often archers from Crete, were granted Roman citizenship upon discharge. Soldiers now took an oath to the emperor himself instead of to the people and senate of Rome.

As Rome grew in power and became rich on the proceeds of that empire, fewer and fewer indigenous Romans joined the legions. With a constantly increasing demand for manpower, the legions and mercenary troops were increasingly recruited from the provinces conquered by Rome, not as auxiliaries, but as legionaries. A perfect example of this is found in the Romans' conquest of Britain in the first century. To fill the ranks, the Romans recruited many Frisians, then located on the coast of present-day the Netherlands, to serve on the most northern frontier of the Roman Empire.

During the expansion of the Roman Empire, Roman citizenry contributed around 65 per cent of the imperial soldiers. By its decline in the fifth century AD, this had had fallen to just one per cent. In the fifth century AD, Roman generals may still have led the legions of Rome, but its ranks consisted of legionaries mainly from Gaul (present-day France) Goths (from present-day Germany), and others from other conquered provinces. The de-Romanising of the legions and its reliance on foreign soldiers ultimately led to the downfall of the empire.

With Roman Empire's decline, the western world was thrown into a dark age. As if the clock of time had been reset, tribalism grew to dominance once again. What military organization there was became more localised and centred around local warlords. Invasions still occurred, like the Saxon invasion of England, but these were migrations, not the expansion of Empires.

Warlords became kings, and as the western world moved into what is now called the middle ages, military service grew into a feudal system which was to dominate Europe for nearly a thousand years. That system featured a well-armed nobility and a peasantry who were expected to fight when called upon to do so. During this period, we have one of the very first examples of a "mercenary company" in the late 10th century with the formation of the Varangian Guard, who were descendants of Viking bands that had ventured south. They were first hired and paid to serve as the personal bodyguards of the Byzantine Emperor Basil II. The ferocity of these axe-wielding former Vikings was soon put to good use by the Emperor, helping him to suppress a rebellion and thereby retaining his crown. The Guard went on to serve as the personal bodyguards and protectors of Constantinople for more than two hundred years.

On its creation, the Varangian Guard was almost exclusively composed of Vikings, but by the eleventh century, the Guard began to recruit other nationalities into its ranks, including Saxons from England, Normans, Danes and other nationalities. The selection process for entry into the guard was gruelling, and applicants had to demonstrate their proficiency with the weapons of the day in addition to paying an entrance fee in gold. Service in the Guard brought rewards, with many members becoming extremely wealthy and wielding immense power. Perhaps its most famous member was Harald Hardrada, who used the wealth he accumulated during his service with the Guard to buy ships, recruit men, and re-claim Norway's throne before falling in battle in 1066 to the swords and axes of Harold Godwinson's Saxon army.

The Norman invasion of England in 1066 saw the first large scale deployment of mercenary forces since the fall of the Roman Empire. The vast majority of Duke William of Normandy's (William I of England) army were "sell swords," that is, hired mercenaries from Brittany, Flanders, Champagne and Italy. These were professionally trained soldiers working for pay, or the promise of land after the conquest of England.

The army they faced was feudal, except for the "housecarls," the kings personal bodyguards. They were hand-picked, professional soldiers and perhaps, man for man, the best fighting infantry in Europe at that time. Unfortunately for King Harold of England, he just did not have enough of them. Predictably, the more professionally trained and disciplined sell swords of William I won the day. His son, William II, carried on with the practice of hiring sell swords and would later earn the acronym of *militum mercator et solidator*, or "a great buyer and purveyor of soldiers."

It was not until later that the practice moved from the hiring of individual warriors to organized contracting of mercenaries. Perhaps the first recorded use may have occurred in 1101 AD, when Robert of Flanders supplied Henry I of England with 1,000 Flemish knights for service in his campaigns in England and Normandy, reputably for a fee of £500. This was likely the first example of a genuine military contract.

With money or plunder to be had, those who had military training would often hire their services to the highest bidder, individually or in organised groups or companies. There was no shortage of employers, even Popes frequently hired mercenaries. A classic example was Pope Innocent III, who in 1209 hired a mercenary army and launched a crusade against the Cathars, a breakaway sect in Southern France. After the storming of the city of Beziers, most of the inhabitants—Cathars and orthodox Christians—fled to the city's church for safety. Arnaud Amalric, the papal legate in charge of the mercenary army ordered it sealed and burnt, allegedly saying "Kill them all, God will know his own."

A prime example of the mercenary companies of the time were the Swiss mercenary companies. Swiss mercenaries were highly valued for the power of their determined mass attacks in deep columns with spears, pikes, and halberds. They often refused to take any prisoners and had consistent record of victory.

The hiring of Swiss mercenaries was easy because a potential contractor could obtain an entire ready-made Swiss mercenary contingent by simply contracting with their local governments in the various Swiss cantons, which had a form of militia system in which the soldiers were bound to serve and were trained and equipped to do so. During this period, the various kings of France considered it a virtual impossibility to take the field of battle without Swiss pikemen as the infantry core of their armies.

Another example of a mercenary company of that period was the Catalan Grand Company. First formed in 1302 by Roger de Flor, who recruited Spanish veterans of the War of the Sicilian Vespers to form a free company of mercenaries. At the conclusion of the war, he contracted his 6,500-strong company to the Byzantine Emperor Andronicus II. The company was deployed by the Emperor to the Eastern Mediterranean to combat the invading Ottoman Turks and succeeded in forcing the invading Turkish army away from Constantinople. Success on the battlefield by the Company was not matched by their discipline off it, and their penchant for wanton looting, rape, and plunder brought down the wrath of Emperor Andronicus II. In 1305, de Flor and as many as 1,300 of his men were ambushed and killed by another group of mercenaries hired by the Emperor.

The Company did not disband, however, instead the surviving members tried to set up an outlaw state Gallipoli. When that failed, they marched to Greece and found employment with the Duke of Athens. After a dispute over back pay, the Company went to war with its former employer, eventually defeating his army and killing the Duke at the Battle of Kephisos in 1311. The company then went on to rule large parts of Greece for nearly seventy-five years, until an army from Florence finally defeated them and forced them to disband.

The outbreak of The Hundred Years' War—fought from 1337–1453 between England and France—saw an ever increasing demand for well-trained men. This period of history saw the rise of organised "free companies" of mercenary troops, who were used by all sides in the war. Amongst them were mercenary companies of Genoese crossbowmen, who were largely trained and organised in Genoa, and first came to prominence in the First Crusade in the twelfth century. At the Battle of Crezy in 1346, more than 5,000 of them were deployed by the French army to oppose the English longbowmen.

Heavy rain preceded the battle, and the English longbowmen simply removed their bow strings and put them under their water resistant caps to keep them dry—an action that coined the phrase "keep it under your hat." The strings on the crossbows of the Genoese could not be unstrung, the stretch making them useless. When the English archers restrung their bows and sent a rain of arrows towards their opponents, the Genoese retreated and were mercilessly butchered by their French employers.

With the truce of Bordeaux, the Treaty of Brétigny, and later by the truce of Tours, most of the mercenary companies were made redundant. Many were absorbed into their own nation state armies when the war ignited again.

Others moved to Italy, hiring their services to various Italian city states. Perhaps the most prominent was the "White Company" under Sir John Hawkwood, an English warlord, who was knighted for his service during the Hundred Years' War. Its members included mercenaries from England, Germany, Breton, and Hungary. Their proficiency and professional skill with longbows and lances led them to be regarded as one of the more elite mercenary companies to fight in Italy.

Other notable mercenary companies who served in Italy was the German "Company of the Star" under Albrecht Sterz and Hanneken Bongarten, and the Breton and Gascon company of Bertrand de la Salle. By 1410, these "free companies" were replaced by native Italian *condottieri*, with the "Company of the Rose" in 1410 as the last to disappear.

In the fourteenth century A.D. and the advent of gunpowder and firearms, there was a revolution in warfare. Before that time, the common man could not compete with armoured knights or well-trained men at arms until an easy-to-use musket levelled the playing field. To paraphrase the words of Samuel Colt when he produced his first revolver: "Now all men were equal."

For the next two centuries, war changed dramatically as armies grew from a few thousand men to tens of thousands, and as massed ranks of musket-armed infantry replaced heavy armoured cavalry on Europe's battlefields. To meet the highly increasing demand for manpower, ever greater numbers of professional mercenary companies were founded in a highly competitive and expanding market where nations or states now offered contracts for thousands of men at a time. During this age, the Swiss, Germans, and Italians all produced entire companies of professional soldiers for foreign powers.

Perhaps the most feared of all the mercenary companies of the sixteenth century were the German *Landsknechts*. This company was formed by the Holy Roman Emperor Maximilian I (1493 - 1519) who observed the effectiveness of the Swiss mercenary pikemen in wars of independence against the Duchy of Burgundy. Rather than hire the Swiss, he copied them leading to the formation of the *Landsknechts*. They had a well-earned reputation for total ruthlessness and violence, which led one chronicler of the time to remark that the devil refused to allow *Landsknechts* past the gates of hell because even he feared them. It was not unknown for entire regiments to swap allegiances, even in the midst of battle, if offered more gold by the other side.

The English Civil War (1642 - 1646) saw both sides employ mercenaries. Hundreds of foreign mercenaries flooded the country in search of lucrative pay and any opportunities to plunder or rape. Most did not care which side they fought on. This was never more exemplified than by Captain Carlo Fantom, a Croat mercenary. Initially, Captain Fantom fought on the Parliamentary side, but later, in 1643, he switched to the Royalist cause. He was a true mercenary in every sense of the word and was famously quoted as saying that he did not care for causes, but rather he showed up to fight for money and women; continuing on to say his father and grandfather were Roman Catholic and that he fought for the Christians against Turkish troops and vice versa. Before the war ended, he was hanged in Bedford for raping a woman.

In addition, many of the military leaders on both sides of the English Civil War were former mercenaries. Prince Rupert of the Rhine, for example, first joined a Protestant army in the Netherlands at the age of 14. He later fought military campaigns against Spain and Catholic European countries. On the parliamentary side, Thomas Fairfax, third Lord Fairfax of Cameron, had extensive mercenary experience before the outbreak of the civil war. He started his mercenary career in the Netherlands, fighting on the Protestant side against their Catholic opponents.

Spain had recruited foreign soldiers into its army for centuries, forming them into the Foreign Regiments (*Infantería de línea extranjera*). One such example was the Regiment of Hibernia, which was formed in 1709 from Irishmen who fled Ireland in the wake of the "Flight of the Earls", and the penal laws that followed Spain would continue to recruit foreign mercenary soldiers into its army right up until modern times.

In the eighteenth century, the German principality of Hesse-Kassel became the most prominent contactor of mercenary forces in Europe. In 1715, England hired 12,000 Hessian mercenaries to fight in its war against Scotland and France. By 1720, England had entered into a formal contract with the principality, paying it £125,000 per year (over £30,000,000 in today's money) to keep 12,000 Hessian troops on standby to be deployed with its army, and by the end of the decade, that amount would almost double.

The Revolutionary War of 1776 saw Britain deploy more than 30,000 Hessian mercenaries—about a third of its total forces—to fight its rebellious colonies. The formidable German mercenaries were both despised and feared in equal measures by the colonial army. Britain would continue to deploy Hessian mercenaries well into the late-eighteenth century; 12,000 Hessians mercenaries were fielded by Britain in war with France in 1793, and another 1,000 in its bloody campaign in Ireland in 1798. By the close of the eighteenth century, throughout Europe and particularly in Britain, public opinion turned sharply against the use of mercenary forces. The principality lost its best customer and, in 1803, was affiliated with the Holy Roman Empire, and eventually joined the Confederation of the Rhine.

In other parts of the world, it was a different story. In 1805, Lieutenant William Eaton, a United States marine, recruited and led a mercenary army of 400 Christian Greek, Muslim and Arab mercenaries to a decisive victory at the Battle of Dema, and then the capital of the Ottoman province of Cyrenaica (now in eastern Libya). At the conclusion of the battle, Lieutenant Eaton raised the American flag, the first time it was raised on a battlefield outside of North America.

During the South American wars of independence, mercenaries were recruited to fight in Simón Bolívar's army, and many were of Irish descent. John Devereux raised the Irish Legion, which arrived in Venezuela in 1817; however, his unruly troops soon mutinied and were later devastated by multiple epidemic waves. Bolívar noted that he was happy to be rid of them because they wouldn't kill until they were paid.

In Europe, the nineteenth century saw the almost complete disappearance of mercenary forces from the congenital armies, with the French Foreign Legions being the exception to the general rule. The Foreign Legion was created in 1831 to allow the incorporation of foreign nationals into the French Army. From its foundation, the Legion can truly be described as a mercenary force, although it is part of—and deployed in combat—as part of the regular French Army. French citizenship can be applied for once three years' service has accrued, and any legionnaire who is wounded during a combat for France can instantly apply to be a French citizen under a provision known as *Français par le sang versé*, which translates to "French by spilled blood."

Training and discipline in the legion is tough. French legionaries have proven themselves both to be exceptional soldiers and completely ruthless in combat. It is hardly surprising then, as will be seen in the following chapters, that many legionaries go on to become fully fledged private mercenaries after completing their service with the Legion.

With the outbreak of the Crimean War (1854 - 1856), Britain tried to follow the French and Spanish example and recruited men from afar to form the British Italian Legion, the British German Legion, as well as the British Swiss Legion. These combined forces were formed as a result of the Enlistment of Foreigners Act 1854, and were known collectively as the British Foreign Legion. A total of 14,000 men were recruited, although none ever saw active service. The Legion was disbanded after the war.

The American Civil War (1861 - 1866), like all wars, drew mercenary volunteers from around the world to fight on both sides during the conflict, which killed more Americans than any other war. The Union was far more dependent on foreign mercenary volunteers than the Confederate side. Of the 2 million soldiers that fought for the Union during the civil war, about a quarter to a third were foreign-born.

This was primarily because the Union made a concerted effort to recruit foreign mercenary volunteers both in the United States and abroad. Recruitment posters written in Italian, French, Hungarian, and German were widely distributed. Whilst many of these nationals volunteered to fight in the war, the largest bodies of foreign mercenary volunteers were made up of Irish and Germans, recruited both at home and aboard, who made up half of all the foreign soldiers.

Of these, by far the largest foreign ethnic group to fight for the Union were of German heritage, about 216,000 ethnic Germans. This count was roughly half of all foreign-born recruits that fought for the Union. The German Division of the Army of the Potomac was led by Hungarian Major General Julius Stahel; German Brigadier General Louis Blenker and Colonel Felix Salm-Salm, a Prussian prince. The highest ranking immigrant German officer in the Union Army was a German veteran of the 1848 revolutions, Franz Sigal, who was appointed by President Lincoln to the rank of major general.

Irish immigrants and foreign volunteers, many of whom were fleeing hardship, famine and persecution in their native land, made up the next largest contribution of foreign volunteers. Irish volunteers were recruited both in the United States and in Ireland, and volunteers were also drawn from the British Empire. They formed "The Irish Brigade," which took part in almost every major battle in the war and reportedly suffered some of the highest casualties of any Union formation.

Brigadier General Wlodzimierz Krzyżanowski, a veteran of the Greater Poland uprising of 1848, raised one of the first military companies when the war broke out, comprised of entirely Polish immigrants. Later it would join other immigrant companies to form the Polish Legion. Krzyżanowski became a brigade commander during the war, and at its end, he was appointed governor of Georgia.

Other notable foreign mercenary volunteers were the future President of the Swiss Confederation, Emil Frey, who was colonel of the 82nd Illinois Infantry Regiment and was taken prisoner at the Battle of Gettysburg and Hungarian colonel Frederick George D'Utassy, who led the 39th New York Infantry Regiment, also known as the "Garibaldi Guard" which comprised over a dozen nationalities, including Algerians, Turks, Slavs, Swiss, and Spaniards.

The Confederacy tried to undermine the Union enlistment of foreign mercenary volunteers with a concerted propaganda campaign in the United States and abroad. Confederate propagandists alleged that the Union was relying heavily on "foreign mercenaries" and urged them to refuse to serve as cannon fodder for those in the Union too wealthy or scared to fight. As a result, the Union downplayed the importance of immigrant and foreign mercenary volunteers contribution to the war effort, which was considerable.[1]

Apart from nearly being drawn into the war by "The Trent Affair," when a U.S. ship boarded a British flagged ship to arrest two Confederate diplomats *en route* to Britain, Britain stayed largely neutral throughout the American Civil War. Some Britons did enlist in the Confederate forces, with Henry Wemyss Feilden as perhaps the most prominent. Feilden joined the Black Watch at the age of nineteen, and fought in China as well as in the Indian Mutiny between 1857 - 1858. In 1862, he resigned his commission in the British army and joined the Confederacy. He fought with distinction during the war and became assistant adjutant-general with the of the Army of Tennessee under General Joseph E. Johnston and was present at the surrender at Bennett Place.

After the Confederate surrender, Feilden returned to the British Army, and was promoted to captain in the Royal Artillery in 1874. He would later serve in both the First and Second Boer Wars, and was appointed Paymaster of Imperial Yeomanry and decorated for his service in India, China, and South Africa.

The most notorious foreign volunteer in the Confederacy was Swiss born Hartmann Heinrich Wirz (Henry Wirz) who was commandant of the infamous stockade of Camp Sumter, a Confederate prisoner-of-war (POW) camp near Andersonville, Georgia. During his tenure as commandant, nearly 13,000 Union POWs died in inhumane conditions. After the war, Wirz was tried, convicted, and hanged for war crimes. He was the only man on either side in the war to have been judged a war criminal. Many of the US Civil War veterans, both Union and Confederate, later found work as mercenaries for the Egyptian government in the 1870s and 1880s.

During the Mexican Revolution (1910 - 1920), Pancho Villa's *Division del Norte* employed mercenary soldiers-of-fortune who brought valuable experience to the *Division* and could count on a good salary and high rank if they proved their worth. One of these was Ivor Thord-Gray, one of the most outstanding and least known mercenary adventurers of the day. Originally born in Sweden, Thord-Gray first joined the merchant marine and sailed on three ships from 1893 – 1895 before leaving to settle in Cape Town, South Africa, where he worked briefly as a prison guard on Robben Island. In 1897, he took on his first military role when he enlisted in the Cape Mounted Riflemen. There, he was a private and fought in the Boer War between 1899 - 1902. For a short time after the end of the Boer War, he served in the South African Constabulary before being commissioned as a Captain in the Lydenburg Militia. In 1904, he got his first regular commission when he enlisted in Royston's Horse as a Lieutenant and fought in the Bambatha Rebellion in 1905, where his services were recognised with a promotion to Captain.

Thord-Gray moved from South Africa to Kenya were he became a Captain of Nairobi Mounted Police in 1907. He then moved to the Philippines where he was again promoted to Captain in the Philippine Constabulary (US Foreign Legion) and served with them between 1908 - 1909. After trying his hand as a planter in Malaysia, Thord-Gray served a short time in the Chinese Revolution before leaving for Mexico.

Thord-Gray was initially rejected by Villa and his officer staff as a candidate for military service because they were suspicious of his intentions. However, once his skill as an artilleryman became known, he was awarded a commission as the Chief of Artillery along with the rank of first captain. When Villa's forces ran out of munitions, Thord-Gray again proved his worth to the Mexican revolutionaries by successfully acquiring the supplies whilst at the same time evading US authorities and successfully returning to Mexico.

Having gained both the trust and respect of Villa, Thord-Gray was constantly promoted; first to Major, then Lieutenant-Colonel, and Colonel. In 1914, he was made Chief of Staff of the First Mexican Army. With the outbreak of the First World War, Thord-Gray left Villa and hurried back to Europe, joining the British Army in 1914 with an initial rank of Major and second in command of the 15th Battalion Northumberland Fusiliers. He rose to the rank of Lieutenant-Colonel commanding 1/26 Battalion Royal Fusiliers in 1916. Thord-Gray then transferred to the Canadian Army. As a Lieutenant-Colonel in the Canadian Siberian Expeditionary Force, he was deployed in the Russian Civil War in 1918 as part of the Allied intervention.

Thord-Gray transferred again, this time to the Russian "White Army" in February 1919 and appointed a Colonel Commanding Officer of the 1st Siberian Assault Division where he served as a Major General until November 1919. His last appointment was as High Representative of the Provisional Siberian Government to the Allied Expeditionary Corps at Vladivostok. In later life, Thord-Gray became an American citizen and in August 1935 he became the Major-General and Chief-of-Staff to the Governor of Florida.

During the First World War, foreign volunteers joined both the British and French armies. For example, American pilots formed "The Lafayette Escadrille" squadron, but as these were part of conventional forces, they cannot really be considered mercenaries in the truest sense of the word, although the distinction may be a narrow one.

After the success of the Bolsheviks in the Russian Civil War, a large contingent of White Russians fled the country and settled in what is now called Jordan. They quickly offered their military skills to the country's armed forces, initially as mercenary military advisers. Gradually, over a number of years, they became assimilated into Jordanian culture and adopted the Muslim religion, but still continued their tradition of military service. During the Six Day War, Jordan's army was the only Arab army to inflict more casualties on the Israeli army than they suffered. Even today, a large proportion of Jordanian special forces are blue-eyed descendants of those White Russian immigrant mercenary volunteers.

The Spanish Legion, or *Legión Española, La Legión* was established in January 1920 serving as part of Spain's Army of Africa. It is the Spanish equivalent of the French Foreign Legion and was initially known as the Tercio of Foreigners, or *Tercio de Extranjeros.* It was under that name it fought in the Rif War, or *Guerra del Rif* of 1920 – 1926. Foreign recruitment spanned the gambit of all Spanish-speaking nations, but the majority of recruits were in fact Spaniards. Over the years, the force's name has changed first from *Tercio de Extranjeros* to *Tercio de Marruecos,* and it was that name that is fielded in operations targeted at Morocco. By the end of the Rif War, it officially became "The Spanish Legion." The Spanish Legion would play a major role in the Spanish Civil War, fighting on behalf of Nationalist forces against General Franco's fascist forces.

In 1935, right between the first and second world wars, Fascist Italy invaded Ethiopia, where foreign mercenaries and would-be adventurers flocked to the country to help Haile Selassie's forces fight the invading army. At least fifty fought with the Ethiopian forces, another fifty to sixty joined medical units. Amongst the more notable were the Trinidadian pilot Hubert Julian—who nicknamed himself "The Black Eagle"—the White Russian Feodor Knovalove, the Czechoslovakian writer Adolf Parlesák. Austrian Nazis and Belgian fascists also fought with the Ethiopian forces. Most had little or no military experience. Despite this, the Italian invaders attributed any Ethiopian army successes to the activities of foreign mercenaries, exaggerating their numbers from a few dozen to thousands.

The Spanish Civil War (1936 - 1939) saw volunteers from around the world flock to Spain to join the International Brigades. It is estimated that volunteers came from more than fifty different countries to serve in the Brigades. The Paris-based Communist International recruited, organized, and directed the Brigades. There were seven Brigades in all, divided into battalions by nationality: British, German, Austrian, Italian, American, Polish, Canadian, and Hungarian. There were large numbers of volunteers from all locations, but the single biggest contributor was France, which supplied some 28,000 fighting men. The motivation for the majority of the International Brigade was to fight—and often die—in Spain due to an undoubtedly deep-seated hatred of fascism. As the French politician and writer François-René de Chateaubriand famously said, men do not allow their own killings just for their interests. They allow their killings to happen for their passions.[2]

The Nationalist Faction also deployed mercenaries in the conflict: German "volunteers" made up of air force members as well as the army of Nazi Germany who formed the Condor Legion. It used the latest weapons of the time—supplied by Hitler—and was responsible for the infamous bombing of the Spanish town of Guernica. Before the Japanese attack on Pearl Harbour, a former American military officer Claire Chennault, with the direct permission of President D. Roosevelt, organised three squadrons of fighter pilots to combat the Japanese advance in China. Officially known as "The American Volunteer Group," it achieved lasting fame as "The Flying Tigers." Each of the mercenary pilots earned a monthly salary of between $600 - $700, with a $500 bonus for every Japanese aircraft they destroyed.

During the Second World War, "volunteers" flocked from around the world to fight on both sides. Britain recruited foreign pilots to help it fight and win the Battle of Britain. Soldiers from occupied European countries flooded Britain to continue the fight against Nazi Germany. The Poles in particular formed an entire army. In Nazi Germany, the SS recruited "Arian" volunteers from the countries it conquered in an effort to bolster its ranks. Strong contingents came from France, the Netherlands, Norway, and other Scandinavian countries. Near the war's end and with its back to the wall, the SS became less discriminating and recruited non-Arians and Muslims into its ranks. As with the volunteers of the First World War, those who fought in the regular armies of the both sides probably could not be considered mercenaries in the purest sense of the word. The end of the Second World War and the beginning of the Cold War would introduce a gradual global expansion in the use of true mercenaries and mercenary units. The age of the modern mercenary had begun.

Chapter Two

Yemen
1950 - 1970

Yemen is a mostly mountainous country that is strategically located at the southern entrance of the Red Sea. The country's mostly Muslim inhabitants speak various dialects of Arabic, and the vast majority of whom lived as impoverished peasants. Its centuries-old location, at the crossroads of both ancient and modern trade and communications routes, has made the country a target for foreign invasion and intervention.

In 1962, Colonel Nasser of Egypt's eyes turned to Yemen. Nasser had seized power in a military coup in Egypt in 1952 and was formerly elected president in 1956. Nasser's popularity in the Arab world had soured after his nationalisation of the Suez Canal and his ultimate military and political triumph in the subsequent Suez Crisis.

In September 1967, Colonel Abdullah al-Sallal and a pro-Nasser activist led a popular coup against the incumbent Royalist and pro-Western government of Imam al-Badr. The ultra-nationalist Colonel al-Sallal and his military backers then announced the creation of the Yemen Arab Republic. Royalist forces that supported the Imam took to the hills and began an insurgency—which was supported by Saudi Arabia and Jordan—against the new Republican regime. Almost immediately, Nasser deployed Egyptian soldiers into the country to "secure" the revolution. Before the war's end, Egypt would deploy as many as 80,000 men—one-third of the entire Egyptian army's strength—into Yemen. The resulting conflict became known as the North Yemen Civil War and lasted until 1970.

Nasser and new Yemeni leader al-Sallal almost immediately began to give diplomatic and material support to anti-British republican forces in Aden, were British forces were engaged in their own bitter insurgency war. Billy McLean, a former decorated member of the Special Operations Executive (SOE) and a serving conservative MP made a secret reconnaissance of the country. His report sent a shock wave through the government. Egyptian forces, well-armed by the Soviet USSR, were launching a scorched earth campaign against the Royalist forces, reportedly even using poison gas. Without help, the Royalists would be crushed in a matter of months.

Following McLean's report, the British Government made the decision to begin a covert military operation against the newly founded Yemen Arab Republic. The British Government sought and received support for this covert operation from both the Saudi Arabian and Jordanian governments.

It was decided by the then government, at an early stage, that there would be no direct official involvement by British Special Forces, and that this was to be a secret war. To lead the operation, the government allowed McLean to approach Jim Johnson, a recently retired commander of 21 SAS, a reserve regiment of Britain's own 22 SAS regiment. McLean first approached him at White's, the London Gentleman's club, and asked him to form a covert army to aid the Royalist side in the Yemen civil war. Johnson's reply was reportedly laconic "Well, I've nothing particularly to do in the next few days. I might have a go."

Johnson recruited Tony Boyle, an ex-RAF pilot to help him and both, with the approval of the British government, approached Lieutenant Colonel John Woodhouse, commander of 22 SAS requesting that he "lend" them some personnel. Over the next four years, both serving and ex-SAS personnel were recruited—as well as French mercenaries—to operate a covert war in Yemen. The selected SAS "volunteers" were given official leave to take part in the operation. This is what is called in the SAS a "deniable operation." The SAS personnel knew that the operation had been sanctioned by the government who could not *officially* acknowledge the presence or involvement of the SAS.

A similar deniable operation was undertaken by the SAS in Northern Ireland in the early 1970s when members of the SAS B Squadron were "de-badged" to undertake covert operations in Northern Ireland. The government officially denied that it had any SAS troops in the province until their official deployment in 1975.

David Sterling—one of the founders of the SAS—set up a cover company called Stirling's Television International Enterprises Company to run the operation that was funded by both Saudi Arabian and Jordanian money. The London office of the adjutant of 21 SAS volunteers (TA) was utilised as a clearing ground for the British mercenaries, who were reportedly paid

£150 per month (equivalent to over £3,800 at today's rates). A system of safe houses was set up in Bahrain to funnel the mercenaries into Yemen, and the entire operation was co-ordinated by MI6.

To lead the Anglo/French mercenary force, Colonel David Smiley was specifically recruited by McLean. Smiley was a former highly decorated Second World War officer (LVO OBE MC & Bar) and had severed with the SOE during the wars in Albania and Thailand. After the end of the Second World War, Smiley joined the Secret Intelligence Service (MI6) working on anti-communist missions to Poland and Albania. He was once beaten up and expelled from Poland.

In 1958, he took command of the Sultan of Oman's forces against local insurgents and led both the SAS and local forces in a series of dramatic and successful military operations in the deserts and mountains. Later, overall command of the combined mercenary force passed to Lieutenant Colonel Johnny Cooper, who was already a legend in the SAS and one of its founding members. He was highly decorated, being awarded the Distinguished Service Medal (DCM), was twice mentioned in dispatches and rendered a Member of the British Empire (MBE) for SAS operations in the Malaysian jungle. "Johnny" Cooper was a natural leader, tough, resourceful and ruthless when he needed to be and exactly the right man to lead the mercenaries on the ground in Yemen.

Separately from the recruitment of serving and ex-SAS men, a parallel recruiting drive was under way in Paris. With specific agreement of the French government, Roger Faulques, an ex-Foreign Legionnaire, began recruiting French and Belgium mercenaries to serve in Yemen. Faulques had an almost mystical standing within the French armed forces. He had been a maquis resistance fighter in 1944, before joining the regular French forces and then took part in the last battles of the Second World War in the French First Army. He was promoted to corporal and received the *Croix de Guerre*—France's highest military award—at the tender age of 20. He later entered one of France's most elite military academies and was promoted in 1946 to 2nd Lieutenant where he was assigned, at his own request, to the Foreign Legion in its 3rd Foreign Infantry Regiment.

He then served in the First Indochina War as Lieutenant with the 1st Foreign Parachute Battalion until its destruction in 1950. On 26 February, 1948, he was in command of a group of legionaries when they were ambushed on Route Coloniale, where half of his command were killed

in the ambush. Faulques led the survivors in hand-to-hand fighting until he was wounded in both feet by a machine gun bullet. He was evacuated under fire by his legionaries and would later be appointed a Chevalier of the *Légion d'honneur* and held five citations.

After recovering from his wounds, Faulques returned to action. Whilst leading a platoon in the evacuation of Cao Bang, he was seriously wounded four times and left for dead. After lying on the ground for three days, he was captured by the Vietminh, who believed his wounds to be mortal and repatriated him to the French authorities. Faulques was mentioned in dispatches and eventually made an Officer of the *Légion d'honneur* for exceptional services. Faulques eventually recovered from his wounds and served with the French forces in Algeria as an intelligence officer.

Given official leave by the French army, he would go on to fight as a mercenary not only in Yemen but also in the Congo and Biafra. Smiley was later to observe that the French and Belgian mercenaries under his command alternated between the Yemeni and Congo theatres since "in the Congo they had women and alcohol at will but were rarely paid, while in Yemen they were paid but were deprived of women and alcohol."[1]

The combined force of British and French mercenaries that emerged from the recruiting drive would never exceed fourty-eight, but their impact on the civil war in Yemen was too far exceed the numbers involved. Once in country, first David Smiley and then Johnny Cooper set about training the tribesmen fighting for the Imam. Initially, money and weapons were supplied by Saudi Arabia and Jordan. Jim Johnson organised much of the early flow of cash and weapons. Travelling extensively through the Middle East, he was able to persuade Saudi Arabia and Jordan to both fund the operation and supply arms. Often, he personally carried luggage stuffed with guns and explosives, his passage through customs carefully orchestrated and choreographed by the intelligence services of Britain, Saudi Arabia and Jordan.

With the money and weapons obtained by Jim Johnson, the Anglo/French mercenary force directed and often led the tribesmen on ambushes against the Egyptian forces. Where they could not lead an operation directly, they used bribery as an effective tool to insure success, handing out both money and arms in instalments in proportion to the successes achieved. The swashbuckling French mercenary Bob Denard brought Smiley to see the aftermath of one such ambush, and recorded: "The sight was indeed impressive. The Royalists had set their ambush in a valley between sand dunes and basalt rocks that looked like small volcanoes on the surface of the moon and the grim relics of the battle littered the sand on either side of the track. There was a wrecked Russian T34 tank, and the burnt out shells of several armoured personnel carriers and I counted-with my handkerchief to my nose-more than fifty decomposing bodies, half-buried by sand and half eaten by jackals. I saw also six decapitated corpses—executed Republicans, they told me."[2]

The various detachments of mercenary units set up a reliable radio network—something that had been lamentably lacking before their arrival—to co-ordinate the actions of the Imam's forces, casualty evacuations, and the distribution of money and weapons shipments. The Anglo/French mercenaries led Royalist tribesmen to ambush Egyptian columns, which were restricted to the few roads that were in the country. On Smiley's advice, the Anglo/French mercenary-led force began to concentrate on Egyptian supply routes, with devastating results. As it became more active and effective, it needed more weapons. Back in London, Jim Johnson turned to an unusual source for help: Mossad, the Israeli secret service. Surprisingly, he found them very receptive to the idea of supplying the Yemeni Royalist forces with arms.

From the Israeli viewpoint at the time, there were a number of benefits to supplying arms to Cooper's mercenary-led forces in Yemen. Firstly, Nasser's Egypt was its main enemy at the time. Anything that caused an attrition to his forces directly and, in the process, weakened Nasser's standing in the Arab world, directly helped Israel. Secondly, Mossad could gain valuable information about the Egyptian Army's operational procedures, weapons, and combat effectiveness.

On 31 March, 1964, a light aircraft commanded by Israeli Lieutenant Colonel Arie Oz, made its way in darkness towards a small landing strip. Guided by Cooper's elaborate radio system, it avoided the Egyptian military camps and spotted a series of small fires, lit by the British members of the mercenary unit. Into the darkness sixteen parachutes opened, each containing a crate filled with much-needed weapons.

With the weapons supplied by Israel, the mercenary-led Royalist forces launched a three-pronged attack against the Egyptian forces facing them. In one of the attacks, fifty Egyptian soldiers surrendered. The Royalist forces eventually surrounded between 3,000 - 5,000 Egyptian troops in garrisons on the eastern slopes of the mountains and desert, who had to be supplied entirely by air. One thousand Egyptian soldiers were estimated to have been killed in the operation.

Over the next year, the British and French mercenary-led force of tribesmen ran amok, penetrating as much as 20 miles inside Yemen, they attacked supply routes, ambushed, and destroyed whole Egyptian army units and quite simply, ran Nasser's much-vaunted army ragged. By the end of 1965, according to official Egyptian army figures, 15,194 men were killed in action in Yemen.

Before the deployment of mercenary forces into Yemen, there had been unverified reports that the Egyptians used poison gas. The SAS contingent in the Anglo/French mercenary force were able to obtain indisputable proof by collecting samples taken from casualties of the attacks and sending them for forensic analysis, proving the rumour true and publishing it to the world. The subsequent report suggested strongly that the gas had been produced in China.

As a result of the mercenary-led Royalist's antirational campaign, a ceasefire was declared in August 1965. The Anglo/French mercenary force strictly observed the ceasefire and restricted its role to supplying medical aid and maintaining communications. In late 1966, the ceasefire broke down and the Royalist forces re-started military operations. Neither side could achieve a military breakthrough, and the war stagnated into a stalemate; however, events elsewhere were to break it.

In 1967, what became known as The Six Day War broke out between Egypt and Israel, and the Israeli army and air force launched a surprise attack against Egypt. At the start of the war, about 68,000 Nasser's best troops and many of his Russian-supplied MIG fighters were still bogged down fighting in Yemen. There can be little doubt that the mercenary-led activities of the Royalist forces in Yemen directly contributed to the Israeli victory in the short war.

After Egypt's defeat in the six day war, Nasser decided to pull troops out of Yemen, and in November, Britain withdrew from Aden. Perhaps the most fitting tribute to the effectiveness of the British and French mercenary force was made by President Nasser as he described his involvement in the Yemen Civil War as "My Vietnam." The withdrawal of Egyptian troops did not stop Britain's covert war in Yemen, and the British and French mercenary force continued to support the Royalist forces for almost two years. In 1969, two mercenaries from Watchguard—run by David Stirling—were killed while leading a band of royalist tribesmen in Northern Yemen. Both men's bodies were decapitated and their heads displayed in various villages.

In late 1969, both the Saudis and Jordanians—allegedly under American pressure—cut off their supplies of money and weapons to the Royalists, and British and French mercenaries withdrew from the country. There was a bitter sense of betrayal amongst the departing mercenary force, particularly the members of 22 SAS who were "on leave." Not only had they recently lost two close comrades in the most brutal of fashions, loyalties and friendships had built up over the years with the Royalist tribesmen they led, and who would now be abandoned to their fate.

Deprived of money, weapons, and mercenary support, the Royalist forces accepted the inevitable and a treaty was signed ending hostilities. Yemen became North Yemen Republic, and Al-Badr escaped to England where he died in March 1969. In 1970, the private mercenary group Watchguard made a proposal to King Faisal of Saudi Arabia that it be commissioned to create a task force to infiltrate North Yemen to carry out massive sabotage raids. Before the Saudis could accept or reject the proposal, the plan was vetoed by the British government.

Africa
The Congo
1960 - 1965

From 1950 to the mid-1970s, there was a new wave of decolonisation in Africa. One unforeseen result of this rush to freedom from the colonial yoke was a series proxy of Cold War confrontations between the then-Soviet Union and the United States. The first of these was in the former Belgian Congo, which gained its independence on 30 June, 1960.

Prior to independence, the Congolese elected a president, Joseph Kasavubu and a prime minister, Patrice Lumumba. The American administration under President Eisenhower hoped that under them, the Republic of the Congo would form a stable, pro-Western, central government. Within days, those hopes vanished as the newly independent Congo spiralled into chaos. On 5 July, 1960, Congolese soldiers in the

Force Publique mutinied against their white Belgian commanders at the Thysville military base, and it quickly spread to other bases, with violence soon breaking out across the entire nation.

The Congolese government made a direct appeal to the United Nations to provide troops and demanded the removal of Belgian troops. On 13 July, the United Nations authorized the creation of an intervention force, the *Organisation des Nations Unies au Congo* (ONUC) that also demanded the withdrawal of all Belgian troops.

Two days earlier, the wealthy Katanga province declared its independence from the Republic of the Congo, followed in August by the South Kasai province. Lumumba responded by requesting assistance from the Soviet Union, which promptly deployed both advisors and military support. The Soviets' involvement had split the Congolese government and led to an impasse between Lumumba and President Joseph Kasa-Vubu.

Belgium, with United States' support, backed the *Katangese Gendarmerie* who had started the rebellion in Katanga province. In Paris, Roger Faulques and Captain Yves de La Bourdonnaye were given leave by the then-army minister Pierre Messmer to organise support for the rebellion. Faulques recruited Bob Denard and other former French Algerian War veterans to join him. Once in the country, he led a mercenary force of about 1,000 men, comprising mercenaries from France, Britain, Rhodesia, South Africa, and other voluntary irregulars.

The deadlock between Lumumba and President Joseph Kasa-Vubu was broken by Colonel Joseph Mobutu of the Congolese National Army (CNA) who orchestrated a *coup d'état* on 14 September, and ordered the Soviets out of the country. Patrice Lumumba was kidnapped and later assassinated by the Katangese with the Belgium's direct support, and the indirect support of the American CIA. Katangese military officer Moïse Tshombe then declared himself president.

Officially, the Falques' mercenaries were hired by European mining companies in Congo-Leopoldville as "security guards," but in actuality they were under the direct command of President of Katanga Moïse Tshombe. For a short time, Falques mercenary unit served alongside another called "4 Commando" and led by Lieutenant Colonel "Mad Mike" Hoare. This mercenary unit had been hastily formed from Second World War veterans, former members of the Rhodesian Light Infantry (RLI), and ex-members of the Israeli Army. The Commando only saw action from 7 to 11 April, 1961, before disbanding, but its leader would make important contacts that would be of immense value to him later.

Lumumba's death led to an international outcry, and whilst in the Congo with Soviet support, a rival government, "Free Republic of the Congo" was founded in the eastern city of Stanleyville by Lumumba supporters led by Antoine Gizenga. Katanga, however, declared itself independent under the leadership of Moïse Tshombe. In response to the international outcry over Lumumba's death and the involvement of mercenaries in the Congo, a 4,700-strong UN force comprising mainly of the 99th Indian Infantry Brigade under the command of Brigadier-General Raja, were deployed as UN peacekeepers.

The Indian brigade—without the knowledge or approval of Swedish born UN Secretary General Dag Hammarskjöld—launched "Operation Morthor" (Hindi for smash and grab) and attacked. Despite the fact that they faced a numerically superior force of professional soldiers from various nations, Faulques organised a skilful defence. After a brutal assault by Indian troops on a lightly defended post office in the Katangan capital of Elisabethville on 13 September, 1961, that killed all of its Katangan occupants, Moïse Tshombe ordered Faulques to go on the offensive.

Faulques' counter offensive resulted in the siege of Jadotville. His mercenaries and 3,000 – 5,000 Katangan troops surrounded by a force of 155 Irish soldiers under Commandant Pat Quinlan—fought furiously until they ran out of ammunition. After five days, on 17 September, Faulques himself accepted their surrender. Despite the fact that the UN force inflicted heavy casualties on Faulques' forces, his brilliant counter offensive resulted in the UN operation ending up a strategic failure.

Swedish-born UN Secretary General Dag Hammarskjöld was highly critical of mercenary involvement in the Congo, but on 18 September, 1961, Hammarskjöld was *en route* to negotiate a ceasefire in the Congo when his aircraft crashed, killing all aboard. The circumstances surrounding the crash remain controversial to the present day, with claims and counter claims. A 1962 Rhodesian inquiry concluded that pilot error was to blame, while a later UN investigation could not determine the crash cause. The CIA claimed the KGB was responsible, whilst others have pointed the finger at a Rhodesian mercenary by the name of Van Risseghem as being the perpetrator of the fatal crash. The real truth will never really be known.

Following Hammarskjöld's death, the UN forces again went on the offensive. In December 1961, they launched Operation Unokat to regain control of the situation. Again, Falques designed the defence strategy, but the overwhelming superiority of the UN forces eventually persuaded Tshombe to sign the Kitona Declaration, and an uneasy peace followed. Violence flared up again in 1962 and UN Secretary General Thant authorized yet another offensive, Operation Grandslam. Swedish air support and heavy mortar fire engaged Faulques' mercenaries who suffered heavy casualties, allowing Swedish peacekeepers to enter the Katangese capital Elizabethville. They were quickly followed by the Indian brigade of General Raja, securing the capital by 28 December. Tshombe, realizing that his position was untenable, sued for peace on 15 January, 1963. Two days later, he signed an instrument of surrender and declared the Katangan secession to be over. The UN forces then expelled Faulques' mercenary force from the country.

The UN forces departed the Congo in 1964, just as a revolt by half-crazed superstitious warriors who called themselves *Sambas* (lions) was beginning to engulf one provisional town after another. What became known as "The Simba Rebellion" began as a communist-inspired revolt in the Congo province of Kwilu. Cuban revolutionaries—including Che Guevara—entered the country to support the rebellion. It quickly spread and turned into a limited civil war. Moïse Tshombe had, by this time, returned from exile and was appointed Prime Minister in April 1964.

Four months later, Simba rebels marched on the province's capital of Stanleyville, and murdered, raped, and pillaged everyone and everything in sight. Neither the United Nations nor the United States showed any appetite for armed intervention. Tshombe instructed Jerry Puren—a French mercenary who worked with him in Katanga—to raise a mercenary force. Puren started the process of recruiting and placed himself in charge of air operations with Alastaire Wicks, a former member the Rhodesian SAS, as second-in-command. The former leader of "4 Commando," Lieutenant Colonel "Mad Mike" Hoare, was selected to be the operational leader on the ground.

A former territorial officer born of Irish parents in Calcutta, India, Mike Hoare served with distinction in the 2nd Reconnaissance Regiment of the Royal Armoured Regiment in Burma during the Second World War. He fought in the Arakan campaign in Burma and at the decisive battle of

Kohima that stopped the Japanese advance into India. He left the British army with the rank of major. A small man physically, he was described by those who met him as both "dapper" and "charming."

The mercenary force that was to be called "5 Commando," also nicknamed "the Wild Geese" was recruited in both South Africa and Rhodesia. Mercenaries from around the world flooded to answer newspaper advertisements. The unit would eventually comprise former soldiers and adventurers from South Africa, Britain, Rhodesia, Belgium, and Germany.

The German recruits were almost all former Second World War veterans, many of whom arrived wearing the Iron Crosses they received in the war. One of most notorious of these was Siegfried "Congo Killer," Muller whose vicious brutality toward the native black population made him a hated figure in West Germany, particularly amongst socialists and student activists.

Contracts lasted for six months, and basic pay was advertised at US$280 per month, plus US$420 danger pay and 37,000 Congolese francs as pocket money for the month. NCOs earned basic pay of US$400, and senior officers US$1,100 per month. Compensation of US$19,000 was payable to next of kin in the event of a soldier's death. Hoare chose as his second-in-command a dour Yorkshireman, John Peters, a former British army sergeant who served in "C Squadron" of the Rhodesian SAS. Peters' cold-blooded ferocity in battle would make him a legend in the coming operations.

Colonel Vandewalle was sent to the Congo by the Belgian government to oversee operations and, after some pressure from the government, was given permission by Tshombe to take overall control of the mercenary operation, including aircraft supplied by the CIA. After several weeks of training, "5 Commando" went into combat and operated mainly in daylight in "flying columns" of jeeps and armoured cars. An elite 100-man flying column, comprised of Hoare's best recruits, was known as "Force John-John" and was led by John Peters. It was frequently used to lead advances and initiate attacks. In one rare night attack, Force John-John, under Peters, attacked a Simba convoy near the Sudan border. In the initial assault, a lucky shot by Peters hit a jeep full of ammunition and blew it to pieces. Hoare later recorded: "The battle lasted ten minutes at the end of it Force John-John had annihilated the whole of the enemy column and captured eleven trucks and mountains of ammunition"[3]

In a later engagement in the town of Niangarn, Simbas launched a counter attack against Hoare's forces. Peters, throwing a hand grenade into the middle of them, led the counter attack into a mass of Simba's shouting the only French he knew: *Advance les mercenaries*' which saved the situation and eventually, after bitter fighting, routing the Simba forces.[4] With the aid of men like Peters, Hoare's rapidly trained but poorly organised "5 Commando" was instrumental in crushing the Simba uprising in just two months.

The rebellion crushed, Simbas resorted to taking hostages. Many were held in the provincial capital Stanleyville. The European hostages, in particular, received barbaric treatment from their captors, including the raping of minors, murder, and even cannibalism. Hoare's flying columns took an important role, in conjunction with Belgium Para Commandoes, in Operation Dragon Rouge, which resulted in the relief of the city and the saving of many lives. Tragically, many of the European hostages were mutilated and murdered before help could arrive.

Following the relief of Stanleyville, 5 Commando worked with the *ANC* Congolese troops to clear eastern Congo of Simba rebels. In one operation, their swift advance almost captured Che Guevara himself, who escaped in the nick of time to Tanzania. 5 Commando's main backer, Tshombe, was ousted as Prime Minister on 13 October and replaced by Evariste Kimba who, in turn, was very quickly ousted by Mabuto in a coup. With their main political support gone, Puren and Tshombe left the Congo to live in exile in Belgium.

Mike Hoare and Alistair Wicks also left the Congo after choosing to not renew their contracts. John Peters, by then the commanding officer of 5 Commando, continued to pledge his and the unit's loyalty to the government and continued operations in southern Congo. Tshombe's removal led to two mercenary revolts. The first was by mercenaries under the command of Jean Schramme in conjunction with the Baka Regiment of the ANC, who planned a to re-install Tshombe in a counter-coup. Jean Puren (still in Belgium) and the mercenary leaders of 5 Command refused to take part in it.

On 23 July 1965, the planned coup took place, and the mutinous Baku Regiment of the ANC as well Schramme's mercenary units rose up to support the exiled Tshombe, killed the ANC commander, and took control of the radio station in Stanleyville. Bob Denard quickly notified the government and called for support to put down the counter-coup. After a stalemate, there was a recognition the rebellion had failed, and a truce was negotiated where surviving Katanga troops were given amnesty. Jean Schramme and the surviving mercenary officers were transported to prison, and Mobutu remained secure as president.

The second mercenary revolt was actually initiated by Jean Puren whilst he was still in Belgium. This was more carefully planned and again led by Jean Schramme, and this time, Bob Denard supported it and was also heavily involved. Their intended counter-coup was initially successful, but the ANC quickly recovered and counter attacked, eventually forcing 150 mercenaries, 800 Katanga soldiers, and 1,500 women to flee across the Rwandan border, where they were disarmed and interred by the Rwandan army. In other parts of the country, many mercenaries were summarily executed, and those European mercenaries who survived were evacuated by the Red Cross.

As a result of the two mercenary revolts, Mabutu ordered all recruitment for 5 Commando to cease immediately and 5 Commando was officially disbanded in April 1966. The legacy of 5 Commando is mixed, whilst many in Europe and the West in general saw it in a somewhat heroic light after it saved European hostages during the Simba revolt. However, reality was somewhat different. Whilst some members such as John Peters were undoubtedly heroic, the unit had a well-documented history of unsanctioned killing, torture, looting and rapes in Africa. Hoare perhaps best described the men he led in his written account of the activities of 5 Commando, calling them "appalling thugs."[5]

Biafra
6 July 1967 - 15 January 1970

In July 1967, the Nigerian state of Biafra—led by Lieutenant Colonel C. Odumegwu Ojukwu—declared independence from Nigeria, which was led by General Yakubu Gowon. The resulting civil war was called the Nigerian-Biafran War or, more simply, the Biafran War.

The war was characterised by unspeakable brutality, especially on the Nigerian side, which horrified the world. A graphic example of this was recorded by a British television crew in the later stages of the war. A rake-thin Biafran man had been detained by a Nigerian military patrol, hog-tied, and thrown in a ditch, all the while pleading in broken English "me no Biafran soldier, me no Biafran soldier." The Nigerian officer kept saying he was a Biafran soldier, when the television reporter asked him what was going to happen to the wretched man, the officer casually turned his machine gun toward the pleading man and poured a stream of bullets into his helpless victim.[6]

There was, from the very onset of the conflict, a large-scale military imbalance between the numerically superior, better trained, and better equipped Nigerian forces and the Biafran rebels. Outgunned and outmatched by the Nigerian forces, Biafra hired mercenary support in an attempt to redress the balance. France supported the rebellion in the oil-rich, newly declared independent Biafra. With the active support of both the French Government and French Security Services, Roger Faulques began recruiting and organising a mercenary unit to go to the country. One early recruit was a former comrade of his from the French Foreign Legion called Rolf Steiner.

A German by birth, Steiner joined the French Foreign Legion at 17 and saw combat in Vietnam. He was wounded a number of times, was twice demoted in rank from sergeant to private for insubordination, and twice promoted back up to the rank of sergeant. Steiner went on to fight with distinction in Egypt during the Suez Crisis and in Algeria before joining the underground OAS and where he became involved in a plot to overthrow General De Gaul, for which he served 9 months in prison.

Faulques, Steiner, and more than 50 other mercenaries flew to Port Harcourt via Lisbon. On landing, all were immediately commissioned as officers in the Biafran army. Not long after they were in the country, the ever aggressive Faulques led his combined Biafran troops and mercenary force on an unauthorized attempt to retake the city of Calabar. The attack ended disastrously, with heavy losses to the accompanying Biafran troops. As a result of the failed operation, Faulques and most of the white mercenaries left the country. Steiner stubbornly remained.

Steiner, because of his superiority in rank, assumed command of the 4th Commando Brigade of the Biafran Armed Forces, a unit comprising some 3,000 men. A Welsh mercenary, Taffy Williams, was appointed as his second-in-command and given a separate unit comprising about 100 Biafran troops. Born in Wales in 1934, Williams received military training in South Africa and fought in the Congo as part of "Mad Mike" Hoare's 5 Commando. Williams went on to serve two tours in Biafra where he rose to the rank of Major in the Biafran army. He was noted for his leadership and almost suicidal bravery in combat. Many of the Biafran troops he led were devoted to him and thought him bulletproof. In one engagement, in early 1968, Williams and his hundred Biafran fighters managed to keep two battalions of Chadian mercenaries serving with the Nigerian Federal Army at bay for twelve weeks armed only with antiquated weapons.

One of Steiner's few achievements was to establish a brown water navy by converting some Chris Craft Boats into gun boats. Steiner went on to successfully use them in raids for weapons and supplies, and led mercenary and Biafran forces with some initial success against the Nigerian forces. This instilled in them a believe, based on their experiences in the Congo, that their involvement in the conflict would compensate against the superiority of the Nigerian forces; however, it would prove a disastrously wrong assumption. Whilst in the Congo, they had largely faced undisciplined local militias and even the UN troops, with the exception of the Irish, but were unable to match the French-led mercenary force in direct combat. The Nigerian army was a far more formidable opponent, as its troops were regulars, British-trained and well-disciplined. They had an excellent officer core and many officers had passed through the rigorous officer course at Sandhurst.

Faced with such a professional army, Steiner's mercenaries had only a limited impact on the war. This was never more greatly illustrated than in the period between 15-29 November, 1968, when Steiner—in an operation code named "Operation Hiroshima"—led 4 Commando and a large contingent of Biafran soldiers in an ill-fated attempt to recapture Onitsha from the Nigerian 2nd Division. The operation was a disastrous failure, with well over half of 4 Commando troops killed and many more wounded. Significant numbers of hard-to-replace Biafran soldiers were also killed. After the disaster, Steiner suffered a nervous breakdown, and was arrested and expelled from the country.

His position as head of 4 Commando was filled by Taff Williams. Under Williams' leadership, deprived of weapons, regular food, and any reasonable prospect of victory, the small white mercenary group that was left fought on regardless of the odds. Those odds grew darker with every passing week. There is no doubt that they carried on not for a monthly pay check, but in a genuine commitment to the Biafran cause, perhaps a rare quality in any mercenary. Williams summed up the motivation of many of the mercenaries who stayed when he said of the Biafran troops he led: "I've seen a lot of Africans at war, but there's nobody to touch these people. Give me 10,000 Biafrans for six months, and we'll build an army that would be invincible on this continent. I've seen men die in this war who would have won the Victoria Cross in another context."[7]

Britain had always supported the Nigerian side during the war and increased that military aid as the war intensified. Bolstered by this support, Nigerian forces launched their final offensive against the Biafrans on 23 December, 1969. The Biafran towns of Owerri fell on 9 January, and Uli on 11 January. The Biafran leader Ojukwu fled into exile, leaving his deputy Phillip Effiong to handle the details of the surrender, which was signed on 14 January, 1970 in Lagos, ending the war. Taff Williams stayed to the bitter end and was the last white mercenary to leave the country.

The Anyanya Rebellion
1955 - 1972

Anyanya Rebellion—also known as the First Sudanese Civil War—was a civil war fought in one of the poorest, most undeveloped countries in Africa: Sudan. The war was to rage between 1955-1971 between the northern part of Sudan and the southern region. The war began on 18 August, 1955, when members of the British-administered Sudan Defence Force mutinied in Torit, before moving on to Juba, Yei, and Maridi. Poorly armed and unorganised, the southern Sudanese were little threat to the outgoing British colonial power or the Sudanese government that replaced it. Disorganisation, bitter inter-faction fighting, and poor logistics supplies, particularly weapons, plagued the Anyanya Rebellion from its infancy until the end of the conflict. In the late 1960s, Israel was in a bitter war with Egypt, and in order to prevent Sudanese forces from aiding Egypt in the conflict, in May 1969 it dispatched a military mission, commanded by David "Tarzan" Ben-Uziel, to supply arms to Anyanya rebel forces. The Ugandan government also supported the Anyanya Rebellion, and it was to Idi Amin, the then-commander of the Ugandan Army, that Rolf Steiner offered his mercenary services in 1969.

Because of Steiner's reputation from the Biafran conflict, Amin was convinced that he could reinvigorate the Anyanya Rebellion and dispatched Steiner to the war zone. According to Steiner's own account of his time fighting in the Anyanya cause, not only did he provide them with military training, he helped to resolve internal bickering between the various southern tribes and used his agricultural and medical skills with civilians to improve their quality of life.[8]

The truth is, however, somewhat different. On arriving in southern Sudan, Steiner quickly became involved in the internal problems that plagued the Anyanya since the beginning of the rebellion. Whilst theirs was an ineffectual existing leadership, there were two main contenders jousting to overthrow it: Colonel Joseph Lagu, and General Emilio Tafeng. In August 1969, Steiner focused his support on Tafeng, and planted a story in the Ugandan papers that the *revolution brought down "the nominally in-control Anyanya government, the Nile Provisional Government, and that the people were rallying to Tafeng."*[9] By November 1969, he had become Tafeng's *de facto* military advisor, with the rank of colonel in charge of more than 20,000 men.[10]

Already struggling against the superiority of the government forces, the Anyanya rebels cause now descended in factual in-fighting—caused in part by Steiner, who made outlandish promises to Tafeng about future weapons supplies from Uganda and the west.[11] Steiner believed that if he could establish Tafeng as the leader of the Anyanya cause, Tafeng would appoint him as chief of staff of all Anyanya forces.[12]

Whilst the internal in-fighting continued, Steiner set about training Tafeng's troops. His training techniques could sometimes be brutal and eccentric, such as firing his gun near the feet of sentries he caught sleeping at night, making recruits ride leap swings through fires, and making trainees sit in a circle with their feet facing a mortar tube whilst he fired a round.[13] Although ill-equipped and barely trained, Steiner led Tafeng's forces in an attack on the strategic Sudanese Army post at Kajo Keji. Lacking heavy weapons or mortars, the Anyanya rebel force proved no match for the better armed defenders and were thrown back with heavy casualties.[14]

Following the defeat, Steiner returned to West Germany for a short time. When he returned, despite the calamity of the disastrous attack on Kajo Keji, Tafeng still had not lost faith in him and gave him personal protection of about 800 men. A great part of Tafeng's continual reliance upon Steiner was his belief that the German mercenary would deliver on his continual promises of arms shipments.

In May 1969, General Gaafar Nimeiry overthrew the previous central government and became president of Sudan. He immediately launched an offensive against the Anyanya rebellion in southern Sudan. It was at this stage that the internal fighting with the Anyanya rebel cause proved the undoing of Tafeng, who found his forces trapped between the government forces and the faction led by forces loyal to Colonel Joseph Lagu. This resulted in the collapse of Tafeng's forces in April 1970. Tafeng disbanded what was left of his forces and recognized the authority of Lagu, who had always been hostile towards Steiner's involvement in the Anyanya cause.

Following the collapse of Tafeng's faction, there was a brief pause in the government offensive, but this resumed with renewed vigour in September 1970, which resulted in several Anyanya camps, including the camp at Morta where Steiner was based before being overrun by the Sudanese Army. The Israelis were still supporting the Anyanya cause, and by October 1970 had decided that Lagu was the most "able" of the Anyanya leaders, they considered Steiner more of a problem than an asset.

The Israeli assessment of Steiner was no doubt based on his failures both in the field and his consistently unfulfilled promises of arms supplies from the Uganda and the west. The fact that he served in the German army during the Second World War may also have influenced their decision. The Israeli's view of Steiner was borne out by the observations of an American documentary filmmaker Allan Reed who interviewed Steiner in 1970 and recalled, "He wanted to be king. We found him sitting on the ground in this little hut, and he was patching up some infected wounds that some kids had, there was a whole long line of them. He said the only time he was ever happy was when he went into battle. His eyes lit up when he talked about it. He told me that he thinks of himself as a seventeenth-century man. It seemed to me that he was there building himself a little kingdom."

Further, Reed stated that Steiner claimed he was working for MI6 and the Central Intelligence Agency, but Reed was sceptical saying that Steiner failed to deliver any goods. "Any major Western intelligence agency could at least get him some machine guns or munitions...It was really quite strange. It was quite a pathetic looking place."

The locals later told Reed that the previous year, Steiner ordered them to build an airfield, saying that masses of arms and relief aid from the West would then be flown in. Of the airfield that had been built in 1969, Reed recalled: "So the people chopped down the trees and built a grass runway. It was completely overrun with weeds. The people said that no planes had ever come."[15]

Lagu hostility to Steiner would in all probability have resulted in him dispensing with his services, but in any event, the matter was taken out of his hands by the Israelis, who refused continued support unless Steiner left the country. Israeli agent David Ben-Uziel remarked: "I told Lagu either Steiner leaves or we get out."[16]

Dismissed by Lagu, Steiner decided to return to Europe but was arrested *en route* in Kampala, Uganda. Under interrogation, he refused to implicate his benefactor, Idi Amin, in his activities in southern Sudan and was extradited by plane to Khartoum. On 8 January, 1971, Steiner was charged with crimes against Africa and convicted. Steiner was initially sentenced to death, but this was commuted to twenty years imprisonment. Severely tortured whilst in prison, he was released after serving three years, after which he returned to Germany and retired.

With the help of Israel, Lagu was eventually able to oust the existing Anyanya leadership and, for the first time in the rebellion, unite the various factions under the banner of his Southern Sudan Liberation Movement (SSLM). With the assistance of outside agencies, such as World Council of Churches (WCC) and the All Africa Conference of Churches (AACC)—both had built trust in each of the combating forces—Lagu was able to negotiate a peace deal that led up to the Addis Ababa Agreement of March 1972, effectively ending the war.

An estimated half a million people died over the seventeen years of the civil war. The Addis Ababa Agreement may have brought the war to an end, but it did little to settle the festering grievances of the south Sudanese, particularly the Anyanya people who had suffered terrible atrocities and repression throughout the conflict. These unresolved grievances would see a re-igniting of the north/south conflict during the Second Sudanese Civil War (1983 - 2005) and led ultimately to the formation of the independent state of South Sudan.

Despite Steiner's own assertions as to his importance in the Anyanya rebellion, his contribution seems to have been marginal at best. Certainly that is the opinion of British historian Edgar O'Ballance, who later wrote:

"Steiner had hardly made any impression in the south, which in general seemed embarrassed by his former presence there, but in view of his experience, some of his comments on this semi-secret war are of interest."[17] Steiner gave his own reasons for his failures in south Sudan, saying the Anyanya guerrillas fought well when they fought against one another, but "less well against the Sudanese Army," and that they were "cowardly."[18] Readers should decide for themselves as to where the truth lies.

Chapter Three

Africa Angola 1975 - 1976

In August 1970, an operation was organised by the security firm Watchguard, run by Colonel David Stirling. The plan was to raid Libya's main prison in Tripoli—known as "The Hilton"—free supporters of the exiled King Idris, and foment revolution against the new ruler, Colonel Muammar Gadaffi.

"The Hilton Assignment," as it came to be known, was aborted by Stirling after opposition from the Central Intelligence Agency and the Italian secret police (SID) who saw Colonel Gadaffi as an anti-Communist ally. John Banks, a former private in the 2nd Battalion of the Parachute Regiment, had been summarily discharged from the army because of "Services No Longer Required," was reputably involved in recruitment for the aborted operation.

In May 1975, an advertisement was placed in *The Daily Mail* and *The Daily Mirror* that read "Ex-commandoes, paratroopers, SAS troopers wanted for interesting work abroad. Ring Camberly 33456." Those who answered the advertisement were met by John Banks. In the briefing that followed, Banks outlined a sabotage operation into Rhodesia, which had Unilaterally Declared Independence (UDI) from Britain, from bases in Zambia.

Unbeknownst to Banks, one of the former SAS men who attended, Andy Dennison, had been accepted into the Rhodesian Army. In addition, the Rhodesian "C Squadron" still maintained good relations with its parent regiment 22 SAS, even after UDI had been implemented. The former SAS man informed the relevant authorities and the intended operation ended in shambles. Banks was to go on and play a pivotal role in one of the most disastrous, shambolic, and horrific mercenary interventions of the twentieth century, when a group of white mercenaries were sent to intervene in the civil war in the African state of Angola.

The Angolan Civil War erupted almost immediately after the country gained its independence from Portugal and was fought mainly between two former liberation guerrilla armies: the communist Peoples Movement for the Liberation of Angola (MPLA) and the anti-communist national Union for the Total Independence of Angola (UNITA).

UNITA was led by Jonas Savimbi. The author met him briefly in the late 1970s in Angola and found him to be both a charismatic and highly intelligent man. His UNITA troops' loyalty to him was almost Godlike. A third former liberation guerrilla army was the pro-western National Front for the Liberation of Angola (FNLA), led by Holden Roberto, who was to be the main recipient of the mercenaries that would be sent to Angola. As with past African civil wars, the Angolan Civil War was seen as a new "hot phase" of the ongoing Cold War. The USSR gave military and economic support to the communist MPLA, whilst Cuban and East German troops trained and fought with the MPLA on the ground.

In January 1976, the CIA began to channel hundreds of thousands of dollars to the FNLA. With the funding from the CIA, Holden Roberto set about hiring mercenaries from his base in Zaire. The first four were British paratroopers, all former members the 1st Battalion. They were Costas Georgiou, Nicholas Mervyn Hall, Charlie Christodoulou and Mick Wainhouse, and none ever rose above the rank of private. Only Christodoulou (whose nickname was "Shotgun Charlie" because he always carried a Spanish-made shotgun) had been honourably discharged. The others had all ended their military careers in prison: Georgiou for an absurd post office robbery in Northern Ireland in February 1972. Georgiou, and another member of 1 PARA were armed with British army weapons and made their getaway in an army bus. Georgiou was quickly arrested by the military police, and at his subsequent court martial, was described by his own defending Counsel as "a potential candidate for Broadmoor Hospital." Georgiou was immediately sentenced to five years in prison.

The backgrounds of these four men arriving as mercenaries in war-torn Angola is so comical it might be a work of fiction. After placing an advertisement in British newspapers on behalf of the four former paratroopers, Hall had been contacted by London representatives of

Holden Roberto and flown to his base in Zaire. After an initial meeting, he was given £20,000 and told to return to Britain and begin recruiting mercenaries to fight for the FNLA. Back in England, Hall contacted John Banks, the mercenary force he compiled for the aborted "Hilton Job" was now put into action, and among the mercenaries that answered his call was a former sergeant in the 22 SAS, Peter McAleese. Two weeks later, Hall's mercenary band departed for Angola.

Georgiou went to Angola in advance of Hall's gathering mercenary force as an unpaid medical orderly. He was by this time using name "Tony Cullen." Many journalists were to go on and refer to Georgiou as "Colonel Callan" in the mistaken belief that the ex-paratrooper was inspired by the TV series of that name. In fact, Tony Cullen was a former friend from 1 Para. Georgiou eventually adopted the Callan *nom de guerre*. It was this early stage that Georgiou came to the direct attention of Holden Roberto. When an MPLA attack threatened to overwhelm the hospital that he worked in, Georgiou and another mercenary called Lyndon Sheehan first rallied the FNLA troops, then led them in a successful counter attack.

Impressed by the swift victory, Holden Roberto immediately promoted Georgiou to Colonel and gave him overall command of the FNLA forces. A short time later, Hall and the first group of British mercenaries arrived, and Hall promoted himself to Major under Georgiou. Within 48 hours of the British mercenary unit's arrival in Angola, Georgiou led his men in disarming and massacring a group of FNLA fighters, who he reportedly killed just for the "fun" of it. In another incident—recounted to the author personally by one of the few British mercenaries to return from Angola alive—one of the British mercenaries had captured a weapon, and Georgiou asked him if he had test fired it. When the mercenary answered "No," Georgiou called over an FNLA soldier, made him stand to attention and shot him dead, then returned the weapon with "It works OK."

Quite apart from the CIA-funded British mercenary operation in the United States, David Bufkin began a recruiting campaign in *Soldier of Fortune* magazine. A thoroughly disreputable character, Bufkin was a former U.S. Army soldier with a criminal background. He managed to get about a dozen American mercenaries into Angola, all of whom were either killed or captured by MPLA or Cuban forces.

In all, three batches of British mercenaries were dispatched by Banks to Angola between 1975–1976. A great number were fantasists, with no military experience; many shot themselves or others accidentally and were more a danger to their own side than the enemy. Many, like Georgiou himself, were racists who actually hated and despised the black troops they commanded. A fellow mercenary described him as "a homicidal maniac," and further, as a man who spent a great deal of time "killing blacks just for fun."[1] Under Georgiou's inept, racist, and psychopathic leadership, Bank's mercenaries systematically undermined and damaged the morale and fighting ability of the FNLA troops they were supposed to support.

One notorious incident that occurred during the ill-fated adventure happened after a group of Bank's ill-trained new "mercenaries" accidentally ambushed a vehicle containing four other members of Georgiou's outfit. Georgiou went into a psychotic frenzy, and personally shot dead one of the men, Phil Davies. The rest he handed over to his "sergeant major," Sammy Copeland. Copeland was another former member of the Parachute Regiment, and he and six other mercenaries loaded the unfortunate men into a truck, drove them to the countryside, ordered them to strip, and then machine-gunned them to death. Mike McKeown, one of the few who escaped, recalled "The men knew their time had come, my pals leaped out of the truck and dashed across a field, looking for cover in the tall grass. The boys who went down like cattle were my mates."[2] Fourteen men died in the atrocity.

Following the massacre, Mike Hall and the former 22 SAS man Peter McAleese held a drumhead court martial, and Holden Roberto himself attended. Copeland was sentenced to death by firing squad, as it was being formed he attempted an escape, was initially wounded, then according to Pete McAleese, "Casually, one of the mercenaries walked over, drew a pistol and shot him dead."[3] "Shotgun" Charlie Christodoulou also faced the court martial but was acquitted and sent to the front line without pay. On 14 February, 1976, Christodoulou, two British and two American mercenaries were killed in an ambush by Cuban forces. It was later estimated that he was involved in the murder of at least 167 members of the FNLA.

It is estimated that Banks sent about ninety-six British mercenaries to Angola. The MPLA forces they faced were mainly battle-hardened veterans of their colonial bush war with Portugal. They were better organised, better led and were fighting for a cause they believed in. On their own, they could have probably dealt with the inept mercenaries

Banks sent. With the dispatch of some 35,000 Cuban troops in November 1975, both the FNLA and the British mercenaries' fate was finally sealed.

A number of mercenaries were captured by the combined MPLA/ Cuban forces and put on trial. Ten were imprisoned, but four were executed: American Daniel Gearhart (who had been recruited by David Bufkin), British mercenaries John Derek Barker, Andrew McKenzie, and Costas Georgiou himself. During the trial, evidence was presented that Georgiou and Christodoulou had been responsible for killing 170 of their own FNLA troops. All four were executed by a military police MPLA firing squad on 10 July, 1976. In accounts given by two former British mercenaries Chris Dempster and Dave Tomkins, McKenzie was the only one of the four killed outright. Georgiou and Gearhart were only wounded by the firing squad and a *coup de grace* had to be administered by the officer in charge. Barker, another former paratrooper, fainted and was shot after waking up on a stretcher.[4] The executions brought an end to the tragedy.

Africa
The Comoros
1975

As the debacle in Angola unfolded in 1975, the swashbuckling Bob Denard was undertaking the first of four mercenary-led coups in the Comoros, a group of islands at the northern end of the Mozambique Channel of the Indian Ocean between Madagascar and the southeast African mainland, about 180 miles off the eastern coast of Africa, which had unilaterally declared independence from France on 6 July, 1975.

In the first coup, Denard ousted Comoros' first President, Ahmed Abdallah. He went on to make a failed coup in Benin in 1977, then served for a time in Rhodesia with the ill-fated, all-French 7 Independent Company. In between coups, Denard amassed a personal fortune in the Comoros in property, business, and hotels. His final coup was recorded in a UN report on mercenary activities published on 7 January, 1996:

"B. Islamic Federal Republic of the Comoros: On 28 September, 1995, the Islamic Federal Republic of the Comoros was again attacked by mercenaries who once more seriously infringed the right of the people to self-determination and the constitutional stability of the country. As on earlier occasions, the coup was led by the French mercenary,

Bob Denard, whose real name is Gilbert Bourgeaud and who, at the head of a handful of twenty or so mercenaries of various nationalities, held President Said Mohamed Djohar hostage in barracks close to the presidential palace. They also seized the radio and television stations, and with the support of a few hundred Comorian soldiers, managed to take control of the capital, Moroni, for a few days."

After a week of national confusion and uncertainty, the Prime Minister of the Comoros, Caambi-El Yachourtu, who had taken refuge in the French Embassy, prevailed upon France to send troops to the Comoros under the 1978 Franco-Comorian defence agreement in order to put an end to the foreign aggression and restore the rule of law. In connection with this legitimate intervention by France, the French Minister for Foreign Affairs, Mr. Hervé de Charette, said that, in the normal course of events, Bob Denard would be placed under arrest. On 5 October, the French military force of just under 1,000 men gained control of the Moroni airports and gradually the whole city, while Prime Minister Caambi-El Yachourtu announced the formation of a twelve-member government of national unity. Realizing that further resistance was futile, Bob Denard, who by then controlled only the Kandani military barracks where he had taken refuge, surrendered to the French forces and was subsequently taken to the island of Reunion. Denard, who is charged with assassination of a President of the Comoros, was serving a five year conditional sentence for his part in a mercenary attack on Benin in 1977; it is therefore somewhat surprising that he managed to get out of France to lead another coup in the Comoros.

Because of the sentence he was serving, Denard was not supposed to leave France, where charges were also pending against him for the assassination of the President of the Comoros, Ahmed Abdallah Abderemane, on 26 November, 1989. Consequently, the judge in charge of the case, Chantal Perdrix, issued to Interpol an international warrant for Denard's arrest. Denard was taken prisoner on 5 October, 1995, by the French force which put an end to the mercenary coup and was handed over to the appropriate authorities for trial by a French court.[5]

Denard would be prosecuted twice in French courts over his activities in the Comoros, and both times he received suspended sentences. It was always suspected but never proven that he acted with the approval of the French government, who used the Comoros as a convenient base to circumvent the embargo on apartheid South Africa. In his autobiography, Denard said, "Often, I didn't exactly have a green light from the French authorities, but I went on the amber."[6] Denard died on 13 October, 2007, at the age of 77.

Africa
Rhodesia
1965 - 1980

On 11 November, 1965, the southern African state of Rhodesia made a Unilateral Declaration of Independence (UDI). Britain, the former colonial power, refused to recognise the declaration and imposed sanctions that were internationally recognised. For fourteen years, the minority-led white government fought a bitter bush war against two guerrilla movements, the Zimbabwe African National Liberation Army (ZANLA) and the Zimbabwe People's Revolutionary Army (ZIPRA), the respective armed wings of ZANU and ZAPU, which began in earnest in December 1972.

During the entire bush war, the Rhodesian military augmented its limited resources of manpower by recruiting foreign mercenary volunteers. Mostly, these served in units like the Rhodesian Light Infantry (RLI) an airborne unit that had its own overseas recruitment programme. One member of 2 Para—who the author served with—was directly recruited in this way. Bob "Shoulders" Smith—so nicknamed because of his awkward gait, caused by an upper torso being out of proportion to the rest of his body—served with 11 Troop, 3 Commando RLI, as the troop corporal from 1975 - 1977.

Foreign mercenary volunteers also served in almost all of the combat arms of the Rhodesian armed forces. An estimated 300 Americans, many former Vietnam war veterans, served with the Rhodesian forces as well as volunteers from Britain, Australia, Canada, Holland, France, and Germany. Many had a racist agenda and were completely opposed to the idea of governments led by black people. Others were motivated by anti-communism, some for a desire to see combat, a few were just psychopathic and wanted a semi-legal cover to kill.

One combat unit was unique in the history of the Rhodesian Army, as it was an exclusively expatriate unit: the 7 Independent Company. Exclusively

French, its members were almost all former French paratroopers or former Foreign Legionaries. It was only in existence from November 1977 through May 1978, and at its height numbered about 200 strong and was at one time commanded by Bob Denard. The experiment of creating an entirely expatriate French fighting force proved to be disastrous: 7 Independent Company proved to be undisciplined, it was involved in at least two friendly fire incidents that caused several fatalities, and was so indiscriminately brutal that the local population the Rhodesians—no strangers to brutality themselves—disbanded it in May 1978.

Amongst the mercenaries from around the world that flocked to serve in Rhodesia was the former Angolan mercenary and ex-22 SAS man Peter McAleese, who joined in 1977, and went on to serve with 'C' Squadron Rhodesian SAS. One member of the Rhodesian SAS who the author served with him during the Rhodesian bush war described McAleese in simple, if somewhat brutal terms: "He's killed more people than I've met."

The author himself served in Rhodesia in 1977 - 1978, with South Africa's elite special forces unit No. 1 Reconnaissance Commando, who were deployed into the country to support the Rhodesian special forces. The author found the majority of the foreign mercenary volunteers serving with their special forces to be highly committed to the Rhodesian cause. A typical example was Robert Callen MacKenzie.

Robert Callen MacKenzie turned down an appointment to the United States Air Force Academy and joined the US army at 17 to fight in Vietnam. During his military service, he became airborne-qualified and completed a jungle warfare course. On his first tour in Vietnam, he took part in the attack on Mother's Day Hill, but during the assault, he suffered a severe bullet wound and spent a year in hospital. The US army classified him as 70 per cent disabled, and he was permanently retired. In 1970, MacKenzie—determined to see military service—moved to Rhodesia and underwent the rigorous selection course for 'C' Squadron Rhodesian SAS. He served until 1980, rising from trooper to captain and SAS Squadron Commander. He was twice decorated, receiving first the Rhodesian Bronze Cross for "gallantry and determination in action," and the Silver Cross for "conspicuous gallantry and leadership in action."[7]

The author served for a short period with Mackenzie in Rhodesia in 1978, and found him to be intelligent, professional, and in combat, quite fearless. Known unofficially as "Captain Mack," he inspired a personal loyalty from the men serving under him, both native Rhodesian and foreign volunteer, that was quite extraordinary.

Andy Dennison, the ex-22 SAS man who betrayed John Banks' plot to send mercenaries into Rhodesia, went on to serve with distinction with the Rhodesian African Rifles. He rose to the rank of Major, and was decorated three times for bravery including made a Member of the Legion of Merit and Bronze Cross of Rhodesia for outstanding bravery whilst being seriously wounded. In July 1979, whilst off duty in a bar near Victoria Falls, a guerrilla attack happened nearby. Dennison grabbed his personal weapon and rushed outside to engage the enemy and was tragically shot dead by a black Rhodesian police officer.

With the Lancaster House agreement in 1980, the Rhodesian Bush War effectively ended. MacKenzie, McAleese, and many other foreign mercenary volunteers moved to South Africa and joined various units in the South African Defence Forces before departing for mercenary endeavours in other parts of the world.

It is estimated that between 800 - 2,000 foreign mercenary volunteers served with the Rhodesian forces during the Bush War, although the exact number will never be known. In the author's firm opinion, the Rhodesian recruitment and deployment of foreign mercenary volunteers was a major factor in its ability to continue the fight for as long as it did.

Africa
Togo
1978

After the reformation in 1950 the British SAS Regiment, its former members' considerable talents were continually in demand for mercenary operations. Mainly, they provided training or protection, and occasionally they fought in actual combat, but never sold their lethal skills as assassins. One of the few recorded exceptions to this general rule occurred in Togo in October 1977. A dozen or so ex-SAS members were hired by a retired Canadian officer to assassinate the President of Togo as well as his deputy. News of the impending assassination plot leaked out and came to the attention of MI6. The then-Cabinet Secretary, John Hunt, in a secret memo, informed the Prime Minster, Jim Callahan:

"They are thought still to be in this country. Clearly everything possible has to be done to prevent the operation being launched."[8]

MI6 contacted the SAS team leader and "persuaded" him to cancel the operation. The ex-Canadian officer at the centre of the plot fled to Switzerland. It would be another decade before ex-SAS members would be involved in a direct assassination attempt.

The Seychelles Coup Attempt 1981

When the Republic of Seychelles achieved its independence in June 1976, within a very short period of time, the leftist-leaning prime minister Francis-Albert René launched an armed coup against the more moderate President James Macham. In 1979, René discovered a CIA backed plot to oust him and promptly expelled several Americans suspected of involvement in the plot.

Later in 1979, René won internationally recognised elections, after which he pursued a socialist agenda as part of which South African landing rights to the country were withdrawn and there was a sharp deterioration of economic ties between both countries. René frequently warned that Macham's sympathizers were conspiring to use mercenaries to stage a counter coup, but these warnings were mostly dismissed by critics of the regime, who accused René of exaggeration or even fabrication as an excuse to jail political opponents.

In 1978, Macham approached the South African government through exiles based there, seeking support for a counter coup to oust René. René's hostile stance to the apartheid regime made them willing to sanction and support the counter coup. They set aside a number of their own elite reserve special forces unit, 2 Recognisance Commandoes (2 Recce) to take part in the operation. To lead and organise it, they directed Macham's representatives to "Mad Mike" Hoare. The South African government security agencies and SADF code named the attempted coup as Operation Angela. Hoare began recruiting mercenaries. In all, fifty-four were recruited, including twenty-seven members of the SADF (including the members of special forces the South African government had set aside), nine ex-Rhodesian soldiers, seven ex-Congo mercenaries from Hoare's old 5 Commando days, one South African Security agent called Dolinchek, and three civilians.

Hoare informed the assembled mercenary force that US$5 million would be raised for the operation, but only US$300,000 was at that moment available. The rest of the mercenaries' salaries were to come from the Seychelles Treasury once the coup was successful. Hoare dispatched nine members of his mercenary force to the island of Mahe in the Seychelles as an advance guard. Their purpose was to identify potential targets and rally support from dissident Seychellois soldiers. The main force, disguised as a visiting rugby players on holiday, arrived in a chartered plane on 25 November, 1981. Hidden in their luggage, under toys that were supposedly due to be handed out to local orphanages, were disassembled AK rifles.

Hoare's operational plan was for his mercenary force to rendezvous with the advance team then disperse around the island. After several days in hiding, when President René was holding a cabinet meeting, they would strike, seize the parliament, airport, radio station and other key installations. Once in control of the radio station they would broadcast that they had seized power on behalf of Macham. However, the plan almost immediately began to fall apart.

After disembarking from their aircraft, the majority of Hoare's mercenary force had made its way undetected through customs when a suspicious security officer began to search one of the two remaining mercenaries luggage. To his astonishment, he discovered it concealed an AK 47 rifle and raised the alarm. Faced with a tough-looking group of angry looking men, both customs officers ran for the exit. One of Hoare's men quickly pulled his own disassembled AK 47 from its concealed compartment, assembled and loaded it and shot the escaping customs man before he could reach the other side of the building. Still, the alarm was raised by other security staff.

Hoare's mercenary force attempted to continue with the coup, erecting a road block and mounting an unsuccessful attack on the nearby Pointe La Rue Barracks, during which one mercenary was wounded. The Seychelles security forces counter attacked with two armoured vehicles, which blocked and occupied the airstrip, and confined Hoare's mercenary force to the airport's buildings.

One of the armoured vehicles was driven to the terminal forecourt, but Hoare's mercenaries shot the vehicle's tires out, improvised Molotov cocktails and set it ablaze. The vehicle's commander, 2nd Lieutenant David Antat, emerged from the top and fired at the mercenaries, who counter attacked, and killed him.

During the height of the ensuing gun battle between Hoare's mercenaries and the Seychelles security forces, an Air India jet landed at the airport, damaging a flap on one of the trucks strewn on the runway. Hoare arranged a ceasefire to enable the aircraft's passengers to evacuate the combat zone. Seychelles security used the lull to pour more reinforcements into the area. After nearly six hours of fighting, Hoare realised that his position was hopeless. A decision was made to hijack the Air India jet. After boarding it, Hoare ordered the captain to fly him and his men to South Africa. During the flight, Hoare asked the captain if he could open the doors of the aircraft to allow his men to dispose of their weapons and was told this was not possible in a modern jet aircraft.

In the author's opinion, even if the attempted counter coup had not been foiled by the vigilance of the security guard at the airport, it is highly unlikely that it would have succeeded. The Seychelles exiles who proposed the counter coup assured both the South African government and Hoare that they would be assisted by a 400-strong "local resistance force" on the ground. In reality, no such force existed, and in the absence of such assistance, it was highly unlikely that Hoare's small force could have achieved its objectives.

From the total coup force, one mercenary was killed—SADF 2 Recce member Johan Fritz—and two were wounded. One Seychellois soldier, 2nd Lieutenant David Antat, was killed and a police sergeant was wounded. Back in the Seychelles, seven members of Hoare's advance team were arrested, charged with treason, and put on trial. Four—Aubrey Brookes (Rhodesia), Jerry Puren (South Africa) and Britons Bernard Carey and Roger England were all sentenced to death. Martin Dolinchek was sentenced to twenty years imprisonment, and Robert Sims was sentenced to ten years imprisonment. Charges were dismissed against Susan Ingles, Sims' common-law wife.

Following came negotiations between South Africa and the René regime in the Seychelles as well as a US$3 million payment made directly to President René. As a result, all six of the convicted mercenaries were pardoned by René and deported to South Africa in mid-1983. On landing in Durban, South Africa, Hoare and his mercenaries were arrested and charged under the Civil Aviation Offences Act, in relation to their hijacking of the Air India flight. After the intervention of the

South African government, which invoked Section 29(1) of the General Laws Amendment Act. This section effectively barred twenty-five of the accused and/or witnesses, who were all current or reserve members of the SADF, from providing evidence on matters concerning their involvement in SADF operations before 24 November, 1981. Only eight were set to face trial.

There was, of course, an international outcry at the South African stance. Claims were made in many political centres around the world that South Africa was condoning aircraft hijacking and air piracy. As a result, charges were levelled against all the mercenaries involved. Following a five-month trial in July 1982, Hoare was sentenced to ten years imprisonment. The trial judge observed on sentencing him that he was an unscrupulous person with "a highly cavalier attitude to the truth." The other mercenaries received sentences ranging from five years to suspended sentences.

Hoare was released from prison in May 1985 after serving just three years of his ten-year sentence as a result of a general amnesty announced in December 1984 by President Pieter W. Botha. He died of natural causes on 2 February, 2020 in a care facility in Durban at the age of 100. The apartheid South African Government always denied any knowledge or involvement in the attempted counter coup. After apartheid ended, as part of the Truth and Reconciliation Commission, there was an investigation into the Seychelles attempted counter coup, the Commission found:

"...that the attempt to overthrow the Seychelles Government was an operation undertaken by senior operatives of the NIS and the Department of Military Intelligence with the collusion of elements within the SADF. As such, it was a violation of international law and an infringement of the sovereignty of the Seychelles government. The death of a Seychelles citizen in the operation was a gross human rights violation.

For these acts, the Commission finds the following to be accountable in their capacities as heads of agencies of the state directly involved in the operation:

- Prime Minister P.W. Botha
- Minister of Defence General Magnus Malan
- Head of the office of Chief of Staff Intelligence: Lieutenant General P.W. van der Westhuizen, and The National Intelligence Service."[9]

The Maldives
1980 - 1988

The Maldives, in Southern Asia, is an archipelagos country in the Indian Ocean. Until 1979, the Royal Air Force had maintained a staging post on an atoll called Gan. From 1980 onwards the Maldives had remained steadfastly no-aligned, despite the international tensions in the politically sensitive area following the fall of the Shah of Iran and the Soviet invasion of Afghanistan.

In 1980, nine ex-members of 22 SAS, having been promised payment of £10,000 each, attempted a coup. The plan, such as it was, was for the team to seize the National Security Service headquarters and armoury in the capital of Male. This was, to say the least, ambitious as the mercenary team were only armed with a few .22 pistols and were relying on the element of surprise to succeed.

The team travelled to the Maldives posing as business men on a diving trip, but their cover quickly dissolved, given the absence of wives or girlfriends. Plus, they stood out like a bacon sandwich in a synagogue amongst the upper-class foreign tourists.

The Maldivian Government got wind of a mercenary "assassination squad" on the island and the team hurriedly abandoned the plot before they could be detained by local security services. In 1981, two of the alleged coup members, Harold Stanley Davidson, a former SAS staff sergeant, and Philip Anthony Sessarego, a former SAS corporal, signed confessions admitting their roles in the attempted coup. In the "confessions," Ahamed Naseem, brother-in-law of former Maldives President Ibrahim Nasir, was named as the mastermind behind the attempted coup.

The attempts by the nine ex-members of 22 SAS to stage a coup in 1980 was a half-baked, hairbrained idea and had more of the farce about it than a serious attempted coup. A far more determined attempted coup took place on 3 November, 1988, when Tamil mercenaries from the Sri Lankan rebel group the Peoples Liberation Organisation of Tamil Eelam (PLOTE), also known as "The Tamil Tigers" launched a concerted effort to overthrow the Maldives government.

Landing at dawn by speedboat from a hijacked Sri Lankan freighter, eighty PLOTE mercenaries and another eighty that had already infiltrated the capital Male earlier, quickly seized control of most of the capital. The coup was foiled by the direct military intervention of the Indian Army, code named Operation Cactus.

Indian paratroopers landed and quickly engaged the PLOTE mercenaries, in the ensuing gun battle nineteen Indian troops, eight members of Maldivian security services, and eleven Tamil PLOTE mercenaries were killed before the remaining PLOTE mercenaries surrendered. Businessman Abdullah Luthufi was named as the mastermind behind the plot, but was never prosecuted.

Afghanistan
1980 - 1985

In 1980, the Soviet Union invaded Afghanistan. In late 1981 Lieutenant Colonel Michael Rose, later General Sir Michael Rose, told the assembled rank of 22 SAS—of whom the author was one—that government approval had been given for the deployment of the SAS into Afghanistan to aid Afghani fighters in the war against the invader. The government, fearful of the political implications should SAS troops be killed or captured, cancelled the deployment.

Instead, they turned to a private British security firm Keenie Meenie Services (KMS) to undertake the task. The term "Keenie Meenie" was originally a Swahili term for the sinuous, unseen movements of a snake in tall grass and later became synonym for the slave trade. The term was adopted by the SAS in Aden to refer to any undercover work and therefore was further adopted by KMS on its foundation. KMS was originally founded in 1975 by Brigadier Mike Wingate Gray, Colonel Jim Johnson, Major David Walker and Major Andrew Nightingale, and provided bodyguard protection for British diplomats in Buenos Aires.

Before deployment into Afghanistan, the first KMS six-man infiltration squad received advance training at the SAS headquarters in Stirling Lines Hereford. Unfortunately, due to an Afghani traitor, the Soviets were pre-warned about the intended infiltration of the KMS unit and successfully ambushed it. After a fire fight, five escaped but one was killed. The Soviets identified him from papers on the body as Stuart Bodman. This proved to be a false identity and the actual identity of the KMS operative was never made public.

The Soviets also recovered a miniature satellite dish, a transmitter, and a computerised keyboard amongst other military equipment, which they displayed with undisguised glee to the world's press. Following the failure of the infiltration operation, KMS restricted its activities to training Afghani fighters outside of Afghanistan's borders. In the aftermath of the incident, in the British Parliament, MP Ron Brown asked the Secretary of State for Foreign and Commonwealth Affairs if "Mr. Stuart Bodman has received any public funds from his Department or represented Her Majesty's Government in Afghanistan in any capacity?" Sir Geoffrey Howe answered "No."[10]

Sri Lanka 1983 - 2009

The Sri Lankan Civil War fought between Singhalese-dominated Central Government and the minority Tamil population had its origins in violent anti-Tamil pogroms following the country's independence from Britain in 1948. The conflict broke out in earnest in July 1983 and lasted until 2009. The main Tamil rebel group, the Liberation Tigers of Tamil Eelam (LTTE)—also known as "The Tamil Tigers," led by Velupillai Prabhakaran—fought a bitter, prolonged war of attrition against the numerically superior Singhalese armed forces.

The aggressive and often suicidal attacks of the (LTTE) insurgents—many of who carried vials of poison around their necks to commit suicide rather than surrender—forced the Sri Lankan government to recruit and train a specialised counter insurgency unit to deal with them. This unit was named the Special Task Force (STF).

From the beginning of its formation in 1983, the STF was an elite unit. Although officially a police unit formed from the existing police force, it was and is, in reality, a heavily armed paramilitary unit that specialises in counter terrorism and counter insurgency operations. Initially, it was locally trained by the Sri Lankan army, and volunteers taught members how to use and handle infantry weapons as well as being given basic jungle warfare training. The first elements of the unit deployed into the North of Sri Lanka to help protect police stations from attacks by the LTTE separatists.

Training for the STF dramatically improved in 1983, when a group of former British SAS contract mercenaries were employed by the Sri Lankan government to train the unit. The British contract mercenaries trained the STF in sophisticated counter terrorism and counter insurgency techniques. The training took place in Katukurunda wing of the Sri Lankan Police College, and by the end of their one year contract, the British contract mercenaries had turned the STF into a highly effective paramilitary counter insurgency unit and the Katukurunda wing of the Sri Lankan Police College into a sophisticated training complex.

The author has spoken to many of the former British SAS contract mercenaries who served in Sri Lanka through this period. As the STF became better trained and began to go on more offensive operations against the LTTE separatists, their trainers received constant pressure to accompany them on operations; not to observe and advise, but to actually lead and take roles in actual combat. All refused, pointing out that they were contracted to train, not fight. At the end of their one year contracts, all but a very few left Sri Lanka and in 1983, Keenie Meenie Services (KMS) took over STF training.

It would seem that the KMS contract mercenaries did not have the same qualms about accompanying and taking part in STF operations. Whether this was part of their initial contract or whether contracted soldiers simply went off the reservation, the author cannot say. The fact that British contract mercenaries took part in combat operations would not, in itself, have raised much concern in Britain and around the world. After all, these mercenaries, with the explicit approval of the British government, have been contracted to fight in other combat zones.

In Sri Lanka, problems arose because of the combat activities of the STF, which was accused of several human rights abuses, including torture, summary executions without trial of rebel prisoners, and killings of unarmed Tamil civilians.[11] These atrocities, if true, were not only witnessed by the KMS contract mercenaries, but allegations have arose that they actually participated in many of them.

To give but one example of the massacres attributed to the STF, on 27 January 1987, STF officers were accused of raiding a prawn factory in the village, and shooting dead its workers, including seven boys ranging in age from 12 to 14 years old. The killings were dubbed "The Prawn Farm Massacre." According to the victims' relatives, the night before the massacre, locals witnessed government helicopters circling the area. The next morning, helicopters were seen dropping troops off, as they went on to slaughter dozens of Tamils. Some workers were taken to nearby road and shot dead. Forty people, who had been hiding in a nearby farm, were also killed.[12]

From witness evidence, it seems clear that KMS mercenaries flew the helicopters involved in these atrocities as *The Asia Times* reported in 2002: "The British pilots were seen flying helicopter gunship and air planes to bombard and attack innocent Tamil civilians in the Northern province, especially on the Jaffna Peninsula. These British mercenaries were paid a monthly salary of around £2,500 per person and other fringe benefits in order to actively participate in killing and maiming innocent Tamil civilians."[13]

Following the publication of the book *Keenie Meenie: The British Mercenaries Who Got Away with War Crimes* by Phil Miller, the Metropolitan Police launched an investigation into the activities of KMS in Sri Lanka, the first time British mercenaries were investigated by the Met, which is the UK force that's responsible for investigating accusations of war crimes or human rights abuses. No prosecutions were ever made as a result of the investigation.

KMS ceased operations after its involvement in Sri Lanka, and a new mercenary company, Saladin Security, took over many of its contracts. The KMS founder, David Walker, a former high-ranking officer in the British SAS has denied explicitly that any KMS personal were involved in war crimes in a statement issued in 2022 by a representative on his behalf stating: "The allegations that David Walker or staff of KMS Limited were complicit in war crimes in Sri Lanka in the mid-1980s is categorically denied. [Saladin Security] is an entirely separate company from KMS and had no involvement in Sri Lanka. Mr. Walker was neither a shareholder nor director of KMS. The [War Crimes] Unit has not yet asked for assistance from Saladin or Mr. Walker, but they will be happy to cooperate if asked."[14]

The Sri Lankan conflict ended with the defeat of LTTE rebel insurgents in May 2009. The fighting killed an estimated 100,000 people and left about 20,000, mostly Tamils, missing. At the end of the war, the United Nations accused both sides of atrocities, especially during the conflict's final stages, and in 2020, Sri Lanka's president acknowledged for the first time that those who had disappeared were, in fact, dead.

Africa
Sierra Leone
1991 - 2001

In 1961, Sierra Leone gained its independence from Great Britain. Siaka Stevens became prime minister in 1968. A populist, Stevens officially connected the country's diamond mines to political power and profit. He nationalized the diamond mines and encouraged illicit mining to gain even more political power. Stevens and a Lebanese businessman called Jamil Mohammed eventually took control of the diamond mines. At the end of Stevens' seventeen years in power, his successor, Joseph Momoh, took control of Sierra Leone. Momoh was politically inept, and placed even more responsibility into Mohammed's hands. As a result, illicit diamond mining flourished in Sierra Leone. By 1991, due to the open political corruption, blatant illicit diamond mining made the country vulnerable to armed rebellion.

A civil war broke out on 23 March, 1991, when the Revolutionary United Front (RUF), 100 fighters from Liberia and Sierra Leone, led by Foday Sankoh, an ex-army sergeant, invaded east Sierra Leone. The RUF was supported by the special forces of Charles Taylor's National Patriotic Front of Liberation (NPFL). Sankoh claimed he represented the oppressed poor and promised a greater share of the country's wealth to them, but the reality was very different, indeed. In the next nine years, the RUF and NPFL would unleash a reign of terror characterised by drugged child soldiers and a campaign of indiscriminate violence that would see women and children with their limbs hacked off. Rape of women and girls was also a widespread atrocity. RUF members of the RUF primarily perpetrated this brutal tactic as a tool of war to terrorize the civilian population into submission and break apart families and communities.

By March 1995, the RUF advanced to within twenty miles of Freetown, the capital of Sierra Leone. It was at this time the mercenary company Executive Outcomes entered the conflict. Based in South Africa, Executive Outcomes fielded a force of 500 military advisers and a force of 3,000 trained and well-equipped combat soldiers backed by tactical air support and transport.

Many of the black troops deployed by Executive Outcomes were former members of the South Africa's apartheid era crack anti-guerrilla unit, 32 Battalion. The Sierra Leone Government paid Executive Options $1.8 million a month—with funds coming primarily from the International Monetary Fund—to conduct its military campaign.

Executive Outcomes

Simon Francis Mann, a former officer in the Scots Guards and the 22 SAS Regiment, had formed the Executive Outcomes mercenary company in 1993. In the same year, Executive Outcomes carried out its first major mercenary operation. After the valuable oil tanks at Kefekwena in Angola were overrun by UNITA rebels in 1993, the then-president of Angola, Jose Eduardo dos Santos, hired them to retake the facility. Executive Options hired many ex-members of South Africa's crack mixed race anti-insurgency unit, 32 Battalion, to carry out the mission.[15]

The operation was not as simple as the planners had expected: thousands of UNITA troops had moved into the area and put up fierce resistance to the mercenary assault. Several mercenaries were wounded and three died in action, and over two dozen chose to terminate their contracts and were evacuated after just a few days. Those that chose to stay on were paid a bonus of $3,000. Executive Options then went on to play a significant role during this episode of the Angolan conflict, influencing both its course, duration, and the final victory of the government forces.[16] Mann would later claim that his operations in support of the government of Jose Eduardo dos Santos in Angola had netted him more than £10,000,000.[17]

Executive Outcomes mainly employed ex-members of the South African (SADF) special forces, almost exclusively former members of either the Reconnaissance Commandoes, or 32 Battalion. Their reliance on these battle-trained former special forces troops was well founded. As the reader will know from the introduction in this book the author was a former member of Reconnaissance Commandoes. In his opinion, whatever the reader's opinion is of the apartheid regime in South Africa, these two units—with the exception of the British SAS and America's Seal Team 6—were the finest special forces in the world.

The Reconnaissance Commandoes comprised of 4 Commandoes: No. 1 Commando was the regular front line unit, No. 2 Commando was a reserve unit whose members were called up for major operations, there was no No. 3 Commando, No. 4 Commando was a specialist boat unit and No. 5 Commando was a mixed-race unit.

32 Battalion was also a mixed-race unit; many of its original members were ex-Portuguese special forces who had fought in Mozambique during its colonial war. Both units had a gruelling six month selection course comprising a selection phase, a bush craft tracking and survival phase, and a weapons and tactics phase, at the end of the which most new members were "bloodied" in an actual operation.

One exception to the general employment of ex-SADF members by Executive Outcomes was a former Fijian member of 22 SAS, Kauata "Big Fred" Marafano MBE, who the author had the privilege of serving with in his two tours with the SAS. A well-respected veteran of military campaigns ranging from Aden through Borneo to the Falklands War and Northern Ireland, the citation for his MBE encapsulated everything that needed to be said about "Big Fred." It read:

"It is doubtful whether any officer or NCO can equal the number of operations which WO1 Marafono has volunteered for and taken part in. On all, his standards of leadership and gallantry have been a positive inspiration to subordinates and superiors who have come into contact with him. Many anti-terrorist techniques currently in use in Northern Ireland and in the UK are the result of his unstinting work and clear vision."[18]

Executive Outcomes in Sierra Leone

As a fighting force, Executive Outcomes proved to be particularly effective in launching a successful military campaign against the RUF. In only ten days, it drove the RUF rebel forces back sixty miles. Eventually, with the support of local militia units, it recaptured many of the diamond fields originally captured by the RUF. In the next seven months, they recaptured almost all the territory taken by the RUF, destroyed its main base of operations and forced the RUF to admit defeat and sign the Abidjan Peace Accord on 30 November, 1996. A period of relative peace followed, allowing the troubled country to hold both parliamentary and presidential elections, which were eventually won by Ahmad Tejan Kabbah.

"Mac" MacKenzie and the Sierra Leone Commando Unit (SLCU)

Quite apart from the Executive Outcomes operation, in January 1995, the country's leader, Valentine Strasser, began to organise a force to counter the RUF, and his right hand man Major Tarawali contracted sixty Gurkhas of the mercenary company Gurkha Security Guards (GSG) to train 160 green troopers to form the nucleus of an independent strike force to be called the Sierra Leone Commando Unit (SLCU).

To lead them, Tarawali hired Robert Callen MacKenzie, the former American commander of 'C' Squadron Rhodesian SAS. MacKenzie arrived in Sierra Leone in late January 1995 and, whilst scouting for a possible location for a training camp, stumbled upon a village that had been devastated in an RUF attack. The RUF were still in the vicinity. MacKenzie and two GSG members, Borlace and Tarawali, persuaded their reluctant green troops to pursue them by leading from the front. The RUF broke and ran, instilling an immediate fighting spirit into the SLCU. On 17 February, 1995, MacKenzie was leading a convoy of his SLCU deep inside territory controlled by the RUF when it was ambushed. MacKenzie successfully led his combined Gurkha and SLCU in a counter attack that forced the RUF to flee into the undergrowth.

This success was, however, to have tragic consequences, deluding the Sierra Leone high command as to both the effectiveness of the SLCU and the ineffectiveness of the RUF. As a result, they ordered MacKenzie to attack the RUF base camp in the Malal Hills. MacKenzie objected strongly to the proposed attack, pointing out that the SLCU was not yet ready to face major combat and that the Gurkhas—whom he was ordered to take with him—were contracted for training alone and not for combat.

Despite his objections, the orders stood. MacKenzie reluctantly agreed to carry out the assault. Gathering what little intelligence he could, MacKenzie prepared for the assault. Prior to the assault itself, jets borrowed from the Nigerians were to drop cluster bombs on the rebel positions to soften them. However, they bombed the wrong hill. Alerted by the bombing, the RUF were ready and waiting for MacKenzie's assault.

MacKenzie was, as always, leading from up front with Tarawali and Lieutenant Andy Myers of the GSG. The attacking force immediately came under a deadly hail of fire. Tarawali perished in the very first volley, and his body was initially recovered but then dropped by fleeing SLCU troops, who trampled Gurkha medics travelling behind the advancing party in their panic.

MacKenzie ordered a retreat, but as he began to organise it, the senior Gurkha medic saw MacKenzie take two rounds through his legs and one through his back. MacKenzie dropped his rifle and fell. As Lieutenant

Myers attempted to give him assistance, he too was shot. Neither were ever seen again. Intercepts of RUF radio traffic later revealed that they had taken Tarawali's and MacKenzie's bodies, but there was no word on Myers. He would be later presumed dead at 9:00 on 24 February, 1995. "Mac" MacKenzie died as he had lived: as a professional soldier to the end.

Fred Marafano in Sierra Leone

Executive Outcomes left Sierra Leone in 1997, after which the RUF resumed its activities. The nine-year civil war claimed over 75,000 lives, caused 500,000 natives to become refugees, and displaced about half of the country's 4.5 million people. Finally, in July 1999, the RUF and the President of Sierra Leone, Ahmad Tejan Kabbah, signed the Lome Peace Accord. The RUF, under pressure from the UN and the US government, agreed to surrender its forces in exchange for a share in Sierra Leone's government.

The accord brought only short-lived peace: on 6 January, 2000, just seven months after it was signed, RUF again revived its attacks despite its promises to surrender its forces; but the RUF never did. Due to the continuing conflict, the UN issued a ban on non-governmental diamonds for Sierra Leone. "Big Fred" Marafano stayed in the country after Executive Outcomes left and in 1997, formed his own security company, Vanguard International, which worked to support the Sierra Leonean government forces against the RUF rebels. He was intensely committed to the cause of the Sierra Leone people in their struggle against the RUF's barbarity.

In 2000, he provided support during the daring SAS led Operation Barras, launched to free Royal Irish regiment soldiers held by the "West Side Boys" militia. Just three months shy of turning 60 years old, he hovered overhead providing top cover from a Hind gunship. The operation was a total success, but sadly, one SAS corporal was killed as the hostages were being evacuated.

When Marafano left Sierra Leone in December 2006, around his neck was a necklace that contained a lion's tooth, confirming his position as an honorary member of the Kamajor, which was a militia that comprised local hunters of the Mende tribe in Sierra Leone. He died of natural causes in March 2013, aged 72, and is buried in the SAS Regimental plot in Hereford.

Chapter Four

Cuba
1950 - 1980

In the 1950s, the blatant corruption and oppression of the military dictatorship of Fulgencio Batista was clear for all the world to see. Most of the country's sugar industry was in US hands, and Batista exploited its commercial interests by negotiating lucrative commercial deals with the American Mafia. His secret police kept order by carrying out wide-scale acts of violence, torture, and public executions. Rebels took to the hills, determined to oust the brutal and corrupt dictator.

One American decided to put his military training to good use by becoming a mercenary and joining the fight to oust Batista. His name was William Alexander Morgan. Morgan was born in Cleveland, Ohio on 9 April, 1928, and joined the US Army after the Second World War, serving with B Company, 35th Infantry Regiment, in Japan, where he became highly skilled with firearms. During that time, he went absent without official leave (AWOL), was arrested, escaped custody by overpowering a guard, then was recaptured and court martialled. In 1941, he was dishonourably discharged from the Army and served two years in federal prison.

Violently opposed to the Batista Regime, Morgan left behind his wife and child in 1957 and travelled to Cuba. On arriving he made contact with and joined a guerrilla force operating in the Escambray Mountains in central Cuba called the *Segunda Frente Nacional de Escambray* (SFNE). Morgan set about training and leading the group in operations against Batista's soldiers, and his military training and weapons expertise enabled him to lead the group in many successful ambushes. As a result, he was promoted to *comandante* and given command of his own column. He explained his motivation in an article in *The New York Times*:

> "I am here because I believe that the most important thing for free men to do is to protect the freedom of others. I am here so that my

> son, when he is grown, will not have to fight or die in a land not his own, because one man or group of men try to take his liberty from him. I am here because I believe that free men should take up arms and stand together and fight and destroy the groups and forces that want to take the rights of people away."[1]

Castro's leading revolutionary, Che Guevara, joined Morgan's group in the mountains in December 1958. Within days, their combined forces had captured the city of Santa Clara on 31 December, 1958. Twelve hours later, Batista fled the country. The combined guerrilla group then went on to take the city of Cienfuegos on 1 January, 1959. Just two months later, Morgan was warned by officials of the US Embassy in Havana that his participation in the revolution was putting in jeopardy his US citizenship. In August 1959, Morgan was instrumental in smashing a counter coup by the Dominican Republican strongman Rafael Trujillo. He had initially promised Trujillo that he would lead the coup, but instead informed Castro of it. In September 1959, the US State Department revoked his citizenship.

Morgan decided to settle in Cuba and married a fellow Cuban revolutionary, Olga María Rodríguez Farinas. He renounced his US citizenship on 24 September, 1959, and developed a business of frog farming. He sold the legs to restaurants, the skin for fashion accessories, and the rest for grinding down for cattle feed. The business was highly successful: he employed over 600 workers and exported 50,000 pounds of frozen frog legs every month to the US.

When the French freighter *La Coubre* exploded in Havana Harbour on 6 March, 1960, killing over 100 people, an American called Jack Lee Evans linked Morgan to the explosion. Morgan denied any involvement and attended the memorial service in Havana along with Castro and Che Guevara. However, this show of solidarity between the erstwhile revolutionary comrades would not last. Throughout the struggle to overthrow Batista, Morgan always maintained vocally that Castro and Che Guevara were not communists, but patriots fighting to free their country from dictatorship.

When both Castro and Guevara began to show their true colours—imposing on Cuba a strict communist doctrine and subjecting many of his former guerrilla comrades who opposed it to arrest, mock show trials and execution, it was all too much for Morgan. He decided once again to take up arms against the new oppressor and began to organize the smuggling of weapons to the counter-revolutionaries in the Escambray mountains.

Betrayed by informants, Morgan was arrested on 19 October, 1960, on the direct orders of Castro and, after a short show trial, he was executed by firing squad on 11 March, 1961. He was only 32 years old. Both Fidel Castro and his brother Raul attended the execution. In 2002, Morgan's body was returned to the US, and in April 2007, his citizenship was posthumously restored.

One month after Morgan's execution in Havana, a mercenary debacle occurred in Cuba that would ultimately lead the entire world to the precipice of nuclear war. The Eisenhower administration distrusted Castro's close ties with Nikita Khrushchev, the then-leader of the Soviet Union. In response to the perceived threat only 80 miles off US soil, Eisenhower gave the Central Intelligence Agency (CIA) the green light to begin planning for the military removal of the new Cuban regime.

Before becoming President, John F. Kennedy was briefed on the plan by the CIA, which involved the training of Cuban exiles into an effective fighting brigade, deploying them into Cuba where it was anticipated that Cuban people and elements of the military would rise up in support of the planned invasion. The ultimate goal was to overthrow Castro and establish a non-communist government that was friendly to the United States. What Kennedy was not told was that the CIA task force that was in charge of the paramilitary assault did not think it could succeed without becoming an open invasion that was supported by the American military. President-elect Kennedy never saw the brief that included the assessment.[2]

In March 1960, the CIA erected training camps in Guatemala and began recruiting and organising in preparation for the planned invasion. Brigade 2506, as it was named, was made of Cuban exiles, composed mainly of determined but inexperienced youths who dreamed of "liberating Cuba from Castro" and who fled Cuba after the revolution to form the armed wing of the Democratic Front (DRF). US military personnel also formed part of the unit and conducted training. From the very onset, the invasion plan—which depended heavily on surprise to succeed—was doomed to failure. The invasion plans, despite the CIA's efforts to keep them covert, became common knowledge among Cuban exiles in Miami, many of whom had relatives who had volunteered for Brigade 2506. Cuban intelligence quickly learnt of the mercenary training camps in Guatemala. In addition, in as early as October 1960, the American press reported widely on events as they unfolded.

The invasion plan proposed to Kennedy was ambitious, involving two air strikes against Cuban air bases, before a 1,400-man invasion force invaded under cover of darkness to launch a surprise attack. There were additional plans for paratroopers to be dropped in advance of the invasion to disrupt Cuban forces. Simultaneously, a smaller force would land on Cuba's east coast to create confusion.

The site chosen for the invasion was a remote, swampy area on the southern coast of Cuba, where it was hoped that a night landing might allow mercenary forces to land with little or no opposition. It would also help to hide any US involvement. Strategically, the site could not have been more badly chosen, as it was more than 80 miles from Cuba's Escambray Mountains, the only possible refuge if anything went wrong. On successful landing, the mercenary force planned to advance across the island to Matanzas and set up a defensive position. The United Revolutionary Front would then send leaders from South Florida and establish a provisional government, headed by José Miró Cardona, a former member of Castro's government.

In February 1961, shortly after his inauguration, President Kennedy authorized the invasion plan. Almost immediately, the plan started to go wrong. On 15 April, 1961, eight bombers—obsolete Second World War B-26 bombers painted to look like Cuban air force planes—left Nicaragua to bomb Cuban airfields. The subsequent air strikes missed almost all their targets and left most of Castro's air force intact. As news broke of the attack, newspaper photos of the planes used in the attack showed that they were repainted US planes, revealing to the world the US support for the invasion. As a result, President Kennedy cancelled a second air strike.

On 17 April, 1961, Brigade 2506 landed on the beaches along the Bay of Pigs. Che Guevara played no role in the subsequent fighting, because a day before the invasion, a marine-laden warship faked an invasion off the West Coast of Pinar del Rio and drew forces commanded by Guevara to that region. From the first minutes of the invasion, the mercenary force came under heavy fire, initially from local farmers and villagers, armed in advance, who took up arms and bought crucial time for Castro's main Revolutionary Army to arrive.

Cuban planes that should have been destroyed prior to the invasion, bombarded the invaders, sank two escort ships, and destroyed half the exile's air support. In addition, bad weather hampered the ground force, forcing it to work with soggy equipment and insufficient ammunition. Then the Cuban Revolutionary Army counter attacked with roughly 20,000 troops. Heavily outnumbered and out-gunned, the situation for the invading mercenary force became critical. Despite his intention to keep US involvement in the invasion a secret, under pressure from the CIA, President Kennedy gave permission for American pilots to fly six aircraft over the beaches. Pilots were instructed that if they were shot down and captured, they should describe themselves as mercenaries and that the US would "deny any knowledge of them."[3]

The "air umbrella" that Kennedy authorised arrived too late and was not sufficient for the task set for them. All of the planes were shot down by intense Cuban anti-aircraft fire. The mercenary invasion was crushed later that day. A few of Brigade 2506 escaped by sea, 1,200 surrendered, and more than 100 were killed. Cuban losses numbered over 300, 176 of whom were farmers and villagers who took up arms once the invasion began. Four US airmen perished, and it wasn't until 1976 that the men were awarded medals in ceremonies that their families were encouraged to keep secret.[4]

The captured members of Brigade 2506 were kept captive in appalling conditions for twenty months. After negotiations with the US, in exchange for $53 million worth of baby food and medicine, Castro agreed to their release. The first plane load of Brigade 2506 survivors landed in the US on 23 December, 1962. On Sunday, 29 December, what was left of Brigade 2506 held a ceremony in Miami. The Brigade's flag was handed to President Kennedy, who assured attendees that the flag would be returned to the brigade in a "free" Havana, a promise never fulfilled.

The Bay of Pigs mercenary invasion was a disaster both in its planning and execution. The mercenary force trained by the CIA was simply not up to the task set for them. It reality, the plan could not have succeeded without full participation of US ground and air forces, something Kennedy was simply not willing to even consider. In the aftermath of the disaster, the Kennedy administration, determined to make up for the failed invasion, initiated Operation Mongoose, a plan to sabotage and destabilise the Cuban government and economy. The plan also included sometimes impossibly ludicrous plans to assassinate Castro, including a plot to utilise exploding cigars. This had the effect of pushing Castro's Cuba into even closer ties with the Soviet Union. Ultimately, allowing them to deploy nuclear missiles in Cuba and leading the whole world to the brink of nuclear war was what the world would come to call "The Cuban Missile Crisis."

China/French Indo China/Laos/Vietnam "Air America" 1950 - 1975

Origins

What does an American President do if he wants to extract an agent inside a hostile country without starting a war, or carry out deniable air operations in support of a foreign country's war, or carry out air operations in a country his armed forces are forbidden by treaty from entering? The answer is simple: you convince your intelligence service (CIA) to buy an airline, staff it with contractors (mercenaries) and get them to undertake the task. The resulting organisation became known as "Air America."

There is a complex history about who actually owned Air America; in fact, it was owned by the American government and managed, at least initially, by the CIA. Later, civilian CEOs managed operations. The company's origins date to 1946 when it was named Civil Air Transport (CAT). The owners were General Claire Chennault and Whiting Willauer. Chennault led the famous mercenary squadron called "The Flying Tigers" during the Second World War.

Civil War erupted in 1945 between Chiang Kai-Shek's Nationalists and the Chinese Communist Party led by Mao Tse-tung (aka Chairman Mao), and CAT flew missions in support of the Nationalists and helped them flee to Formosa in 1949 when they lost the war on mainland China. Following the relocation of the Nationalist forces, CAT no longer had a mission and was almost bankrupt. Chennault turned to the US State Department to purchase the airline. The CIA was immediately interested, seeing CAT as a means of intelligence-gathering operations in China. However the State

Department did not want clear ownership of a Chinese company, so the CIA devised a plan for indirect ownership.

Ultimately, CAT was purchased by a U.S. Government-owned corporation in Delaware, which in turn create a subsidiary to disguise the actual owner. The subsidiary was named CAT, Inc. CAT was to have multiple customers over the coming years that included the USAF, the CIA, the US Army Special Forces, and the French Republic, all of which provided income to the airline while keeping the ownership of the company secret. During the Korean War, CAT took part in Operation Book Lift for Far East Material Command. Although the operation was short-lived, CAT pilots performed particularly well, although at least five pilots died during operations.

China

In a covert operation in November 1952, two mercenary CAT pilots, Norman Schwartz and Robert Snoddy—both Second World War decorated veterans—were assigned to extract an agent from Manchuria in Communist China using a newly-developed extraction technique: flying at a low altitude and slow speed with a hook designed to snag on a specially-designed harness worn by the agent. Tragically, the Communist Chinese were forewarned and laid an ambush and shot the air craft down. Schwartz and Snoddy were killed in the resulting crash. CIA agents Richard Fecteau and John Downey were on board the crashed plane, survived and were captured. Both were sentenced to imprisonment for twenty years. Nearly two decades later they were released and made their way out of communist China.

French Indo China

During the colonial war in French Indio China—later Vietnam—France requested American military air cargo support. Then-President Eisenhower was reluctant to involve the US military in a war that was unpopular both at home and in France. Instead, CAT Inc. was given a contract to carry out the mission. After secret training in the Philippines, CAT pilots flew C-119 planes, a military plane that they flew against FAA regulations, in support of the French Army in Indio China. The planes were painted in French colours to further disguise American involvement in the conflict.

Flying supply missions into combat zones in any war is inherently dangerous, and several CAT pilots and crew were wounded during operations. In 1954, whilst supplying French forces on the ground at the pivotal battle of Dien Bien Phu, two CAT pilots—James McGovern and Wallace Buford—were shot down and killed by Viet-Minh anti-aircraft fire. The US Government never acknowledged their deaths. On 24 February, 2005, French president Jacques Chirac posthumously awarded James McGovern and Wallace Buford the Legion of Honour award along with the rank of knight (chevalier), and six other surviving CAT pilots were similarly decorated. The partial remains of both McGovern and Buford were recovered in Laos at war's end.

Indonesia

The Permesta, a rebel movement in Indonesia, started military rebellion against the government, led by left-leaning President Sukarno, in East Indonesia on 2 March, 1957. The centre of the movement was in Manado, and the movement was led by Colonel Ventje Sumual. In 1958, the Eisenhower administration's eyes turned towards Indonesia. Eisenhower believed that under Sukarno, Indonesia might become a communist state and wanted to aid the Permesta, but could not directly use the US military. The solution as always was to turn to CAT Inc. In 1958, a number of CAT Inc. pilots were dispatched to the Philippines to support the rebellion. They flew B-26 planes painted black with the markings obscured, in both supply and bombing runs in support of Permesta rebel ground forces. One of the CAT Inc. pilots involved in the operation was Allen Pope.

Pope was a highly decorated Korean War pilot, and had been awarded three Air Medals and the Distinguished Flying Cross. On leaving the USAF, he joined CAT Inc. in 1954. Pope was shot down (but survived) on a bombing run before being captured in 1958. Initially sentenced to death by an Indonesian military court, Bobby Kennedy intervened and a negotiated amnesty was arranged in 1962. After his release, Pope left CAT Inc. In 2005, he was one of the six living CAT Inc. pilots that were awarded the Legion of Honour by French President Jacques Chirac.

Laos/Vietnam

In the early 1960s, first Eisenhower and later John F. Kennedy saw Laos was the "key to the entire area of Southeast Asia," fearing a Pathet Lao

Communist takeover of the country could create a domino effect that would result in the fall of neighbouring countries—including Thailand—to communism.[5] US Special Forces had been in Laos, training Lao troops, since 1959 under Project Hotfoot, and President Kennedy sent a carrier task force to the Gulf of Siam in April 1961 to support the incumbent government.

Under the terms of the 1962 Geneva Accord, an agreement between the United States, the Soviet Union, China, North Vietnam, Burma, Cambodia, Thailand, South Vietnam, France, India, Poland, Canada, and Laos, all American troops departed Laos. Despite signing the Geneva Accord, North Vietnam remained in Laos, using the country to transport troops and supplies along the Lao-Vietnam border into South Vietnam to attack Americans and South Vietnamese troops.

The CIA decided—with the direct approval of the Presidency—to conduct a covert and clandestine operation inside Laos to halt the flow of North Vietnamese troops and equipment into Vietnam. For logistical support, they turned to Air America. Between 1962 and 1974, Air America provided logistical support both for the Royal Lao Army and Hmong Army, commanded General Vang Pao. In addition, it inserted and extracted U.S. personnel, flew photo reconnaissance missions and search-and-rescue missions for American pilots downed throughout Southeast Asia. In January 1968, two Russian-built AN-2 Colts bombed a U.S. Air Force radar site, and the crew of an Air America helicopter loaded with supplies observed the attack. Ted Moore, the helicopter pilot, flew alongside one of the attacking aircraft, and his mechanic, Glen Woods, shot down the plane using a survival rifle. It was the first time a helicopter had ever downed a military fixed-wing aircraft.

Controversy exists to this day on Air America's role in drugs trade in Southeast Asia. Undoubtedly, its planes carried drugs during the covert war in Laos. One of the main rebel forces used by the CIA to fight the Pathet Loa communist rebels was the Hmong mountain population, which depended on poppy cultivation for hard currency, which was used to fund their war. Air American pilots have been accused of directly profiting from the drug trade[6] or of turning a blind eye to it. Historians still differ on whether or not the CIA and Air America were wilfully involved in the opium trade.[7]

Wherever the truth lies, what cannot be denied is the bravery of the Air American pilots on the ground, especially in the rescuing downed

American and Laotian pilots in hostile country. Air America suffered many casualties during such operations. The war in Laos ended in 1974, after which many Air America pilots left the airline, a few went to Vietnam, where their work was more administrative, including assisting in the final evacuation from Saigon. Within a year of the end of the Vietnam war, the US Government sold Air America assets, with profits going to the US Treasury. In twenty-five years, Air America suffered approximately 186 killed in action, with 35 per cent occurring between 1969 and 1973.[8]

El Salvador 1980 - ?

In the 1980s and 1990s, the United States saw Central and South America as its own "back yard." In its attempts to prevent the expansion of communism, American administration after administration was willing to provide financial and military support to some of the most despicable and brutal regimes ever seen in history. This was never truer than in the Central American country of El Salvador.

The civil war that erupted in the country the 1980s saw the FNLA leftist guerrilla movement, recruited mainly from the peasant class in the country, supported by the Soviet Union, fighting a brutal alliance of countries, oligarchs and generals that, with US support, ruled the country for decades. The main aim of the unholy government alliance was to keep peasants illiterate and impoverished. What resulted was a vicious, bloody, dirty war.

At least 75,000 Salvadorans—although the true figure will never be known—were killed in the fighting. Most were unfortunate victims of the military and its death squads. Massacres were commonplace, as the government forces pursued "scorched earth" policies. Peasants were shot *en masse*, often while trying to flee. Student and union leaders had their thumbs tied behind their backs before being shot in the head, their bodies left on roadsides as a warning to others. Although officially banned from taking part in military operations, twenty-one American "advisors" were killed whilst fighting alongside government forces, and over 5,000 served in the country during the civil war.[9]

American and other foreign mercenaries fought on both sides during the bitter conflict. One of those who fought on the guerrilla side was American

Carroll Ishee, who had been active in movements opposing United States participation in the Vietnam War and in civil rights organizations, before leaving his wife and 12-year-old daughter in his home town of New Orleans, to go to El Salvador. There, in 1981, he joined one of the leftist FNLA guerrilla groups fighting the government forces and fought with them for two years.

In August 1983, he was killed in a helicopter attack by US-led government forces near the town of El Flamenco. His reported last words were: "Tell my wife, my daughter and my American people that I have died fulfilling my obligation." He was the second American mercenary to be killed in the conflict. In early May 1982, David Anderson had been killed in the same area. They were part of an estimated two dozen American mercenaries who fought on behalf of the leftist guerrilla movements during the conflict.[10]

After the FNLA confirmed Ishee's death, the Salvadorian army issued the following announcement confirming "foreign meddling" in the war on behalf of the guerrillas: "As with this mercenary, there are many directors of various nationalities that are in charge of ordering the destruction of the people's property that has cost the Salvadoran people so much sweat." The communiqué then went on to list the names of eight other foreigners "in key posts of the terrorist directorate from West Germany, Belgium, Venezuela, Colombia and Mexico."[11]

Unlike William Morgan in Cuba, Carroll Ishee is not recorded to have had any military training or skills prior to his joining the FLNA. It is also clear that he received no payment for risking his life in a combat zone. He and the other American and foreign volunteers that fought for the FNLA in El Salvador have been described as "Internationalists Mercenaries"[12] but whether they can truly be described as such is debateable.

On the other side of the equation, US Vietnam veterans *did* travel to El Salvador on a number of occasions to provide military and medical training to Salvadoran troops. The group was made up primarily of the editors of the gung ho mercenary magazine *Solders of Fortune*, including Alexander McColl, a colonel in the US former special forces. The group's "expenses" were paid by the magazine. They denied being mercenaries, instead describing themselves as "adventurers."

Whilst in country they carried handguns for "self-defence" and were reported to have accompanied Salvadorian troops on combat missions.[13]

The group's activities in El Salvador did not have official US approval, but seemed to have the tacit support of the US government. When asked to comment about the Soldier of Fortune group, embassy spokesman Donald R. Hamilton was quoted as saying, "We want to encourage private, voluntary efforts to help the Salvadorans."[14]

The group of mercenary ex-Vietnam veterans worked closely with the Atlacatl Battalion of the Salvadorian army and trained them on sniping, explosives, and weapons maintenance. Later pictures published in *Soldier of Fortune* magazine showed a Salvadoran soldier and two members of the magazine group crouching in the brush around the bodies of two dead "Gs." ("Gs" are enemy guerrillas) The picture was a trophy photograph reminiscent of a hunter displaying a kill.[15]

The Atlacatl Battalion, named after a legendary indigenous figure from the Spanish conquest of El Salvador who fought against the Spanish conquistadors, was established in 1981. It was an airborne, rapid-response unit and was directly implicated in almost every massacre during the civil war—including the El Mozote massacre the El Calabozo massacre as well as the 1989 murder of six Jesuit priests. When the Chapultepec Peace Accords ended the civil war, the Battalion was disbanded in 1992.

Nicaragua 1979 - 1990

The attempts to undermine and overthrow the Marxist Sandinista government in Nicaragua by the United States authorities between 1979 and 1990, if written as a piece of fiction, would in all probability be rejected by any reputable publisher as being too improbable to be worth publishing. Unfortunately, for the land of the free and the home of the brave, they happen to be true.

The United States occupied Nicaragua in 1912 in what was termed "The Banana Wars." Following the departure of US forces, the brutal and corrupt regime of the Somoza family came to power. The Sandinista National Liberation Front (aka FSLN) ousted the last of the Somoza family dictators Anastasio Somoza Debayle in 1970 after a year-long military campaign. In the United States, the Sandinista victory was seen as a direct threat to its economic, political, and military influence in the region. In 1983, President Reagan stated that "The defence of southern frontier was at stake."[16] and the US imposed severe sanctions and embargoes on Nicaragua which had a crippling effect on its economy. It also decided on direct military intervention on the ground.

What followed was a decade-long proxy war between an exiled mercenary group that was called "The Contras" and financed, trained, and armed by the CIA and the Sandinista government, and backed by the Soviet Union and Cuba. It would mire the Reagan administration in scandal with allegations of drug smuggling, illegal arms shipments to Iran, and atrocities committed on a colossal scale by the Contra mercenary forces as directed and sanctioned by the CIA.

What would eventually became known as "The Contras" was actually made up of an amalgamation of three distinct groups: ex-guardsmen of the Nicaraguan National Guard who served under the ex-dictator Somoza; anti-Somozistas who supported the revolution but felt betrayed by the Sandinista government; and finally, groups of Nicaraguans who had no actual involvement in the revolution, but opposed the Sandinistas for various reasons.

The US through the CIA saw these desperate groups as a potential guerrilla army that could be used against the Sandinista government. With the assistance of Argentinian Intelligence, they sought to unify them. By June 1985, they were able to unify most Contra groups into the United Nicaraguan Opposition (UNO) and when the UNO dissolved in 1987, it was replaced by the Nicaraguan Resistance (RN).

The training of Contra mercenary force was undertaken by both CIA paramilitary "contractors," many of them gung ho veterans of the failed Bay of Pigs invasion of Cuba, and British ex-members of the 22 SAS, supplied by Keenie Meenie Services (KMS). The resulting mercenary force they put into the field to overthrow the Sandinistas achieved little in the way of military success on the battlefield, but it was good at spreading terror. During the course of the conflict and following guerrilla manuals provided by their trainers, Contras launched a systematic wave of terror inside Nicaragua, assassinating civilian leaders and government officials, and by attacking soft targets such as schools, health clinics, and Sandinista cooperatives.

These atrocities were not the work of isolated bands of Contras who had gone off the reservation. Nor were they committed because the Contras themselves were inherently undisciplined savages. They were, in fact, part of a carefully laid out campaign of terror outlined in a manual prepared especially for the Contras by the CIA called *Psychological Operations in Guerrilla Warfare*. The ninety-page book of instructions recommended "selective use of violence for propagandistic effects," and to kill (i.e. "neutralize") government personnel. Further, they were taught to "direct demonstrators into having clashes with authorities, to provoke shootings or riots leading to the killing of one or multiple people," who then would be seen as martyrs. Then, the situation should be taken advantage of immediately against the Government to create greater conflicts. The manual also recommended: "Selective use of armed force for PSYOP, psychological operations, effect. Carefully selected, planned targets—judges, police officials, tax collectors, etc. — may be removed for PSYOP effect in a UWOA, unconventional warfare operations area, but extensive precautions must ensure that the people 'concur' in such an act by thorough explanatory canvassing among the affected populace before and after conduct of the mission."[17]

The manual came to public attention after it was revealed by the *Associated Press* on 15 October 1984. Newspapers in America and around the world labelled it a "murder manual." The then-Contra leader, Edgar Chamorro, was forced out of the movement following the public furore over the publication of the manual. He would later testify in an affidavit to the World Court that the CIA "did not discourage" such tactics. In actuality, the Agency severely criticized Chamorro when he admitted to the media that the FDN regularly kidnapped and executed civilians and agrarian reform workers. Chamorro added that the Contras were told the only way to defeat the Sandinistas was to... kill, kidnap, rob and torture them.[18]

In 1984, the CIA officer in charge of the of the covert campaign, Duane "Dewey" Clarridge admitted the Contra campaign of terror and assassination, but defended the actions of both the CIA and KMS in a secret briefing to the House Intelligence Committee by stating "After all, this is war—a paramilitary operation."[19] The actual brutality of the Contra campaign of terror was brought home to the American people in 1985 when *Newsweek* magazine published a controversial series of photos taken by Frank Wohl, a conservative student admirer of the Contras, entitled *Execution in the Jungle*.

In the series, the victim dug his own grave, scooping the dirt out with his hands. He then crossed himself. Then a Contra executioner knelt and stabbed a knife into his throat. A second Contra stabbed him twice, once in his jugular vein and then his stomach. When the victim was finally still, the Contras threw dirt over the shallow grave and walked away. They claimed the photos were faked, pointing out that they had stopped wearing the blue uniforms worn by the Contras in the photos. Rejecting claims that the photographs were faked, Frank Wohl stated "They were wearing them when I left."[20]

Not content to just train the Contras, the CIA paramilitaries were accused of taking a direct and active part in the campaign by blowing up refineries, pipelines, and the mining ports. In one series of sabotage raids between January and March 1984, three harbours in Nicaragua were mined by the CIA, damaging at least seven vessels including a Soviet freighter and a Dutch dredger.[21]

KMS's involvement in the training of the Contras only came to light during investigations into what was to be called the "Iran Contra Scandal." Investigators in Washington opened a safe which had once belonged to the disgraced White House aide, Lieutenant Colonel Oliver North, and found a scrap of paper with a handwritten diagram on it. The diagram was a sketch of the network of private companies he had used to pump arms and money around the world from the desert battlefields of Iran to the steamy jungles of Central America. Down in the right-hand corner of the sheet of paper, under the title "Overseas Op Arms," North had written three letters: KMS.[22]

Otto Von Bismarck, the Iron Chancellor of Prussia, famously said, "A war needs three things, money, money and money." The initial US funding for the Contras came directly from President Reagan who, on 4 January, 1982, gave the CIA a $19 million budget[23] to allow them to arm, cloth, feed, and supervise the Contras. This was to be the CIA's most ambitious paramilitary project since the Bay of Pigs debacle. Later, the US Congress approved military aid, and in the fiscal year 1984 it approved $24 million in Contra aid. The Contra's failure to win either a military victory inside Nicaragua or widespread Nicaraguan support for its policy to overthrow the Sandinista government eventually led the US Congress to outlaw American assistance to the Contras to overthrow the Nicaraguan government."[24]

Determined to keep on financing the Contra movement, the CIA turned to other sources of finance. Between 1984 and 1986, the Reagan administration raised $34 million, which included $2.7 million from other countries and $2.7 million from private sources to fund the Contras. This secret assistance programme to the Contras was run by Lieutenant Colonel Oliver North under the direct orders of the National Security Council and was called "The Enterprise."

The Enterprise had its own airplanes, pilots, airfield, ship, operatives, and secret Swiss bank accounts. One of its pilots, a former US Marine named Eugene Hasenfus, was shot down in Nicaragua in 1986 whilst on a weapons supply run. He was convicted of terrorism and other charges and sentenced to thirty years in prison, but was pardoned and released later that year. The Reagan administration denied any kind of connection to him, and there were also well-documented reports that the Contra terror campaign in Nicaragua was funded, in part at least, by drug running.[25]

The illegal and accountable activities of The Enterprise ultimately led it into the illegal arms trade, with weapons and munitions being supplied to Iran, in direct contravention to official US embargoes and ultimately into the Iran Contra scandal of 1986 - 1987. Lieutenant Colonel Oliver North was indicted in March 1988 on sixteen felony charges. He was ultimately convicted of only three: ordering the destruction of documents, accepting illegal gratuities, and aiding and abetting in obstructing a congressional inquiry. On 20 July, 1990, North's convictions were vacated.

On the ground, an offensive planned by the Contras in 1986 never materialised, and the various Contra groups were limited to sporadic, but often deadly, acts of random terrorism. The Contra's CIA advisors managed in 1987 to obtain heavier weapons for them, including Redeye surface-to-ground missiles, which enabled them to engage the Mi-24 helicopter gunships that had been supplied to the Sandinista government by the Soviets. It was only when the Contras were thus re-armed in October 1997 that they were able to launch large-scale raids into Nicaragua and engage in military, as opposed to terrorist, operations. Despite the new weaponry, after heavy fighting and casualties on both sides, the Contras were still unable to hold any territory inside Nicaragua. The Sandinista government also faced internal problems after it implemented a draft, resulting in riots and street clashes. Ultimately, after the US withdrew military funding to the Contras, both sides entered into negotiations.

The Contras agreed to voluntary demobilization in early December 1989. In the elections that followed in February 1990, Violeta Charmorro's

UNO party won an upset victory of 55 per cent to 41 per cent over Daniel Ortega's incumbent Sandinista party. Many observers put the victory down to the US's threat not to lift sanctions unless Charmorro won. Estimates vary on the total casualties in the civil war from between 10,000 - 43,000 killed. The best estimate, using the most detailed battlefield information, is 30,000 killed.

In Britain, the revelation that a British mercenary company had been involved in the training and supervision of the brutal Contra campaign inside Nicaragua led, in 1997, to Labour MP Dale Campbell-Savours asking the then-Prime Minister a parliamentary question:

"To ask the Prime Minister on what occasions since 1979 representatives of Her Majesty's Government discussed the use of Keenie Meenie Services or Saladin Security with Colonel Oliver North and if she will make a statement?"

The Prime Minister's response was:

"It has been the practice of successive governments not to answer questions about the details of discussions which may have taken place with foreign governments."[26]

Chapter Five

Myanmar
1980 - 1990

Since independence from Britain in 1949, the Karen National Liberation Army (KNLA) a military branch of the Karen National Union (KNU) has been fighting a war for the self-determination of the Karen people of Myanmar (formerly Burma) against a succession of oppressive military governments. Foreign mercenary volunteers, particularly those from France and Australia, have fought for the Karen cause throughout their military campaign. At least three French mercenaries have been killed in action fighting for the KNLA. The first was Jean-Phillipe Courreges, who was killed in 1985 when 150 Karen rebels attacked a Burmese military outpost near the Thai border.

The second was Olivier Thiriet, who was killed by shrapnel on 10 May, 1989, while fighting alongside Karen insurgents against government troops in the Kawmura area of southeast Myanmar near the border with Thailand and Guillaume. In the same attack, an Australian mercenary, identified as Martin Donnelly, an ex-member of the Australian SAS who used the alias "Sonny Wingate" whilst fighting there, suffered shrapnel wounds and was treated in a medical facility in the Thai border town of Mae Sot. The last French mercenary volunteer, Guillaume Oillic, was killed in 1990. One Japanese mercenary volunteer has also claimed to have fought with the KNLA but this has never been independently verified. (See later in this chapter "The Bosnian War").

The most notorious foreign mercenary volunteer to fight for the Karen cause was an Australian called David Francis Everett, a former member of the Australia's Special Air Service Regiment (SASR) which he joined at the age of 21. He would later claim the selection course for the SASR was the hardest thing he ever did in his life. After spending more than three years with the SASR, in 1986 Everett travelled to Myanmar and joined the KNLA, using the alias "Steve."

While operating with the KNLA, Everett used the skills he developed in the SASR to train the Karen fighters in shooting and marksmanship. His most significant contribution was to the field of explosives. As an SASR-trained explosives expert, he introduced the KNLA into the use of claymore anti-personal mines, an easily improvised and devastating close-range weapon that throws dozens of small pieces of shrapnel into an enemy formation. The Karen then used them effectively against government forces.

In 1987, Everitt returned to Australia where he got married. For four years, he led a relatively normal life, but his desire to help the cause of the Karen people in Myanmar still burned brightly inside him. He took flying lessons with the intention of smuggling weapons into Myanmar. Then, in 1991, in order to raise funds for the Karen rebellion, he led a three-man team in an armed robbery attempt at the home of a theatre manager in Perth, Western Australia. Everett, James Reynolds—who was also an ex-member of SASR—and another unknown accomplice who was suspected by police to be ex-SASR, forced the manager to open his safe in front of his very pregnant wife.

After stealing the contents of the safe, all three fled, but Everett and Reynolds were quickly captured by the Australian police, with the third accomplice escaping capture and whose identity remains unknown. Reynolds committed suicide in prison, but Everett was released on bail and fled the mainland to Magnetic Island of the North Queensland Coast. After returning to the mainland he would later attempt three more robberies. In the last, he set off a one-ton explosive that is still the largest explosion in Australia's criminal history. Everett was finally caught in 1991, whilst awaiting trial he escaped custody by faking his own kidnapping with a .22 automatic rifle he had buried in his backyard years earlier. He was recaptured twelve months later after the largest police manhunt in Australian history. In prison, Everett studied for a Bachelor of Arts degree, where he majored in journalism and international relations. By 1999, he graduated with Honours in Strategic Studies. Everett died on 13 May, 2013.

From the author's research, the foreign mercenary volunteers who served with the KNLA did so for no payment. Their motivation for fighting, and sometimes dying, in the Karen cause seems to have been out of a deep commitment to their struggle for self-determination. The Karen insurgency is still ongoing today against the present repressive military regime in Myanmar. On 17 May, 2021, the KNLA launched a new offensive taking back the major military camp of Thay Baw Bo south of Myawaddy from the government forces, which they occupied since 1990.

Columbia
1989

In the early 1970s, Pablo Escobar began his criminal career in Columbia by working for various drug smugglers and often kidnapping for ransom. By 1976, Escobar founded the Medellín Cartel, which distributed cocaine to the United States. It was he that first established smuggling routes into the United States and creating an enormous demand for the drug by 1980. This, in turn, fuelled a drug war between the Medellín Cartel and other Columbian drug cartels. This drug war led to massacres and the murders of police officers, judges, locals, and prominent politicians; and it made Colombia the murder capital of the world. By 1989, the drug wars were at their highest point.

In the summer of 1988, David Tomkins, a mercenary who had been involved in ill-fated mercenary intervention in Angola, through a contact in the arms trade, was introduced to an officer from the Colombian army. Tomkins was asked to put together a team to destroy the headquarters of the *Fuerzas Armadas Revolucionarias de Columbia* (FARC), a communist terrorist group, which was supported by Cuba and had been responsible for a sustained terror campaign inside the country. To fund its terrorist activities, FARC had been producing and smuggling cocaine, which brought it into conflict with the various drug cartels that operated within Columbia.

The Columbian officer informed Tomkins that the proposed "operation" was being funded by the notorious Colombian drug baron, Gonzalo Rodriguez Gacha. Gacha was the head of the Cali drug cartel, and the main and bitter rival of Pablo Escobar's Medellín Cartel. Tomkins was offered about $2,000 (£1,250) per week plus a share of any loot found at guerrilla headquarters. Tomkins quickly agreed to the proposal and set about recruiting a team of mercenaries, one of the first was former 22 SAS mercenary Peter McAleese, who Tomkins had worked with in Angola. They met first in the Booth Hall pub in Hereford, a familiar haunt for both serving and ex-members of the SAS. McAleese quickly agreed to join in a planned attack on FARC. The mercenaries compiled a team of sixteen mercenaries and headed to Colombia; however the military equipment they were promised failed to turn up and the attack was abandoned. Tomkins returned to England in November of the same year.

Three months later, Tomkins was contacted again by his Colombian connections. This time, the planned operation was not against the FARC terrorist group; instead, he was asked to assemble a team of mercenaries to assassinate Pablo Escobar. Tomkins was assured of an unlimited budget, both to pay the mercenaries and buy weapons. He was also promised that there would be no government interference in the endeavour. The US Drug Enforcement Agency (DEA) was apparently informed of the intended operation in advance and approved of it. Former DEA agent Javier Pena is quoted as saying: "When we heard about this plan, of course we wanted him dead. So any effort to kill Pablo Escobar was of course welcomed. We wanted it to happen."[1]

Whether British Intelligence or the British government were aware of the intended assassination plot is unknown. From the author's own knowledge, British Special Forces, especially the Special Boats Service (SBS), were operating in Columbia at the time, training both military and special police units. Again, it is unknown if they approved of the planned assassination by British mercenaries, but it is safe to assume that given their close working relationship with both Columbian intelligence and the American DEA, they at least knew of the plot.

Tomkins again recruited McAleese, and together they assembled a team of twelve British mercenaries. The team were paid a basic pay of $5,000 a month and Tomkins was told a further million dollar bonus was payable for Escobar's head. The mercenary team landed in Cali in March 1989 and received the promised arms, including assault rifles, handguns, explosives, and grenades. A piloted helicopter was also provided, Tomkins later hinted by the Columbian army.

As a staging base, the mercenary team was housed in a luxury villa above the town of Cali. The operational plan was for Tomkins and McAleese's assault team to launch a helicopter attack on Pablo Escobar's private, 7,000-acre estate, *Hacienda Napoles*, 80 miles east of Medellin, where the drug baron had a personal zoo full of exotic animals. The mercenary team, including Tomkins, who had no actual military background, went into a period of intense training in preparation for the assault.

On 3 June, 1989, Tomkins received orders to carry out the assassination. The journey from their base in Cali to Escobar's estate was nearly three hours' flying time across heavy jungle. *En route* to the estate, the helicopter carrying Tomkins and McAleese's assault group flew into a mountain peak because of heavy rain and cloud cover. The pilot was killed instantly, but Tomkins and McAleese survived the crash, although Tomkins was badly injured. It took the mercenary team three days to walk out of the jungle. In June 1989, Tomkins called off the operation and the mercenary team dispersed. Tomkins was arrested in a sting operation by US customs agents in Puerto Rico in 1991, whilst organising a second attempt to assassinate Escobar. As a result, he fled the US. In April 1994, a federal court in the Southern District of Florida indicted the absent Tomkins for conspiracy to violate arms export laws.

When Tomkins returned to the US in 2003 to take part in a chemical weapons survival course so that he could undertake work in Iraq, he was arrested. In 2004, he was jailed for thirty-three months. Pablo Escobar was imprisoned briefly in Columbia but escaped. He died in a shootout with a special police unit on 2 December, 1993. After his death, the Medellín Cartel crumbled and ceased to exist. Unfortunately, the lucrative and ever-expanding market for cocaine insured there were plenty of other drug cartels in Columbia to replace them. Unlike most mercenary ventures, the events in Columbia in 1989 were not, in any sense of the word, a military operation. This is again an isolated example of British mercenaries, especially highly trained former members of 22 SAS being hired specifically for an assassination mission. No doubt many of those who took part in the failed mission comforted themselves by the fact that the intended target was a notorious and brutal criminal drug lord. In the author's experience, very few ex-serving members of the SAS who maintain high moral and professional standards even in the private sector, would ever contemplate taking part in such a dubious, and questionably legal, enterprise.

Bosnia
1992 and 1995

The Bosnian war began with the break-up of Yugoslavia following the succession of Slovenia and Croatia from the Yugoslav federal republic, when the multi-ethnic Socialist Republic of Bosnia and Herzegovina—which was inhabited by mainly Muslim Bosniaks (44 per cent), with minority Orthodox Serbs (32.5 per cent) and Catholic Croats (17 per cent), passed a referendum to gain independence on 29 February 1992.

Although internationally recognized, the Bosnian Serb population, led by Radovan Karadžić, rejected it and instead began to mobilize Serb members of the Yugoslav army into the Army of the Republika Srpska (VRS) to secure Serbian territory. Karadžić's Serb forces were supported by Serbia under the leadership of Slobodan Milošević. As a result of the Serb mobilization, Bosniak and Croat and members of the Yugoslav army formed to create the Army of the Republic of Bosnia and Herzegovina (ARBiH). These were the two main protagonists at the start of the conflict, but as it developed and expanded, other armies and nations were drawn into the conflict.

The resulting civil war began in earnest on 6 April 1992 and ended on 14 December, 1995. The war was bitter, even by civil war standards, with the indiscriminate shelling of cities common place, as was ethnic cleansing of entire towns and villages. Mass, systematic rape was also a significant feature of the conflict and, for the first time since the Second World War in Europe ended, the mass slaughter of innocents. Most of the atrocities were perpetrated by the Serbs, but the Croat and Muslims were certainly not free from having blood on their hands.

As the chaotic and brutal Bosnian War developed, it drew mercenaries from around the world to it like a bright flame attracting a hoard of moths. Some had military experience, most did not. Their motivations, as is always with mercenaries, varied. Most came for treasure, others were idealists driven by either religious or ethnic loyalties, some came for adventure others simply to kill. As a general rule of thumb, mercenaries from Muslim countries served with the Bosniaks, mercenaries from Eastern Orthodox countries served with the Serbs, and mercenaries from Catholic countries served with the Croats. The vast majority of British mercenaries served with the Croats.

Bosniak Muslim Mercenaries

The involvement of mercenaries in a conflict can often have unforeseen consequences, and this was never truer than in Bosnia with the Muslim mercenaries from Afghanistan, North Africa and other Arab countries who entered into the war. Muslim volunteers undoubtedly became involved in the war for mainly religious reasons. Estimates vary on the number of Islamic mercenaries who fought in the conflict, but by the end of the war and having increased their numbers by local recruiting, what became colloquially known as "The Bosnian Mujahideen" had swelled to around 1,500 fighters, who arrived in central Bosnia in the second half of 1992.

Originally, only a few dozen in number, some of the original Muslim volunteers undoubtedly arrived in Bosnia to help fellow Muslims and were involved in humanitarian efforts, such as providing food and other necessities that were being denied to the local population by the Serbs or Croats. Others had more sinister motives, amongst these were many followers of Wahhabism, who maintained contacts with terrorist organizations in Afghanistan, Saudi Arabia, and Iraq, which encouraged the radicalisation of attitudes and actions of the Bosnian Muslim population.[2]

The Muslim mercenary volunteers were mainly based in the city of Tešan, and once entrenched there began to systematically impose a strict and fundamentalist interpretation of Islamic law on the local population. The sale of alcohol and pork was all but banned, couples were forbidden to hold hands in public, girls and older women were ordered to wear the hijab, and it was made obligatory to teach Arabic in schools and to follow the Hanbalite interpretation of Islam.[3]

On 13 August, 1993, the Bosnian government incorporated the Muslim Mercenaries into 7th Muslim Brigade known as "El Mudžahid." Although originally attached to regular Bosnian army, El Mudžahid often operated independently as a separate entity. It consisted of three battalions, and recruits took an oath according to the rules outlined in a pamphlet entitled *Instructions for the Muslim Warrior*, of which 20,000 copies were published in 1993.[4]

Two British mercenaries, Ted Skinner and Derek Arnold, were kidnapped, tortured, and killed whilst training the Bosnian Muslims on 8 February, 1993. Both men claimed to have served with the Army in the past and one had claimed to have held the rank of captain. British Army sources at the time stated "the men's names did not tie up with the regiments in which they were alleged to have served."[5] There was confusion at the time as to what training they offered the Bosnian Muslims; some reports were that they were merely teaching on "military-medical matters," while others that the two were training the Muslims in unarmed combat, including the ways to garrotte enemies.[6] Skinner justified his involvement in the war in the following terms: "Bosnia is a small country being kicked over by everybody. It's being attacked, invaded, its people are being pushed out of their houses, they're being systematically killed and it needs help."[7] The finger of suspicion for their brutal deaths fell on members of El Mudžahid, allegedly jealous of foreign infidels teaching Muslims.

The brutality of El Mudžahid is well documented, as well as its involvement in reprisals for massacres carried out by Croat militias. In one instance, its members kidnapped local Christians and beheaded one, Dragan Popović, and forcing other captives to kiss his severed head. El Mudžahid mercenaries were also involved in direct combat with British troops on a number of occasions in 1993. A British officer described them as "very more aggressive" than the local Bosnian troops.[8] As the war progressed, Bosnian officers realised that the incorporation of the Muslim mercenaries into the Bosnian army was a mistake, recognising that they were responsible for committing atrocities that caused significant damage to Bosnian interests.[9] Throughout the war, there were consistent reports of El Mudžahid mercenaries beheading captured fighters, although many of them could not be substantiated.

Following the war's end, *The International Criminal Tribunal for the Former Yugoslavia* issued an indictment against the Chief of the General Staff of the Army of Bosnia and Herzegovina, General Rasim Delić, which read:

"On July 21, 1995, the El Mujahed unit of the 3rd Army Corps of Bosnia and Herzegovina launched an attack on Krčevine in the municipality of Zavidovići. Soldiers from the Bosnian Serb Army VRS45 were captured and taken to the village of Livade. Two captured VRS soldiers were killed and beheaded by Bosnia and Herzegovina Army soldiers. In Livade, the prisoners were beaten daily and on July 23, 1995, they were taken to the Kamenica camp in the Gostović valley. Within the camp there was a building that was used as a detention centre for captured VRS soldiers. This detention centre was operated by soldiers from the El Mujahed unit. On July 24, 1995, one VRS prisoner was beheaded in the Kamenica camp, and the other prisoners were forced to kiss the decapitated head, before it was placed on a hook on the wall in a room where prisoners were held. The VRS prisoners held in Kamenica camp were tortured and beaten (…). General Delić was warned that El Mujahed soldiers were prone to commit crimes, especially against captured enemy combatants and civilians, and that this unit managed Kamenica camp. Nevertheless, it failed to take necessary and reasonable measures to prevent or punish these crimes."[10]

Hadžihasanović was sentenced to five years in prison but was released on appeal in 2007. The foreign Muslim mercenary volunteers were forced to leave the Balkans under the terms of the 1995 Dayton Agreement, which effectively ended the war. Many dispersed to other countries to continue their Jihad against the West, including Chechnya, Pakistan, and Afghanistan. Two of the five 9/11 hijackers' childhood friends were Khalid al-Mihdhar and Nawwaf al-Hazmi, both were ex-Bosnian Muslim mercenaries. One former Bosnian Muslim mercenary was involved in the murder of American hostage Daniel Pearl in Pakistan.

It has been convincingly argued that the birth of modern fundamentalist Islamic terrorism including Al-Qaeda and ISIS had its birth in Bosnia with the involvement of Muslim mercenary volunteers. In a 2005 interview with US journalist Jim Lehrer, Richard Holbrooke, the chief architect of the Dayton Peace Accords stated that more than 1,000 people belonged to what was at the time called Mujahideen freedom fighters. "We now know that that was Al-Qaeda. I'd never heard the word before, but we knew who they were. And if you look at the 9/11 hijackers, several of those hijackers were trained in or fought in Bosnia. We cleaned them out, and they had to move much further east into Afghanistan. So if it hadn't been for Dayton, we would have been fighting the terrorists deep in the ravines and caves of Central Bosnia in the heart of Europe."[11]

The Croatian Side

As well as receiving direct support from Croatia and the Croatian army, foreign mercenary volunteers from a wide range of countries fought on the Croatian side, including Britain, Spain, Ireland, Spain, Finland, Hungary, Albania, Canada, Sweden, and France. Most of these "volunteers" claimed to have had prior military experience, but in reality, a large proportion were nothing more than fantasists or thrill seekers.

One of the exceptions to this was Eduardo Rózsa-Flores, a Bolivian by birth and a former member of the Hungarian Intelligence Service. He was the first foreign mercenary volunteer to join the Croatian National Guard. He originally arrived in Yugoslavia in June 1991 as a journalist, but while reporting on the war, his car was shot at, and his growing devotion to the Croatian cause prompted him to enter the war directly. He adopted the name "Jorge Eduardo Rózsa" on his enlistment in the autumn of 1991. Rózsa went on to see extensive action, particularly in battles in Slavonia. During the defence of Laslovo he set up the Croatian army's First International Brigade; although termed a "brigade," Rózsa's unit never got beyond a couple of hundred men at its peak. As a result of his performance on the battlefield, Rózsa was awarded Croatian citizenship and accepted into the Croatian Special Forces.

Rózsa was wounded three times in battle and was promoted twice, first to major then to colonel. Unconfirmed press reports linked him to the deaths of two foreign journalists in Bosnia, Swiss national Christian Würtenberg, who was also a member of First International Brigade, and British photographer Paul Jenks. The journalists were investigating Rózsa's alleged involvement in shady drugs and weapons deals and vanished, never to be seen again. Rózsa was officially demobilized on 31 July, 1994 from the Croatian Special Forces.

Eventually, Rózsa was killed by Bolivian police on 16 April, 2009 during a raid in the *Las Americas* hotel in Santa Cruz. He was part of a group of five men who were allegedly planning to assassinate Bolivian President Evo Morales. Árpád Magyarosi was an Irish citizen and Hungarian national; Michael Dwyer, were also killed in the raid. Croatian Mario Tadić, and Hungarian Előd Tóásó were arrested. In 2011, police that performed the raid were awarded the Medal of Valour.

Another exception to the general rule was Irishman Thomas Crowley, who was a former member of the British Army. He joined the Croat forces in 1991 and fought in many battles and was wounded in one. In 1994, Crowley led a training camp for the Croat 114th brigade and helped train more than 2,000 soldiers. He was promoted to Major and was killed in action near Dubrovnik in 1995. In 2012, Crowley was posthumously awarded the Croatian Order of Petar Zrinski and Fran Krsto Frankopan.

Most other British "mercenaries" were an entirely different story. A newspaper headline from the period probably encapsulates the calibre of the British mercenary volunteers who flocked to the country. It read: "Britons flock to fight in Bosnia: Thousands of ex-soldiers and 'untrained idiots and psychopaths' said to be serving as mercenaries with all three sides."[12] A prime example of "untrained idiots and psychopaths" was a serial killer-obsessed northern bouncer, Dave, who apparently wanted to "know what it feels like to kill without guilt."[13] Another was Chris Freeman who wrote the book *War Dogs* under the name Keith Cory-Jones, where one of the few reviews of the book on Amazon read:

"Just to say that I knew Chris (Kit) Freeman briefly prior to him going to Bosnia. His exploits there were also featured in a BBC (I think) documentary. I know that he went to prison in the UK after returning from Bosnia for obtaining money by deception (I was one of the people he robbed) and believe that part of the reason he went to Bosnia was because the British police were looking for him. I wouldn't trust anything that he said to the author. He was certainly in Bosnia but the accounts of his exploits, I imagine, include a lot of fiction and fantasy - he is certainly good at telling a story that is convincing at the time, but which falls to pieces when you take the time to think about it."[14]

Some of these very dubious "mercenaries" did have at least some previous military training. Before going to Croatia, Kirk Davies had served with the Duke of Wellington's Regiment and undertook two tours of Northern Ireland before having his service abruptly terminated by the army. Davies also spent time in prison. His father told him great stories about how he served with the SAS during the war, when in reality, he had only been a driver. When Davies discovered the truth, he threatened to kill his father with a Gurkha knife. On 25 September, 2000, Davies went on a rampage armed with an air rifle and was shot dead by a police marksman in Wakefield, West Yorkshire.[15] Davies claims that he killed fifty Serbs while serving in Croatia as a sniper; their special forces were dismissed by Croatian veterans' organisations as "rubbish."[16]

Despite the Croatians' undoubted need for manpower during the bitter civil war, the inclusion of men of the calibre those outlined above into a fighting unit in a combat zone puts that military in far more peril than their inclusion is worth. Not only do such recruits have no basic knowledge of even the most basic of infantry skills or weapons, their motivation and discipline, essential qualities in any fighting man, were obviously seriously lacking.

As far as the author knows and has researched, no ex-member of the British SAS or any other British Special Forces unit ever fought in combat in the Bosnian conflict. After all, these were highly trained professionals who would require any government or private contractor who wanted them for protection, or training or to fight in a war zone, to pay a high price for training and experience.

One government did have the money to hire ex-SAS soldiers to operate in Bosnia during the war: The United States. A highly regarded ex-senior, non-commissioned officer from 'B' Squadron 22 SAS obtained a contract to provide armed security for American diplomats throughout the entire duration of the war. The team that guarded the diplomats was composed of half ex-members of the SAS and half US Secret Service agents. It bears mentioning that, despite the fact that the US delegation in Bosnia frequently travelled through hostile territory, not a single causality was suffered.

Apart from the somewhat motley collection of British mercenary volunteers, those from other European countries often preferred to form individual units to fight alongside their own countrymen in Bosnia. For example mercenary volunteers from Italy formed the Garibaldi battalion, whilst those from France formed the Groupe Jacques Doriot. Many extreme right-wing fanatics from Germany, almost all of whom had no military experience, joined Rózsa's First International Brigade.

Russian mercenary volunteers primarily fought for the Serbs, but a small group of neo Nazis termed the "Werewolves" fought on the Croat side. Little is known about them or what they actually contributed to the Croatian war effort, but it is reasonable to assume, given their name, that like the majority of the British contingent they did not significantly advance the Croatian cause.

Summing up the general attitude that prevailed amongst these would-be soldiers of fortune, American mercenary Rob Krott, a former officer in the US Army who served as a mercenary volunteer in Bosnia, stated there was a "Rambo syndrome" prevalent throughout the Balkans. After fighting alongside HVO units in Herzegovina, he asserted that "many were more concerned with styling the latest fashions, MTV haircuts, and new earrings than learning to soldier."[17]

Given the motivations of most of the western mercenary volunteers who chose to go to Bosnia, coupled with their lack of training and ill-discipline, it is fair to assume that atrocities were committed by them during the course of war. However only one was ever charged, and eventually convicted, with war crimes. He was a Swede by the name of Jackie Arklöv.

Arklöv was a child of mixed heritage, half-Swedish and half-Black, and by the time he reached the age of 18, he was a committed Nazi and became a devote of the Ustaša: a fascist, ultra-nationalist, terrorist organization of Croatia with a reputation for blood-chilling violence. The Ustaša movement did not start during the Bosnian War. The leaders of the puppet Nazi Croatian State called NDH during the Second World War were called

Ustaše, and the fascist Croats in Bosnia and Croatia adopted the name during the Civil War in ex-Yugoslavia. At the age of only 19, Arklöv left Sweden and initially made attempts to join the French Foreign Legion. Because the Legion was not participating in any wars at the time, he instead travelled to Bosnia where he volunteered for a neo-Ustaša unit called Ludvig Pavlović. Comprised of largely ethnic Croats, its role was described as "special purposes." In practice, this translated into horrendous crimes, such as the ethnic cleansing of local civilian populations.

According to Swedish journalist Magnus Sandelin,[18] Arklöv kept a personal dairy in which he detailed how "he would throw grenades into civilian homes before spraying bullets into anyone who survived the detonation, often blasting extreme heavy metal whilst doing so." He was also said to have recorded that "The murder of Bosniak Muslims was almost as good as an orgasm." Arklöv was also known to have served in concentration camps that were reminiscent of the Second World War, where he committed further atrocities.

Shortly after the ceasefire in Bosnia in 1995, a drunken Arklöv was detained by Bosniak forces and was sentenced to thirteen years in prison for war crimes. Whilst the first year was spent in a Bosnian jail, he was soon returned to Sweden by the Swedish Red Cross. Imprisoned for a short spell in Sweden, he was acquitted of his charges on account of a lack of evidence. Unbeknownst to the Swedish authorities, they were releasing a monster.

In 1999, Arklöv, Olsson, and another neo-Nazi named Andreas Axelsson armed themselves with submachine guns and handguns, and carried out a series of armed robberies, culminating on 28 May with the robbery of the Östgöta Enskilda Bank in the town of Kisa. As the trio escaped with over two million SEK, they were followed by a lone Swedish cop called Kennet Eklund, who the gang attacked with a barrage of hand grenades and gunfire, casing the officer to discontinue his pursuit.

Later, at a road block, two more Swedish cops named Olle Borén and Robert Karlström intercepted the gang. After a shootout, both cops were disarmed and executed at close range with their own guns. The gang escaped, but a few days later were cornered, shot, and arrested in the Swedish town of Tyresö. All three of the neo-Nazi gang were eventually sentenced to life imprisonment.

Russian mercenaries deployed in the Central African Republic © Corbeau News Centrafrique.

Soldiers from the Central African Armed Forces wearing a Wagner Group patch © Corbeau News Centrafrique.

Private Military Contractor, Gunter S., Badakhshan Province, Afghanistan, 2006 © Nanorsuaq.

White mercenaries fighting alongside Congolese troops in 1964.

Lt. Col.Robert C. MacKenzie (standing, wings on hat) with some of the Sierra Leone Commando Unit he was training with the Gurkha Security Guards. Lt Andy Myers is 2nd from left, kneeling. Photo courtesy of Sibyl MacKenzie © Kguirnela.

Special force of the Indian Navy.

Personnel from the Triple Canopy defence contractor await their turn to fire an M240B machine gun for training, Sept. 4, 2011. They are placed in formation, given ammo and ear protection prior to moving on to the live fire portion of training.

Sir David Stirling, an SAS veteran, founded a PMC in the 1960s.

US State Department contract security, International (Green) Zone, Baghdad, Iraq. Contract security, Baghdad © Jamesdale10.

Armed contractors aboard a merchant ship to deter piracy © Hanuma Bhakta.

Wagner Group contractors providing security for President of the Central African Republic Faustin-Archange Touadéra.

The mercenary Dominique Borella photographed in February 1975 on the Bassac front in Cambodia © Rolph31000.

A vehicle of Russian and Syrian mercenaries in Bria, in Haute-Kotto © Moïse Banafio/CorbeauNews.

Young mercenary recruit at Kindu (with Simba bodies in a canoe in the background).

Parade for the delivery of commando patents to the first promotion of the Civil Guard in Kota-Koli.

Congolese soldiers with collected Chinese communist propaganda pamphlets entitled "Pékin Information" meant for mass distribution, December 1964.

Imba rebel wearing animal skins and traditional costume bewitched by "sorcerers" to protect him from harm in battle, December 1964.

Photo taken 2001 during the visit of US Rep. Frank Wolf. Original caption states: *Congolese soldier adjusting automatic weapon*. The weapon is a PK machine gun. These soldiers are from the rebel forces, as stated by Rep. Wolf: *"I traveled nearly 1,000 miles by plane to the towns of Goma and Bukavu in eastern Congo to meet with opposition groups/Automatic weapons are prevalent in both Goma and Bukavu"*.

Member of the Gendarmerie in 1961.

A wounded Katangese gendarme is treated by Swedish medics near Kamina, 31 December 1962.

Member of the South African Special Forces performing a ceremonial parachute jump © NJR ZA.

Whilst serving his sentence, a new investigation into the war crimes Arklöv committed in Bosnia was opened. His trial began on 10 November, 2006, and just over a month later on 18 December, the Swedish court found Arklöv guilty of multiple counts, ranging from wrongful imprisonment and ethnic cleansing to looting and torture.

Overall, western mercenary volunteers, despite the outlandish claims in some parts of the British media about thousands of former soldiers, "untrained idiots," and "psychopaths" flooding into Bosnia, in reality only contributed to about 5 per cent of the total Croatian forces deployed in combat. Some like Crowley and Rózsa were genuine professional mercenaries in the truest sense of the word, and contributed both in combat and training to the Croatian war effort.

On the other hand, western mercenary volunteers like the "obsessed northern bouncer," Dave, Chris Freeman, and Jackie Arklöv were not "mercenaries" by true definition. They had no military skills to sell, no proficiency with weapons or tactics; they were civilians drawn to a war zone by either a psychopathic desire to kill or the thrill of participating in a war. If soldiering is indeed a profession, these were unskilled amateurs playing at war, and for all the wrong reasons.

The Croatian Organisation, founded to commemorate fallen western mercenary volunteers, lists a total number of those volunteers as 461, of which eighty-six were wounded and seventy-two killed (see Annex 1). On those figures more than a quarter of the western mercenary volunteers who participated in the war in Bosnia were either wounded or killed. The likely number of western mercenary volunteers actually involved in the war is probably higher than these figures and, correspondingly, the number of dead and wounded greater. In the author's opinion, professional mercenaries such as Crowley and Rózsa were the exceptions, not the rule; and overall western mercenary volunteers had little impact on the course of the war.

The Serb Side

The Serb side in the Bosnian war attracted mercenary volunteers from mainly Orthodox Christian countries. The bulk of these came mainly from Russia and organized themselves into two principle "Russian Volunteer Units," Русский Добровольческий Отряд ("РДО-1") and Русский Добровольческий Отряд ("РДО-2").

РДО-1 was commanded, recruited, and led by Yuri Belyaev, described in a newspaper article of the time as *a* "baby-faced neo-Nazi from St. Petersburg."[19] The Russian mercenary volunteers were fed, clothed, and armed by Serbs and paid a token salary of $155 a month.[20] Belyaev, like most of the Russian mercenary volunteers, had no military training and was drawn to the war in Bosnia because of his extreme right-wing views. He told a reporter in 1993: "We will also have to go to war in Russia soon. Our party needs officers trained and experienced in warfare. Yugoslavia is a good ground."[21]

Belyaev was indicted in March 1993 in Russia on charges of violating the Russian criminal code that outlaws "stirring up anti-Semitic, racist or ethnic dissent." He also founded the "Popular Social Party" (PSP) in Russia, which promoted the racist policies of Adolf Hitler.[22] The PSP was, at best, a fringe political movement whose numbers never exceeded a few hundred.

Alexander Zagrebov commanded *РДО-2* which was also known as "Tsarist Wolves," because of the monarchist views of its fighters. Separate from these two units, a sub-unit, comprised solely of Cossacks called the "First Cossack Sotnia," was also formed. All three of these formations fought mainly in Eastern Bosnia during the war. Estimates vary on the actual number of Russian mercenary volunteers who served in Bosnia from between 500 to more than 1,500.[23]

Another unit that fought on the Serb side was a Greek mercenary company called the "Greek Volunteer Guard" (GVG), which was formed in Bosnia at the direct request of Ratko Mladić, the Serbian military commander.[24] Its first volunteers arrived in Bosnia in 1995 and consisted of about 100 Greeks with proper military training. Many had ties to the Greek ultra-right-wing movement Golden Dawn.[25] The GVG were based in the town of Vlasenica from March 1995 onwards, as part of the Serbian "Drina Corps."

Vlasenica is only a one-hour car ride from the small Bosnian town of Srebrenica, where in July 1995 the brutal and genocidal killing of more than 8,000 Bosniak Muslim men and boys took place. There were verifiable reports that at the time of the massacre, ten to twelve members of the GVG were present.[26] The Greek flag was raised over the site of the tragedy on the direct orders of Ratko Mladić to honour "the brave Greeks fighting on our side."[27]

One of the Greek mercenary volunteers, Vasilis Schizas, later posted a picture of himself on his Facebook account holding a pig's head with the legend "Srebrenica 1995" depicted on it.[28] The pig's head was regularly used as a threat to Muslims during the war, as the consumption of pork is forbidden to all who follow the Muslim faith. Despite repeated calls for the Greek government to investigate the role of Greek mercenary volunteers in the Srebrenica massacre, in 2011 the Greek investigation was closed, with no one being called for interrogation.[29]

Since the demilitarisation of Japan after the Second World War, few, if any, of its inhabitants have fought in an actual war. One, however, did fight on the Serb side in the Bosnian war: his name was Masaki Takabe. Takabe joined the Japanese Air Force with the intention of becoming a pilot, but was injured during training and was discharged. Determined to become "a fighting man," Takabe made the decision to become a mercenary. His motivation was simple: "In my case, the reason why I became a mercenary is quite simple. I just wanted to be strong. There are many other ways to be strong, but I see real strength in the soldiers fighting at the front line. Thus, the location of battlegrounds didn't matter for me, as long as I could join in."[30] Before fighting in the Bosnia War, Takabe claimed to have fought as a mercenary with the Mujahideen in Afghanistan until 1990, and then with the Karen Liberation Army (see previous chapter), but these claims have never been verified.

Like their western contemporaries, the Russian, Ukrainian, and Greek foreign mercenary volunteers were, from what the author can research, a mixed bunch. Some had previous military training, many did not. Most, though, seem to have been highly motivated by their hatred of Muslims and their support for the Orthodox Christian Serb wish to create "a greater Serbia." Again, like their western counterparts, their relatively small numbers and general ill-discipline meant that their contribution to the Serb war effort was marginal at best. More than 300 foreign fighters perished and are buried in Bosnia.

Professional Military Contract Mercenaries in Bosnia

That is not to say that all mercenary involvement in the Bosnian war was insignificant or had no effect on the war's course. Operation Storm, the last major offensive battle in the Bosnian War ended with a decisive victory for the Croatian army. The offensive was a major factor in deciding the war before Dayton Peace talks. The Croatian offensive forced more than 150,000 ethnic Serbs from their homes and left an "ethnically cleansed" Croatia.

There is considerable circumstantial evidence that suggests a major factor in Croatian victory was the involvement of the American military "contractor" MPRI, who, along with units from the French Foreign Legion, prepared and trained the Croatian Army prior to the offensive.[31] MPRI was reportedly paid $140 million for their contract services. Croatian former Foreign Minister Tonino Picula explained MPRI's role in the training of the Croatian arm in the following terms: "We started at the beginning of the 1990s lacking all kind of assistance. We faced a war of aggression. We needed all kinds of friends to enhance our capability to keep a schedule. I know that it (MPRI) did a significant job in Croatia as a part of US assistance to Croatia during the 1990s."[32]

Based in Alexandria, Virginia, MPRI was founded in 1987 by eight former senior United States officers and was a global provider of 'private military contractors' and military contract services. At its inception, MPRI exclusively employed retired US military personnel. As a result of their success in preparing the Croatian Army for Operation Storm, MPRI won a contract worth approximately $50 million to "Train and Equip" the Bosnian Federation army, which ended in July 1996. The contract was accompanied by an approximately $100 million arms transfer programme.[33]

MPRI have been accused of helping to plan the Croatian occupation and ethnic cleansing of Serb-populated Krajina in 1995. A class action lawsuit for $10.4 billion dollars in compensation was issued against MPRI by a group of Serbs who had lived in Krajina until the Croatian forces drove them out during Operation Storm. The suit alleged that, in their training of the Croatian Army for the offensive MPRI were "participating in genocide." On 26 September 2014, the lawsuit was dismissed, with the US court ruling that the war in the former Yugoslavia was not under its jurisdiction.

Even more troubling was the discovery that during the Balkan Wars (1991–2001), the United States contracted with DynCorp, an American contract mercenary firm, to assist the UN Police Task Force in Bosnia. During their operations, reports emerged that DynCorp employees were buying and trading young women and girls. On 2 June, 2000, US military police raided Dyncorp's facilities, and the US Army confirmed several of the allegations. The information was relinquished to the Bosnian police, but none of the people involved were ever charged with any criminal offence.[34]

The Kosovo War
1998 - 1999

One offshoot of the Bosnian war was the Kosovo War, which was fought between the Federal Forces of Yugoslavia (Serbian and Montenegrin), that controlled Kosovo before and a breakaway Kosovo Albanian insurgent militia that was known as the Kosovo Liberation Army (KLA). Kosovo was actually an autonomous province of Serbia, same as Vojvodina, since the formation of Yugoslavia and also after the civil war in Bosnia and Croatia. It never had the status of the federal state in Yugoslavia such as Slovenia, Serbia, Croatia, Bosnia, Montenegro and Macedonia (now North Macedonia). Fought between 28 February, 1998, and 11 June, 1999, the war was another bitter civil war that only ended with NATO intervention, during which a sustained bombing campaign mounted by NATO aircraft eventually forced the Serb forces to withdraw.

Russian Mercenary Involvement

As in Bosnia, there is evidence that Russian mercenaries fought in the conflict and were accused of war crime as a result. Speaking on 22 June, 1999, Pentagon spokesman Kenneth Bacon confirmed Russian mercenaries had fought on the Serb side during the Kosovo war and that during the seventy-eight days of NATO bombing, a number of Russians had been killed. It remains unclear as to whether the deaths were caused by NATO bombing or because of combat with the KLA.[35]

A *Newsday* report citing ethnic Albanian and Serb intelligence sources accused the Russian mercenaries of war crimes in relation to the ethnic Albanian population. The report also confirmed that German soldiers deployed as part of the NATO forces ordered a group of sixty Russian mercenaries to leave the country. The report also stated that the Russian mercenaries had been organized into a single unit, comprised of either retired or active service military men commanded by a colonel. The unit allegedly operated under the direct control of the Serb "Special Purpose Police" of the Federal Ministry of the Interior in Belgrade. Speaking in 1999, Pentagon spokesman Bacon could not independently confirm the presence or involvement of Russian mercenaries in the Kosovo War: "Our impression is that they were mercenaries, but this is something that I'm sure will be looked into by war crimes investigators, who are now going into Kosovo in considerable numbers to try to figure out what happened and who was responsible for it."[36]

To date, whether or not the Russian mercenaries who intervened in the Kosovo War were regular Russian forces or ex-military mercenary volunteers is unknown. In the author's opinion, going on other Russian intervention since the Kosovo War, they were, in all probability, a mixture of both. Despite the Pentagon spokesman's vow to "look into" the alleged involvement of the Russian mercenaries in war crimes, none were ever identified or prosecuted. This could have been because at the time NATO, arranged for 3,600 Russian troops to join KFOR, the Kosovo Force of Peacekeepers, and any detailed investigation into alleged Russian war crimes might have jeopardised that cooperation with Russia.[37]

American Mercenary Contractors Involvement in Kosovo

Until the start of the Kosovo War, the KLA was classified by the United States as a "terrorist organisation." This apparently did not stop the US supporting the KLA once the war started. There are unverified reports that during the war, MPRI used former US military personnel to train KLA forces at secret bases inside Albania.[38] If the reports of MPRI training the KLA are indeed accurate, it would seem that the American mercenary contractor had no ethical issues as to whom it supplied its military expertise to.

Equatorial Guinea is one of Africa's poorest countries, and its dictator President Teodoro Obiang Nguema seized control in a military coup in 1979. He was—and is—widely regarded as one of the African continent's most brutal dictators. Following its success in the former Yugoslavia, MPRI won a contract to train Nguema's army and private presidential guard. The army and guard successfully protected Nguema from two serious attempts to oust him from power (see Chapter Seven).

Chapter Six

Contract Soldiers and the SAS "Circuit" 1960 - 2022

The rebirth of the modern SAS during the Malayan Emergency left many former members unable to find employment that suited their particular skill sets once their military careers were over. Then there was "The Circuit," so named because of the availability of summer bodyguard jobs in the UK and winter training missions overseas. At first, the main employers of former SAS mercenary contractors were the giants of the British private security industry: Watchguard, Controlled Risks Ltd. KMS, and Saladin. Later, individual former SAS NCOs and officers formed smaller mercenary companies to meet the ever increasing demand for the services of highly trained former SAS soldiers.

There can be no doubt that David Stirling was a visionary. Not only was he the founder of the wartime SAS, but in 1967, he was the first to see the commercial prospects in employing former SAS personnel for mercenary contract service abroad. In 1967 he and several other former SAS officers created the Guernsey-based Watchguard Organisation specifically for that purpose. Watchguard, in effect, started what is now known in SAS circles as "The Circuit."

Amongst Watchguard's first clients was the United Arab Emirates. The company provided security training in its capital, Abu Dhabi. When President Kenneth Kaunda of Zambia suspected a counter coup to his government, he hired Watchgaurd mercenaries for protection and border patrol. In the late 1960s, Stirling's Watchguard made a contract proposal to the royal family in Oman that his organisation should be employed to both train his army and fight against a Marxist-inspired rebellion in the province of Dhofar. The contract negotiations fell through when the British government judged the rebellion as too serious for a private security firm to deal with, and deployed the SAS and other contract regular British soldiers into the country to combat the insurgency.

The resulting Dhofar campaign, called "Operation Storm" by the SAS, lasted nearly seven years and cost the lives of twelve members of the regiment, and the conclusion of the war would have unforeseen consequences for the SAS. Middle Eastern rulers watched with interest and envy at the performance of the SAS in Dhofar, and at the war's end, as many as forty mid-ranking NCOs in the regiment were offered very lucrative contracts to help establish the Special Forces of other Middle Eastern countries—Oman in particular. The loss of this cadre of experienced NCOs left the SAS vulnerable for a number of years thereafter.

One of the most illustrious SAS members to take up the Oman contracts was Julian "Tony" Ball, an ex-member of the Parachute Regiment. Tony, as he always preferred to be called, served as a trooper in "D" Squadron of 22 SAS and had been commissioned into the King's Own Scottish Borderers (KOSB's). Later, he served as an officer in the secretive 14th Intelligence Company in Northern Ireland. He had been decorated twice having been awarded the MBE and MC. His contract of service in the Oman Special forces was negotiated as part of a package organised by KMS. Tony was promoted to Lieutenant Colonel in the Oman Special Forces, but tragically he and another contract soldier, Major Andrew Nightingale, were killed in a car crash in Oman in May 1981.

Controlled Risks Ltd, a subsidiary of the London insurance brokers Hogg Robinson, employed ex-SAS personnel in a dangerous and unique way: in the negotiation of the release of businessmen held for ransom by terrorist organisations. In 1977, the Colombian Marxist terrorist group FARC kidnapped George Curtis, the Vice-President of Beatrice Foods of America. Because of the prevalence of hostage taking in Columbia at the time, his company had taken out hostage insurance, and Controlled Risks Ltd. were contracted to negotiate his release.

Two highly experienced former officers in the SAS, Major Arish Turle, a former squadron commander who had been awarded the MC during the Dhofar campaign, and Captain Simon Adams Dale were dispatched to the country to negotiate George Curtis' release. In Columbia, they made contact with Jim Raisbeck, a prominent Bogota lawyer. Over the next eight months, the three men were involved in difficult and delicate negotiations to free Curtis, at all times cooperating and keeping the Columbian police informed of their activities.

In September 1977, after the payment of a $400,000 ransom and having spent months in a tiny cellar, Curtis was released from captivity. Instead of thanking Controlled Risks Ltd., Turle, and Dale, the Columbian police arrested the two former SAS men on suspicion of being involved in the kidnapping. Both men were held in appalling conditions for eight weeks, but used their time in prison to rewrite Control Risk's "Standard Operational Procedures" (SOPs) in an effort to ensure that what had happened to them would not reoccur in future hostage release situations.

In El Salvador some two years later, two British Lloyds Bank International Bankers, Ian C. Massie and Michael Chatterton, were kidnapped by the Marxist terrorist group "The Armed Forces of National Resistance" (FAKN). Massie was the manager of the bank's San Salvador branch and Chatterton was his assistant. They had been in El Salvador for only three months when they were seized in November 1978 on a street near the bank. Both were held in appalling conditions during their seven months of captivity. SAS operatives from Controlled Risks Ltd. successfully negotiated their release for a ransom of $10 million. This time, thanks to Turle's and Dale's revised SOPs, the negotiators were not arrested by the local police.[1]

Close Protection

The SAS runs its own "Close Protect Course" for serving members. Trainees are taught all aspects of diplomatic security, including close protection, threat assessment, route planning, and building security. It is a highly prized course in the Regiment because, upon completion, one of the most lucrative jobs on The Circuit is summertime bodyguard work in the United Kingdom. Completing the SAS "Close Protect Course" is a valuable asset in obtaining such employment.

In essence, any close protection team is split into three equal, alternating teams: one on close protection, one on building security, and one on rest. Foreign luminaries, such as the royal family of Saudi Arabia or the Sultan of Brunei (both of which the author has worked for during his time on The Circuit) usually have their own permanent security teams which work in concert with the additional security team.

Although well paid, and despite its portrayal in movies and TV, close protection work is intense. You must be alert for dangers to your principal at all times, but ultimately, it's boring work for highly trained combat soldiers like former SAS men. It does, however, have some compensations, close protection teams usually get to stay in some of the finest hotels in Britain, such as the Dorchester in London. Whilst the author was part of the close protection team for the Sultan of Brunei, a notorious gambler, he won a huge amount at the blackjack table and handed out wads of ten and twenty pound notes to the members of his bodyguard team that were present at the win, much to the envy of the part of the team that was on building security and rest!

In addition to offering protection to visiting, usually Middle Eastern, royal dignitaries, several ex-SAS personnel have found niche roles as bodyguards. One former member became a "bodyguard to the stars." Mark "Billy" Billingham, a former member of the Parachute Regiment and 22 SAS, was a mountain troop specialist and became a bodyguard and security consultant for numerous celebrities, including Brad Pitt, Angelina Jolie, Russell Crowe, Michael Caine, and Tom Cruise. Another, Bob Sheppard, made a speciality of protecting journalists in war zones, whilst yet another became head of security for Manchester United.

Jim Davidson, the well-known comedian frequently employed ex-SAS contactors on The Circuit as bodyguards. Davidson had close ties with the SAS, and once organised an all-star celebrity football match for charity against the SAS football team for charity. Unfortunately for the SAS, the celebrities won. Whilst most of the ex-SAS contractors obtained employment through the established SAS mercenary companies, one small team answered an advertisement for a special, long-term, close protection contract in the United States. The principal to be protected was the son of the then-president of Lebanon Rafic Hariri, later to be assassinated in a car bomb attack in Lebanon on 14 February, 2005. His son was undertaking his studies in an American university and needed close protection for the duration of his four-year stay there. The team that was assembled were given diplomatic immunity and were officially part of the Lebanese Embassy in Washington, and the United States authorities granted them permission to carry concealed weapons.

One of the members of the close protection team was Desmond "Des" Howden, a former member of 'B' Squadron 22 SAS and one of the author's colleagues. After starting his contract, Des set his stall out early with his young principal when, after a shopping trip, he attempted to hand the bags containing his purchases to Des. The ex-SAS man's response was brutally frank: "I'm here to protect you, not carry your fucking bags." After that, they both got on swimmingly well.

Another of the team was Charles "Nish" Bruce, another former member of 'B' Squadron SAS. Nish was one of the most outstanding freefall experts not only in the Army, but in the country. He had been awarded the Queens Gallantry Medal (QGM) in Northern Ireland for actions during the ambush of a Provisional IRA assassination team. Sadly, later in life, after a long bout of mental illness, he committed suicide. Fittingly perhaps he chose to go out the way he loved, by freefalling from a plane without a parachute.

Whilst not really part of the actual Circuit, Mohamed Al-Fayed, the late owner of Harrods, employed a permanent close security team of mixed ex-SAS and former members of the Parachute Regiment. One of the ex-SAS members who served on Al-Fayed's team was Bob Horsefell, whose many talents included having a black belt in karate. After Bob gave up The Circuit, he went to be involved in veterans' charities and became an inspirational public speaker.

Another ex-SAS member of the Al-Fayed security team was Frank Collins. Like Bob Horsefell, he had been a member of the anti-terrorist team that stormed the Iranian Embassy in 1980; in fact, Frank was the first SAS man to enter the building. The author had the privilege of working with Frank during a humanitarian medical mission in Malaya in 1984. A born-again Christian, Frank was a deeply religious man who eventually left The Circuit to became an Army chaplain. For reasons no one understands, Frank committed suicide by gassing himself in a car in 1998.

The author worked with the Al-Fayed security team when bodyguarding the Sultan of Brunei and observed that there was considerable tension between the ex-SAS and ex-Parachute Regiment wings of the security team. The tension arose because the ex-SAS members had all been trained during their service with the SAS in close protection, whilst the ex-Parachute Regiment personnel had not.

In addition, most of the ex-SAS personnel had undertaken other private contract personal security work before entering Al-Fayed's employment, and for the majority of the ex-Parachute Regiment members, this was their first close protection work. It was one of the ex-Parachute Regiment members of Al-Fayed's close protection team, Trevor Rees-Jones, who was travelling with Al-Fayed's son Dodi Al-Fayed and Princess Diana the night they perished in a tragic car accident in Paris. Rees-Jones was the sole survivor of the deadly event. Perhaps if it had been an ex-SAS member of the team those tragic events might not have unfolded as they did.

Some former ex-SAS contactors who have passed the course now offer courses for would-be bodyguards, passing on the skills that are needed to obtain employment in today's highly competitive market for trained close protection specialists.

Overseas Training

The winter training teams abroad are, for the ex-SAS men involved in them, far more enjoyable work. 22 SAS prides itself on the quality of its training teams. The author himself undertook such a training team, known colloquially in the SAS as a "Team Job," in Qatar training their special forces. The author found the work there both enjoyable and challenging. The troops we trained went on to perform magnificently in both the First and Second Gulf Wars.

Ex-SAS training teams traditionally took up the slack which the regular SAS, with its limited numbers, could not fill. Saudi Arabia, Kuwait, Qatar, the UAE, and Oman have all been lucrative sources for training contracts for ex-SAS members. The typical training team consisted of about twelve to twenty men, and contracts would usually vary from one to three months. The SAS contractors would offer compressive courses in weapons, special forces tactics, counter insurgency, explosives, and close quarter combat.

Normally, all SAS contract soldiers on a training mission are given temporary officer rank in the army of the contractor. As indicated above, in Oman, contract SAS soldiers were given longer contracts to actually select and train the Omani Special Forces. Many times, as part of their contracts, the SAS contractors would have to set up secret alternative operational centres to which a ruler could take refuge in the event of a coup. In many of these countries, the SAS contractors had to train two separate special forces units, each with a different command structure in case there was a coup and one could be used against the other.

Africa too has been a continual area were ex-SAS contractors have found employment both in the close protection field and training teams. One ex-SAS contactor who worked for a time in Nigeria in the late 1980s and 1990s told the author that the main problem in working in the country was corruption: bribes had to be given to everyone from customs getting into the country to organising police support. The bribe money actually had to be built into the fees that were negotiated for the ex-SAS contractors' overall contracts.

For ex-SAS contract soldiers, overseas training teams are not without risk. On 1 December, 1989, Philippine President Corazon Aquino's government faced an attempted coup by a group of disgruntled soldiers called the Reform the Armed Forces Movement (RAM), who were loyal to the former President Ferdinand Marcos. The plotters almost seized the Royal Palace during the violent uprising, and it was successfully suppressed, but only with American help. Badly shaken by the coup, Aquino decided to hire outside help to train her special forces to deal with any future coup attempts.

In 1990, following intelligence of another impending coup by another dissident group of officers called "Young Officers Union," (YOU) a fifteen-man team of ex-SAS contract soldiers was commissioned by President Aquino. The team's contract required them to train Aquino's government troops in counter-coup techniques, including close quarter combat. The team set about training the government forces and conducted a series of counter-assault drills on the presidential palace, the nation's Congress, and the Manila international airport. The presence of the training team did not go unnoticed by YOU who warned of "drastic action" against the training team, culminating in a letter to the British Embassy that read:

"We wish to inform your office that a group of British mercenaries has been employed and paid for with taxpayers' money by the Aquino regime to train and arm its own Yellow army. Our forces in Manila have closely monitored the various activities of these mercenaries, which are a direct intervention to the country's internal security affairs and a clear violation of Philippine sovereignty. We have the identities of these mercenaries, and we know where they are. We, therefore, ask the British Embassy to order them to leave the country at once or YOU forces will take drastic action."[2]

Loyalist troops were described by the rebels as the "Yellow army" because the colour was Aquino's symbol when she ran against the late former President Ferdinand Marcos in 1986. The ex-SAS contract mercenary team heightened its own security and avoided socialising outside of the secure army facilities they resided in. Professional contract soldiers to the end, they completed their training assignment and left the country without suffering an attack by the YOU militants.

The forces that the ex-SAS contactors trained successfully put down two subsequent coup attempts in 1990: the first, in March, resulted in a siege at a hotel that ended with the government forces successfully storming it. Seven months later, a small group of troops mutinied at an army base but surrendered after being contained by government forces for two days. It would be the last coup attempt Aquino faced.

One overseas training mission was even more perilous for one ex-SAS mercenary contractor. In 1997, the civil war in Sierra Leone had not yet ended, but international recognised elections had taken place. To compound the miseries in that unfortunate country, disgruntled SLA officers staged a coup in May 1997 and established the Armed Forces Revolutionary Council (AFRC) as the new government in the country. The RUF joined with the AFRC to capture Freetown with little resistance. The new government was led by Johnny Paul Koroma, who immediately declared the war "over."

Following the announcement, the country quickly descended into anarchy, with violent armed rebel gangs roaming the capital and countryside, indulging in an orgy of looting, rape, and murder. There was international dismay at the overturning of the civilian government, multilateral armed force from the Economic Community of West African States Monitoring Group (ECOMOG), mostly Nigerian intervened and retook Freetown on behalf of the government, but they found the outlying regions more difficult to pacify.

Ex-SAS contract mercenary Will Scully was on a routine training mission in the country at the time. An ex-member of 'G' Squadron 22 SAS, he served in Northern Ireland, the Falklands, and in the Second Gulf War. Standing well over six foot in height with a muscular build and a shock of blond hair, Scully was probably what every civilian imagined an SAS man to look like. As the chaos engulfed the country, he found himself in a hotel with more than 1,000 expatriates from many nations, being besieged by the rebels who were joined by crazed bushmen in their violent rampage.

A Nigerian army force defending the hotel came under sustained attack from the rebel forces and their bushmen allies. The Nigerians began to panic after five of them were killed—and more wounded—and things looked desperate for those trapped in the hotel. Scully reacted instantaneously to the rapidly deteriorating position, and swiftly made his way to the roof. A quick survey of the situation was all that was needed for Scully to realise that immediate action was needed if the building was not to be overrun.

Grabbing a discarded machine gun, Scully began to engage the advancing rebel forces. Constantly moving from position to position and under continual heavy fire, he held the rebel force at bay for nearly eight hours until a relief force arrived. The rebels, demoralised by Scully's dogged defence, fled at the sight of the advancing relief force, which enabled the evacuation of the occupants of the hotel. For his heroic actions, Scully was awarded the Queen's Gallantry Medal in 1998.[3]

As part of The Circuit, Scully would go on to command aid convoys in Bosnia, and in 2001 protected CNN journalists and helped them set up base in Kabul, Afghanistan. Later, he ran a convoy to Tora Bora and created a base from which the international media covered the US attacks against Al-Qaeda positions hidden in the mountains. During the 2003 invasion of Iraq by the US, he coordinated CNN insertion of equipment into Northern Iraq and proved close protection during the course of the war. In later life, Will Scully became a writer, actor and public speaker.[4]

Some readers who consider the use of contract mercenary soldiers to combat anti-poaching gangs in Africa as not "Military Warfare" in its truest sense. If so, they would be under grave misapprehension. Those contact mercenary soldiers who conduct such operations face, in the armed and heavily armed poaching gangs, many who have terrorist connections, an enemy every bit as merciless as any they might meet on a battle ground in a regular or irregular war.

The point can be well illustrated by recent events in the ongoing war to eradicate the vile practice of illegal poaching in Africa. In April 2020, thirteen park rangers were killed in a rebel ambush in Virunga National Park in the Democratic Republic of Congo. In January 2021, six more were killed and one seriously wounded. The attacks were blamed on a militia group known as Mai-Mai, one of many that operate in the region. Two Mai-Mai militants were also killed in the clash in January 2021.[5]

Although advancing in years, David Stirling, ever the innovator, was the first British mercenary contractor to conceive the idea of using contract mercenary soldiers to combat illegal poaching in Africa, which threatened the very existence of many species of animals. Stirling approached a former senior officer in the SAS, Ian Crooke, with the idea of forming a company specifically to deal with the problem.

The author had the privilege of serving under Ian Crooke during the Falklands War, where he was both the Squadron Commander of 'B' squadron 22 SAS and Second-in-Command of all SAS troops deployed during the war. In 1981, Crooke was dispatched to Gambia with two NCOs as part of a three-man SAS team sent to assess the situation at the request of the President of Gambia who was facing a coup. Senegalese troops had entered the country to suppress the coup attempt and the rebels had seized the President's wife as a hostage.

Whilst getting a briefing at the High Commissioner's residence, Crooke learned that the President's wife had been taken to a nearby hospital. Against the express orders of the High Commissioner, Crooke and his small team went to the hospital and, although unarmed, overpowered the rebel guards and freed her. The Senegalese troops then quickly suppressed the attempted coup. On his return to the UK, Crooke faced the possibility of a court martial after a complaint by the High Commissioner over his "high-handed" disobedience of a direct order. The then-Prime Minister, Margret Thatcher, directly intervened and Crooke was awarded the DSO. Crooke retired from the SAS as Commanding Officer of 21 SAS.

Together, Stirling and Crooke formed KAS Enterprises in 1986, and Stirling appointed Ian Crooke as managing director. In 1987, Prince Bernard of the Netherlands developed a proposal to launch an anti-poaching project in Africa called "Project Lock." There is confusion to this day as to who exactly who came up with that original idea. According to Dr. Hanks, he commissioned KAS Enterprises, whilst David Stirling maintained it was his original idea.[6]

In the event it was Dr. Hanks who put the proposal to Prince Bernhard that even though millions of pounds were being spent protecting rhinos, little was done to halt the horn traffic. According to Dr. Hanks, Prince Bernhard observed that it would be extremely dangerous and a sensitive subject to boot, all while making it clear that it would be opposite to WWF policy to fund this work directly and also that being even remotely connected with such activities would be undesirable. Prince Bernhard readily acquiesced to fund the operation only in a private capacity and on the strict condition that the WWF should remain uninvolved and not even told about it.[7]

In November 1987, Ian Crooke submitted his preliminary proposals to Dr. Hanks, who forwarded theme to Prince Bernhard, who then paid the first instalment of an eventual £500,000 that he had earmarked for Project Lock. An intelligence-gathering phase began in 1988 and developed into a more ambitious project to employ former SAS men for paramilitary anti-poaching work throughout Southern Africa. The active phase of the project got underway in 1989 when Crooke and a team of a dozen ex-SAS members set up a base in a safe house in South Africa, where they organized and set up computer database containing their accumulated intelligence.

For Project Lock, this was when the problems really began to accumulate. Crooke and his team of ex-SAS men quickly established good relations with a number of South African agencies based on mutual self-help. In addition, Crooke's team allegedly purchased weapons for the project from the South African Defence Force (SADF), who were heavily implicated in the illegal ivory trade. Their apparent close ties to the South African regime immediately made them suspect to neighbouring Black African States. When KAS approached conservation officials in Zambia, Zimbabwe, Namibia, Tanzania, and Kenya to persuade them to pass on information regarding the horn trade to Project Lock and to employ KAS to train game wardens, their advances were initially turned down because of KAS' perceived South African connections.[8]

Despite the initial suspicion and refusal to cooperate with KAS on behalf of Black African States, in 1989, KAS succeeded in working with Zimbabwean game wardens, funding a helicopter for anti-poaching operations in the Zambezi Valley. Later that same year, when South African forces were being demobilised prior to independence elections in Namibia, KAS trained an anti-poaching team, and, in mid-1989, KAS also trained game wardens for Mozambique inside South Africa.

As KAS operations expanded, South African Military Intelligence feared that it might be an arm of British intelligence, or that in the course of its anti-poaching operation, it might turn up incriminating evidence of the SADF's involvement in poaching and gun running. A South African intelligence operative, a former police officer called Michael Richards, infiltrated KAS on the direct orders of South African Military Intelligence, by using a false name, papers, and credit cards.[9]

Richard's report to his superiors in South African Military Intelligence warned them that during the KAS' anti-poaching activities, they could learn about South Africa's covert operations in support of UNITA allies in Namibia and Renamo rebels in Mozambique. Richard's report also revealed that Ian Crooke was willing to carry out covert surveillance for South African Military Intelligence on its hostile neighbouring countries. South African Military Intelligence readily took up this offer. In the course of Operation Lock, KAS came across evidence of arms and ammunition smuggling, drug dealing, and the movement of criminals and terrorists, all of which was passed on to the South African authorities.[10]

In July 1989, Ian Crooke's covert intelligence gathering for South African Intelligence was revealed to the world, allegedly as a result of his own indiscreet loose talk. A Reuters correspondent filed a news report insinuating that Project Lock was an "undercover operation" designed to destabilise select Black African states that were funded by South Africa and using as operatives ex-SAS mercenaries."[11] As a result of the news report, KAS operations in Africa were wound up, and Dr. Hanks and Prince Bernhard withdrew from the project in 1989, and KAS ceased training in 1990.

Project Lock was wound up with recreations all round, including KAS's failure to account for its funding, equipment, or rhino horn it purchased during the course of its operations. Subsequently, the World Wildlife Fund tried to distance itself from Project Lock, stating that it had not approved of it and had no role in funding it.[12] KAS was to be embroiled in another scandal in Britain. In a 1993 court case, it was alleged that the head of National Car Parks (NCP) hired KAS Enterprises to engage in some industrial espionage against a rival firm Europarks, UK. The jury were told by the prosecuting Counsel that the operation was initially organised by Ian Crooke, but that he could not be prosecuted because he was living in South Africa.

Despite the failure of KAS and Project Lock, it did set the foundations of the modern day Park Rangers in Africa who carry on the vital and dangerous work of protecting African wildlife from illegal poaching. David Stirling, the founder of both the wartime SAS and modern British contract mercenary companies, died peacefully in his sleep on the 4 November, 1990. Ian Crooke eventually retired to South Africa, still parachuting into his later years before suffering traumatic injuries during a parachute jump and a subsequent stroke. With typical bravery, he learnt to walk and talk again before dying of natural causes on 17 May, 2022.

The author too has helped in a small way as a barrister at law in the ongoing struggle. In April 2017, he was instructed by African National Parks (APN) as their Legal Adviser. APN manages ten parks in seven African countries, and is an international non-governmental organization which seeks to address environmental conservation issues in Africa, especially the decline of many of Africa's national parks. The author drafted their "Voluntary Principles on Security and Human Rights," (VPSHR), their Mission Statement, and their "Guidelines on the Use of Lethal Force by Park Rangers."

From 2010 onwards, The Circuit expanded again to include anti-piracy operations in the Horn of Africa. The phenomenon of what the world calls "Somali Pirates" had humble beginnings. At the beginning of 2000, poor Somali fishermen protecting their tuna fishing grounds attacked the huge commercial foreign trawlers threatening their livelihood. After seizing a number of the trawlers and then ransoming them back to their owners, they quickly realised the commercial prospects of international piracy.

Within a decade, the internal anarchy in Somalia turned its operations into a guerrilla business war with global consequences. Although most Somali pirate attacks do not result in a successful hijacking, by 2008 there were 111 attacks that included fourty-two successful hijackings. By January and February 2009, the rate of attacks were about ten times higher than during the same period in 2008. News indicated that "there have been almost daily attacks in March."[13] By mid-April, there were seventy-nine attacks with twenty-one successful.

The world's navies faced a difficult battle to control the pirates, and western warships operating under a number of authorities including NATO, EU, NAVFOR (European Naval Force), and the US-led Combined Maritime Forces sought to contain the epidemic of Somali pirate hijackings. In addition, naval vessels from China, India, Russia, and Iran also provided warships to patrol the area.

As a result of the confused co-ordination of the international effort and the relatively few warships actually deployed into the vast area under threat, private-security firms stepped into the breach, providing ships with armed security. By December 2011, Nick Maddalena of British shipping-insurance broker Seacurus stated that: "Over 20,000 ships pass through the Gulf of Aden each year. Between 15 and 25 per cent of these ships carry armed security. We give significant discounts for kidnap and ransom insurance if they do—that's providing it's a reputable company, and its people are ex-services."[14]

The rush to provide highly trained personnel onto merchant vessels provoked a boom on The Circuit with many ex-SAS contactors finding lucrative employment. All those employed used firm "rules of engagement" modelled by the British contractors, at least, on those that governed them during The Troubles in Northern Ireland. Other mercenary contractors were not as reticent as the British in using lethal force. On 25 March, 2011 during an attack on the MV *Avocet,* a bulk freighter operated by New York-based Eagle Bulk Shipping Inc. was attacked by Somali pirates in speedboats intent on hijacking it. American contract mercenaries from the US-based private security firm Trident Group successfully fought off the attack after a short, but intense, gunfight.

The gunfight was videoed and subsequently leaked on the internet in April 2012, and the footage fuelled debate over when it was acceptable to open fire in such circumstances. In response to the debate, Trident Group President Thomas Rothrauff stated that, "while it is not visible on the video, return fire from AK-47s on the skiffs barely missed the head of one of his guards. All four ship guards had fired warning shots, and that barrage of gunfire may have provoked a fire fight that masked the sound of return shots from the skiffs on the video," he said. Trident has changed its procedures, and now permits only the team leader to fire warnings.

Rothrauff further stated that "it was likely that the occupants of the skiffs were killed or injured," though he "had no way of knowing."[15] By contrast, during anti-piracy operations in the area between 2010 and 2013, British contract mercenaries used warning shots or non-lethal force to repel attempted hijackings.[16] In many ways, Somali pirates who attacked western ships—even those protected by contract mercenaries—were lucky. On 12 April, 2009, US Navy Seals snipers killed three Somali pirates who hijacked the MV *Maersk Alabama* and held American captain Richard Phillips hostage, after concluding that his life was in immediate danger.[17]

Because of the presence of armed private mercenary contractors onboard ships coupled with a significant increase of naval presence in the area and the development of onshore security forces, by December 2013 there had been a 90 per cent decline in Somali pirate activity."[18]

The problem has not completely disappeared, and even until relatively modern times, the threat of Somali pirate attacks has not been completely eradicated. The Iraq War (see next chapter), Afghanistan (see Chapter Eight) and anti-piracy operations were boom times not just for ex-SAS mercenary contacts on The Circuit, but for ex-British mercenary contactors in general. During the Iraq War boom, those seeking to cash in on it opened offices near the SAS HQ at Hereford. Similarly, during the anti-piracy boom, others opened up offices near Poole, the SBS HQ, in order to sound authentic. Unfortunately, some of the mercenary contactors that these firms provided were not special forces or even highly trained ex-British army, and many were not up to the task that their employers were paying large sums for.[19]

Today, the demand for highly trained ex-SAS contractors in the modern world is not as great as in the boom times. As a result, The Circuit has expanded, and with it, the roles undertaken by those on it. Members now seek opportunities in a large variety of roles, from supporting humanitarian relief operations, the oil industry, overseas mining ventures, as well as sport and the protection of journalists in danger zones around the world.

A prime example of this is "Rusty Firman," another ex-member of 'B' squadron who took part in the famous storming of the Iranian Embassy in 1980. Rusty has worked on a number of interesting jobs, ranging from a diamond mine security consultant in West Africa, to delivering armoured cars to the CNN news crew in Sarajevo during the war, being a security advisor and a bodyguard for the Japanese Embassy in Afghanistan, providing security at the Olympics in Athens for the American swim team, and being the security consultant as well as the personal protection officer for the Japanese Ambassador at the Japanese Embassy in Kabul.[20]

One thing seems certain: with Russian belligerence around the globe, including the present war in Ukraine, coupled with the instability in the Middle East and Africa, the world is getting more dangerous with each passing day. Both ex-SAS mercenary contactors on The Circuit and other future British contract mercenaries should have little difficulty finding employment once their military service is completed.

Chapter Seven

Papua New Guinea
"The Sandline Affair"
1997

Following the end of Executive Outcome's involvement in Sierra Leone in 1996, Simon Mann went on to establish another mercenary company called Sandline International with a fellow ex-Scots Guards Colonel Tim Spicer. Spicer's father had served in the army and he had followed the family tradition, attending Sandhurst and then joining the Scots Guards. He tried for SAS selection but failed the course. Spicer saw combat in 1982 when he was pulled off guard duty at the Tower of London and sent to the Falkland Islands. He took part in bitter fighting in one of the last battles of the war: the Scot's Guards assault on Mount Tumbledown.

He later served in the Gulf War in 1991 and also with the UN in Bosnia. While posted in Northern Ireland in 1992, two soldiers under his command shot an unarmed teenage father of two in the back and killed him. The soldiers were tried and convicted of murder as a result of the shooting. When they were released under the terms of the 1998 Good Friday Agreement, Spicer successfully lobbied and argued for their return to their unit.

Both Spicer and Mann, and the company they formed, would then go on to become involved in what was internationally known as the "Sandline Affair," which had its roots in the more than a decade-long effort by the government of Papua New Guinea (PNG) to terminate a secessionist movement on the island of Bougainville off the Southeast coast of the PNG mainland. At the heart of the conflict was control of Panguna copper mine. The PNG government had received about 44 per cent of its revenue from the mine. Local landowners shut down the Panguna copper mine to protest the environmental destruction it caused and to demand independence.

In 1997, after both Australia and New Zealand refused to provide logistical support for a final assault on Bougainville, the Prime Minister of Papua New Guinea, Sir Julius Chan, decided to seek outside help to suppress the rebellion, and the decision was made to hire mercenaries to deal with it. Chan's Defence Minister, Mathias Jape, was put in touch with Tim Spicer through some overseas contacts. Spicer's initial advice was to continue with the purchase of weapons to give the New Guinea Defence Forces (PNGDF) the necessary firepower to overcome the rebels. However, the head of the PNGDF, Jerry Singirok, dismissed the idea outright and proceeded with a planned assault on the island, codenamed Operation High Speed II. The operation was a disaster, both in planning and execution and, within six days, the PNGDF forces retreated from the island.

In the same year, Spicer put a proposal to Chris Haiveta, the Deputy Prime Minister of Papua New Guinea, that a full-scale mercenary operation could end the Bougainville secession permanently and reopen the Panguna copper mine. Singirok rejected Spicer's proposal out of hand, but Deputy Prime Minister Haiveta invited Spicer to visit Papua New Guinea and assess whether or not such a mercenary venture was possible. In December 1996, after making a preliminary reconnaissance, Spicer confirmed the operation was viable, and his price for the endeavour was US$36 million. He left with an advance payment of US$250,000.

Tim Spicer had his first direct meeting with Prime Minister Chan on 8 January, 1997, and in it he convinced Chan that his mercenary force of forty-four men could, in conjunction with the PNGDF, succeed in ending the Bougainville secession once and for all. Half of the US$36 million Spicer demanded as payment was paid up front, with the remainder due to be paid upon completion of the mercenary operation. Chan never sought the approval of his Parliament for the mercenary operation funding, instead he funded it through the secretive National Security Council. More problematic for Chan, in order to pay Spicer's mercenaries, public services such as education and health would have to suffer cutbacks.

The first of Spicer's mercenaries arrived on Papua New Guinea on 7 February, 1997. Within one week, a total of forty-four had arrived: eight from the UK, five from Australia, and the rest from South Africa. Parallel to the mercenary force arriving, Tim Spicer was having confidential meetings with Deputy Prime Minister Haiveta in which he discussed buying a large stake of Bougainville Copper Limited, the owner of the Panguna mine. The entire mercenary venture—including Spicer's intention to buy a stake in Panguna mine—began to flounder after Prime Minister Chan disclosed his intention to hire mercenaries "for training purposes" to the Australian Foreign Minister Alexander Downer. Downer openly opposed the use of mercenaries against the Bougainville secessionist movement. On 10 February, 1997, the involvement of mercenaries in Papua New Guinea was leaked to *The Australian* newspaper.

In the wake of the revelations, Jerry Singirok publicly condemned the mercenary involvement in Papua New Guinea and began plotting a revolt against Chan. Despite direct pleas from the Austalian government to not to proceed with the mercenary deal, Chan persisted with his plans. On the night of 16 March, 1997 the revolt, code named "Get rid of them quickly" began, but before the night ended, all of Spicer's mercenaries had been disarmed and arrested.

On the following day, Singirok accused Chan and other members of the government of corruption, and evidence of the payments to Sandline and the proposed cuts to public services were leaked to the public. Chan refused to resign and sacked Singirok as Commander of the PNGDF, replacing him with Colonel Alfred Aikung. Although Singirok accepted his sacking, there were nationwide protests in support of him, which grew in intensity as more revelations emerged of Spicer's attempt to buy a stake in Bougainville Copper Limited. Soldiers at the central Murray Barracks began to disobey orders and there were armed standoffs between them and the police.

When the Australians threatened to withdraw financial aid altogether if the Sandline deal was not cancelled, Chan, with some reluctance, terminated the Sandline contract. Weapons, including Mi-24 attack helicopter gunships, piston-engined light aircraft, military small arms, and 600 crates of ammunition that had been purchased for use in the mercenary operation were eventually impounded at the Australian Tindal RAAF base, near Katherine, until the government of Papua New Guinea could arranged for the material to be returned to Sandline.[1] The two attack helicopters remained in storage at the Australian RAAF base until 2016, when they were buried at the Shoal Bay Landfill site.[2]

The termination of the Sandline mercenary contract did not save Chan's political career. After several days of turmoil on 24 March, 1997 Bill Skate, then Governor of Port Moresby, threatened to bring forth a motion calling on Chan to resign. On 25 March, 1997, Chan resigned, and on 22 July, after Federal elections, he was replaced by Bill Skate as Prime Minister. Within one year, Bill Skate was able to successfully negotiate a peace treaty with the secessionist movement on the island of Bougainville. Jerry Singirok was first reappointed and then dismissed in 2000 as head of the PNGDF over charges connected to operation "Get rid of them quickly." In April 2004, he was formally acquitted of all charges laid against him.

Equatorial Guinea coup attempt

In 2004, Simon Mann's Sandline mercenary company became involved in an attempt to oust the brutal dictatorship of President Teodoro Obiang Nguema Mbasogo of Equatorial Guinea. Allegedly, Mann had been persuaded by the Equatorial Guinea opposition leader, Severo Moto, to launch the coup. The plan, later revealed in both newspaper and court documents, involved Mann and two former South African Special Forces officers: Carlos Cardoso and Niek Du Toit.

Carlos Cardoso's role in the coup was to recruit seventy-five ex-South African Defence Force (SADF) members, primarily from within the former 32 'Buffalo's' Battalion and 5 Reconnaissance Commando ranks to launch coordinated attacks in Equatorial Guinea in mid-March 2004. The coup plotters hired two fishing trawlers to operate off the West African coast, and posing as commercial fishing men as a front for the movement of men and arms into the country.

Nick du Toit, at the time a South African arms dealer, was a former army officer in both 32 Battalion and 5 Reconnaissance Commando SADF. His job in the *coup d'état* was to supply the mercenaries with arms, including AK-47s, RPGs, PK machine guns, and mortars. He would be in charge of the advance party of mercenaries who planned to secure the control tower at the Malabo airport and change the frequency to establish communication with an incoming plane from Zimbabwe carrying Mann, the main mercenary force, and additional weapons.

Mann's role was to lead the main body of sixty-five mercenaries. The intended coup plan involved a stopover in Zimbabwe where Mann would purchase sixty-one AK-47 assault rifles, twenty machine guns, 150 hand grenades, ten rocket-propelled grenade launchers, 100 RPG shells and 75,000 rounds of ammunition, then fly on to link up with De Toit's forces on the ground at Malabo airport and launch the coup. Following the plan, Du Toit led a group of fourteen mercenaries as a vanguard to Equatorial Guinea and waited for the signal that Mann was *en route* with the main body and the weapons before seizing the airport control tower.

Unfortunately, the coup plotters had been betrayed, and on 7 March, 2004, police at Harare airport in Zimbabwe surrounded Mann's plane and arrested him along with two colleagues who were on the runway whilst they waited for arms to be loaded on a chartered Boeing 727. The Zimbabwean authorities then tipped off the intelligence services inside Equatorial Guinea and on 9 March 2004, Niek du Toit and fourteen other mercenaries were arrested on suspicion of being the mercenaries' advance party.

Niek du Toit pleaded guilty to the charges against him. He served five years and eight months of a thirty-four-year sentence in a cell measuring 150cm × 210cm. During his incarceration he was beaten, tortured, starved, and kept in solitary confinement for much of his time in prison. His jailers burnt him with cigarettes, beat him with rifle butts and hung him upside down for hours at time. He contracted malaria multiple times and was refused treatment. Of the eighteen mercenaries jailed as a result of the failed coup attempt, only four of them would return home alive. On his release, he retired from mercenary work.

Mann had a less traumatic time in prison, serving three years of a four-year prison sentence in Zimbabwe for arms offences, and was extradited to Equatorial Guinea, where he served less than two years and four months of a thirty-four-year sentence. On 2 November, 2009, and allegedly as a result of heavy bribes, he was given "a complete pardon on humanitarian grounds" by President Obiang. He too, retired as a mercenary after his release.

Mark Thatcher, the son of Great Britain's then-Prime Minister Margaret Thatcher, was arrested by South African police in connection with the failed coup. On 13 January, 2005, he pleaded guilty to helping finance a coup plot in Equatorial Guinea and admitted that he assisted in the transfer of about US$285,000 to the mercenaries. He received a four-year suspended sentence with a fine of about US$560,000.

The informant who betrayed the coup attempt to the Zimbabwean authorities was never conclusively proved. Johann Smith, an ex-commander in the South African Special Forces and internationally renowned security analyst was an occasional advisor to President Teodoro Obiang Nguema Mbasogo. He issued two reports in which he claimed to have warned the American and the British governments in advance of the coup. Smith provided a statement to lawyers representing the government of Equatorial Guinea, and in it recounted that he first heard about the intended coup in November 2003:

"Because I was continuing to work in Equatorial Guinea with government, it was not in my interest that there be a *coup d'état*...I therefore wanted to warn the Equatorial Guinea authorities. I also considered it my duty to warn the authorities in [the] US and England because some of their nationals might be killed. I submitted a report in December 2003 of what I had discovered to Michael Westphal of the Pentagon (in Donald Rumsfeld's department). I expected the US government to take steps to warn Equatorial Guinea or to stop the coup. This was also my expectation as regard the British government, which I warned through two SAS *people I knew, and to whom I sent the report by email, also in December 2003, to their personal email addresses.*"[3] Both the American and British governments denied emphatically that they had any advance knowledge of Mann's planned coup.

In 2009, Nguema repelled another and last attempted counter coup, this by a rebel group that was attempting to free their country from his tyrannical grasp. One rebel gunman was killed in the exchange of gunfire, and the presidential security guards and a few others were thought to have drowned when their boat was sunk by the country's navy.[4] His security services, originally trained by the American mercenary company MPRI, went on to protect Nguema from numerous assassination attempts. Nguema is currently the longest serving president of any country ever and the second longest consecutively serving current non-royal national leader in the world.[5]

Iraq
2003 - 2022

There are many conflicting views of the rights and wrongs of the American-led invasion of Iraq on 20 March, 2003. One view might be that Saddam Hussein was a tyrannical despot who had committed mass genocides against his own people—especially the Kurds and Marsh Arabs—invaded the neighbouring sovereign state of Kuwait without justification, and was a direct threat to the peace and stability of the region who had to be removed from power. On the other hand, some might say that the American and British public were deliberately misled into thinking that Iraq harboured weapons of mass destruction. Others, that war should be the last, not the first, resort of any nation and that Hussein was no direct threat to the west in general and America in particular. Finally, it could be argued that the war was all about oil, and that Saddam Hussein's decision to demand payment for his oil exports in Euros as apposed the universal standard of the American dollar, was the real reason America chose to invade Iraq.

Whatever view is taken of the real reason for the invasion and occupation of Iraq, what cannot he sensibly argued against is that the coalition forces of America, the United Kingdom, Australia, and Poland that crushed the Iraqi armed forces in a lightning war, had absolutely no plan as to what to do after the inevitable victory. This was compounded by the decision to immediately abolish and disband both the ruling Ba'athist party and the Iraqi army, thereby throwing thousands of angry, disgruntled, military trained fighting men into the arms of militants and extremists.

Despite President George Bush's declaration of a "mission accomplished," the resulting insurgency campaign would be brutal and prolonged. US troops would be officially withdrawn in 2011, but that did not halt the insurgency, and, in 2014, the United States became involved once again heading up a new coalition. The insurgency and many dimensions of the armed conflict continue to this very day.

For one group, the appalling tragedy of Iraq was a financial goldmine: they were of course, private mercenary contractors. As the insurgency intensified, coalition troops—especially the US contingent—became overstretched, and the US turned to private contract mercenary firms to fill the gap. The deployment of contract mercenaries also helped keep down the appalling casualty figures in the regular armies deployed, which was rapidly eroding what public support here was for the continued occupation of Iraq.

According to a US Government Accountability Office (GAO) report, by February 2006, there were about 48,000 private military contractors in Iraq, and they were employed by 181 different companies.[6] British mercenaries of all ages, shapes, sizes, and military experience—or lack of it—were Britain's main export to Iraq during the period of the insurgency.[7] This explosion of British mercenary contact companies was helped by the fact that at the time there was no central database of private military and security companies operating from the UK, and no legal requirement to register with any governing body. For the mercenaries involved, the financial benefits were worth the risk of being deployed into an active war zone: many were paid up to $1,500 a day, and a typical western military contract mercenary could earn up to $180,000 a year.[8]

Contract mercenaries also had the advantage of being immune from local prosecution, as a result of Order No. 17 issued in June 2004 by the Coalition Provisional Authority, where all civilian employed by private firms and implementing tasks commissioned by the US authorities within the Iraqi jurisdiction: "...shall not be subject to Iraqi laws or regulations in matters relating to the terms and conditions of their Contracts, including licensing and registering employees, businesses and corporations; provided, however, that Contractors shall comply with such applicable licensing and registration laws and regulations if engaging in business or transactions in Iraq other than Contracts." The United States did not agree to repeal the Order No. 17 until 1 January, 2009.

British Contract Mercenaries in Iraq

After the debacle of the failed coup in Equatorial Guinea, the contract mercenary company Sandline was dissolved. Tim Spicer left Sandline in late 1999 and within a year, launched another contract mercenary company called Crisis and Risk Management. In 2001, Spicer changed the company name to Strategic Consulting International, and formed a partner firm that specialized in anti-piracy consulting called Trident Maritime. In 2002, Spicer, along with Jeffrey Day, an entrepreneur; and former investment bankers Mark Bullough and Dominic Armstrong, formed a new contract mercenary company called Aegis Defence Services.

With the urgent need for contract mercenary soldiers, Aegis finalised a $293 million contract with the Pentagon to coordinate security for reconstruction projects, as well as support for private military companies in Iraq. Aegis would become the second-largest foreign armed force in the country, with more men under arms that the British army had deployed at the time.

Tim Spicer and Aegis were now a major player in the Iraq contract mercenary industry, but as always controversy followed him and his new contract mercenary firm. A disgruntled former mercenary contractor who had worked with Aegis in Iraq posted a "trophy video" in November 2005 that showed two shooting events. In the first, Aegis contractors were seen firing with an automatic weapon at an approaching silver Mercedes. The Mercedes rammed a taxi and sent its occupants running. In the second, contractors fired at a white sedan and ran it off the road. An internal investigation by Aegis concluded that the video was "taken out of context," the actions represented "legitimate operations," were undertaken in compliance with the company's "rules of engagement," and that there was no evidence that civilians were killed. No Aegis employees were disciplined as a result of the video.[9]

British contract mercenaries who the author has spoken to about their time in Iraq avoided the practice of taking trophy videos or trophy photographs. (The trophy video that caused Aegis' problems was reportedly shot by a South African contract mercenary). They're also tight-lipped about what they did or witnessed whilst in the country. One ex-Parachute Regiment contractor who previously worked in Oman and Sri Lanka described to the author in stark terms, "We all have a firm understanding what happens in Iraq, stays in Iraq." He also had a quaint and somewhat controversial solution to the rapidly deteriorating security situation: "Release Saddam Hussein and make him head of police." The author does not know if that advice was ever communicated to the Iraqi authorities. Saddam Hussein was hanged on 30 December, 2006.

More problematic for Aegis, though: in April, 2005, a performance review by SIGIR found that Aegis was not compliant in five areas of its contract, including inadequate employee background checks, and slack verification of qualifications and training. After sampling records of twenty of Aegis's 125 Iraqi employees, the review concluded that the company conducted no police checks on eighteen and failed to interview six; there were no records at all for two of the men. "There is no assurance that Aegis is providing the best possible safety and security for government and reconstruction contractor personnel and facilities," concluded the audit, which recommended stricter enforcement of the contract.[10]

Aegis was also accused of using its contacts in Sierra Leone to hire contractor mercenaries to defend US bases in Iraq for as little as $16 a day, with no checks being made on whether those hired were former child soldiers. James Ellery, a director of Aegis between 2005 and 2015, defended the recruitment of contractors from countries such as Sierra Leone to "reduce costs for the US presence in Iraq." Aegis recruited an estimated 2,500 men from Sierra Leone, at least two claimed to be former child soldiers and threatened to sue Aegis.[11]

These criticisms did not prevent Aegis from expanding its role in Iraq. Aegis was initially awarded a $293 million contract by the Pentagon in May 2004. By December, 2005, that contract was worth in excess of $430 million.[12] After a several month delay due to challenges of the contract award from rival companies, the American Department of Defence renewed the contract with Aegis in September of 2007 for an additional two years and $475 million.

As a result of these large contracts from the US, Aegis controlled the "Reconstruction Operations Centre" in Baghdad, a central "War Room" that tracked and coordinated security contractors moving around Iraq and six satellite offices. The War Room served as an information clearinghouse for security contractors. If a security detail was ambushed, Aegis would coordinate with the military to call in air attacks and ground support to get help to the mercenary contractors under fire. In effect, Tim Spicer's Aegis contract mercenary firm largely controlled the movements of every other mercenary operator in Iraq, deciding who went where, and how.

Because of the immunity from prosecution and the quality of some of the contract mercenaries who operated in the country, there were grave concerns in many circles about indiscriminate shooting carried out, sometimes against totally innocent Iraqi civilians. The majority of the criticism centred around American contact mercenaries, but British firms were not above reproach. In September 2005, Brigadier General Karl R. Horst of the US Third Infantry Division, gave a scathing opinion in general of the contract mercenaries who were then working in Iraq: "These guys run loose in this country and do stupid stuff. There's no authority over them, so you can't come down hard on them when they escalate force. They shoot people, and someone else has to deal with the aftermath. It happens all over the place."[13]

Tim Spicer denied that his Aegis mercenary contractors were aggressive or acting in an unprofessional manner. In October, 2005, he told Jon Swain of the London *Sunday Times,* "We are not trying to fight a war. There are others equipped and paid to do that. We can fight if necessary, but our whole ethos if we are attacked is to return fire and back off. We are not war-fighting people. If we are escorting a client, our job is to run." Surprisingly there is not, even today, any reliable data as to the number of Iraqi civilians or insurgents that were killed by private mercenary contractors who were operating there.

It has to be remembered and taken into account that during the Iraqi insurgency, all foreigners, whether regular army, private mercenary contractor or civilian, were subject to continued and relentless attack. Suicide bombing, especially against vehicle convoys, were an almost daily occurrence. By the end of March 2009, the US Department of Labour confirmed that there were 917 civilian contractors killed in Iraq. This number was updated to 1,537 in the same month just two years later. The total number of casualties was further updated to 1,569 by 20 July, 2012. Whilst not all of these contractors were private mercenary contractors, the dangers for them working in Iraq during this time cannot be underestimated.

The inherent everyday danger faced by private mercenary contractors, especially those posed by suicide bombers, goes a long way to explain—but not excuse—a tendency on behalf of some of them to shoot first and ask questions later, especially as there was no risk of being prosecuted as a result. If you add into this already toxic mix the fact that some of those deployed onto the ground may not have had the appropriate military background to be employed as mercenary contractors in the first place, it goes a long way—in the author's opinion, at least—to explain the comments made by Brigadier General Karl R. Horst.

Given the rush to put boots on the ground and the evident lack of screening by some mercenary contract firms, some people who worked in Iraq should never have been there armed with a gun in a war zone. But not every contractor—British, American, or other nationality—who worked in Iraq was a gun-wielding, money-hungry, trigger-happy lunatic. On the accounts of the vast majority of British contract mercenaries the author has spoken to over the years, they did a difficult, dangerous job in a professional manner. If mistakes were made in the heat of the moment, which they certainly were, they were genuine mistakes, not the work of some crazed psychopath. The conduct of British mercenary contractors in Iraq never reached anything like the debacle of the ill-fated British mercenary involvement in Angola.

As can be gleaned from above, there was a great disparity in the quality of British contract mercenaries who were serving in Iraq. Apart from the giant Aegis company, a myriad of smaller British mercenary companies obtained contracts or sub-contracts to operate there. A big selling point for these companies was to advertise that they were employing ex-SAS mercenary contractors. As can be seen from Chapter Six, many small mercenary contract firms opened offices in Hereford during the Iraq war boom to make those claims more credible.

For this very reason (for British ex-SAS contract mercenaries) the Iraq insurgency was a welcome boost to the established SAS Circuit. Why? Former SAS contract mercenaries were at a premium and that can be explained in the exploits of just one of them. A Fijian ex-SAS contractor who could, without any exaggeration, be described as a living legend, was Sekonaia "Tak" Takavesi, called by all who had the privilege of knowing him simply as "Tak." He was born in Fiji in 1943 and brought up on the Pacific island. He left his tropical home and enlisted in the British Army on 13 November, 1961, joining the King's Own Border Regiment.

Two years later, he underwent selection for the SAS and passed, serving with a number of Fijians in 'B' Squadron. In Aden during the mid-1960s, he and other Fijian members of 'B' Squadron were involved in covert, plainclothes patrols, and dressed as locals, they would blend in and seize targets of opportunity. In one incident, he and fellow Fijian Trooper Talaiasi Labalaba, confronted and shot dead two terrorist gunmen.

In the Oman province of Dhofar on the morning of 19 July 1972, rebel communist insurgents launched a carefully planned attack using 250 of their most élite fighters to capture the small town of Mirbat on the Arabian Sea. The town was a staging area and rest centre for SAS troops fighting in the province. There were only eight SAS men in the base at the time, and the rebels only made one mistake: they didn't bring enough men.

Tak and the eight other SAS men held off the rebel attack until a relief force from 'G' Squadron landed behind the attacking rebel force and all but wiped them out. Tak was seriously wounded but refused to be evacuated until his lifelong friend, Labalaba, was loaded onto the relief medical helicopter. Although Tak survived, Labalaba and Trooper Tommy Tobin perished. Tak was awarded the Distinguished Service Medal (DCM) for his bravery that day. He participated in the Iranian Embassy raid in 1980, the Falklands war, and many operational tours of Northern Ireland. He then retired from the British army as a Warrant Officer First Class.

On leaving, as with most ex-SAS, Tak went on The Circuit on 10 Nov, 2003. At sixty years of age, he was working as a contract mercenary in Baghdad, Iraq, driving two vehicles around the ring road of the city with another ex-SAS contract mercenary, when their vehicles were attacked by at least a dozen Iraqi insurgents. Tak personally recounted to the author what happened next. In the initial ambush, he was shot twice, suffering a bullet wound to the chest and a bullet graze to his head. His vehicle was immobilised and forced off the road. His comrade managed to drive through the ambush.

As Tak sat in his wrecked vehicle, three Iraqi insurgent gunmen approached, intending to take him prisoner—a terrible fate for any contract mercenary in Iraq. Tak put his hands up in a sign of surrender, but as the unsuspecting gunmen got closer, Tak pulled a concealed weapon from the visor above his head and opened fire, killing two of the insurgents instantly and wounding the third. Other insurgents began to fire at his car and Tak was wounded again, this time in the leg. At this crucial time, Tak's ex-SAS comrade, having done a U-turn, re-appeared and began giving covering fire, which enabled Tak to run to his vehicle and make a fighting retreat from the ambush. After a period in hospital, he made a full recovery from his wounds. One senior member of the SAS, who the author talked to about the incident, summed it up in very simple terms: "Did they [ever] pick on the wrong bloke!"

Not every British contractor went to Iraq for money or to guard facilities or people; some went for purely humanitarian reasons. The Mines Advisory Group (MAG), a charitable organisation working in Iraq to make the country safer for its inhabitants, employed expert mine clearance contractors for their operations. Ian Rimell was one. He joined the charity in January 2003 after a long career in mine and bomb disposal with the British Army. On 4 September, 2003, he had cleared a scrap heap filled with ammunition and hidden explosives and later delivered the scrap metal to help with the rebuilding of a local school.

Later in the afternoon, as he was travelling in a vehicle along a main road towards Mosul city, he was shot dead by Iraqi insurgents. An Iraqi colleague, Salem Ahmed Mohammed was critically wounded in the same attack. Ian Rimell was 53 years old, a father of three, and a dedicated humanitarian who worked well with the local people. He was the second British contractor to die in Iraq, but the first to be killed by insurgents. The first British contractor to perish whilst in Iraq was Peter Rudolf, on 21 July 2003. He drowned when he fell ill while on a dive near Umm Qasr. He was working for Sub-Surface Engineer as a diver. By the end of the Iraqi insurgency, at least fifty-eight British contractors would be perish there.

American Contract Mercenaries in Iraq

The history and story of American mercenary contractors in Iraq can be best illustrated by exploring the deployment of just one "Blackwater." The company was formed on 26 December, 1996 by two former US Navy SEALs, Al Clark and Erik Prince, to provide training support to military and law enforcement organizations. SEAL (Navy Sea, Air, and Land) Teams, usually referred to as Navy SEALs, are the Navy's main special operations force and a component of the Naval Special Warfare Command. The Naval Special Warfare Development Group (DEVGRU), previously called "SEAL Team 6" is widely regarded by serving and former members of the British SAS as the only special forces unit in the world that is on a par with Britain's elite unit.

Clark had served both as a SEAL combat swimmer and had also passed the further specialized selection and training course for assignment to DEVGRU. Prince was a former member of SEAL Team 8 who had seen active service in the Middle East and the Balkans. Blackwater received its first Iraq contract, in August 2003, a $21 million contract for Personal Security Detachment as well as two helicopters for Paul Bremer, head of the US occupation in Iraq. It was one of more than sixty private security firms employed by the United States during the Iraqi War to guard installations and officials as well as train Iraq's new army and police, and provide other support for coalition forces. Overall, the company would receive more than US$1 billion in US government contracts. The company was made up of nine divisions and a subsidiary, Blackwater Vehicles.

The story of Blackwater in Iraq is one drenched in blood—not only of Iraqis, many of whom were innocent bystanders—but also of Blackwater mercenary contractors. On 31 March, 2004 at around 10:30 a.m. local time, four armed Blackwater contractors driving two Toyota SUV's were ambushed by Iraqi insurgents in Fallujah. The four mercenary contractors on board were ripped apart by withering gunfire practically before they knew what had hit them. What happened next was an act of savage brutality, even by the blood-soaked standards of Iraq at the time.

The bodies of the four dead contractors were pulled from inside the vehicles, and further beaten, hacked at and burned before being dragged through the streets of Fallujah. Locals cheered as one corpse was attached to a car tow rope and pulled triumphantly through the streets shouting, "*Viva mujahedeen*!" and "Long live the resistance!" A 10-year-old boy was seen grinding his heel into a burned head, yelling "Where is Bush? Let him come here and see this!" In a macabre finale, the remains of two charred, mangled corpses were hung from a green iron bridge across the Euphrates River.[14]

The US Occupation Forces response to the brutal attack was swift. US Marines launched a full-scale assault on Fallujah called Operation Vigilant Resolve, which later became known as the "First Battle of Fallujah." In late 2007, a congressional report by the US House Oversight Committee criticised Blackwater's response to the tragedy, accusing the company of "intentionally delaying and impeding investigations into the contractors' deaths," further concluding that members of the Iraqi Civil Defence Corps, "led the team into the ambush, facilitated blocking positions to prevent the team's escape, and then disappeared."[15] Finally, the report concluded that the attack was masterminded by Ahmad Hashim Abd al-Isawi, an Al- Qaeda terrorist operating in Iraq. Al-Isawi evaded US justice until 2009, when he was captured as a result of a Navy SEAL special operation. After interrogation by US intelligence, he was handed over to Iraqi authorities for trial and executed by hanging around November 2013.

A few short weeks later, Blackwater contractors again came under heavy attack, this time from Shiite militia forces, who launched a sustained and ferocious assault with rocket-propelled grenades and AK-47 on the US government's headquarters in Najaf that was being guarded by Blackwater contractors. After hours of sustained attack, the Blackwater contractors almost ran out of ammunition when they were relieved and re-supplied by a second Blackwater contingent that flew over 70 miles to get there. Two months later, on 5 June, 2004, four more Blackwater contractors,

Americans Jarrod Little and Chris Neidrich, and Poles Krzysztof Kaskos and Artur Zukowski, were killed in an ambush in Baghdad.[16]

The brutality of the attack on the Blackwater mercenary contractors in Fallujah shocked Americans, not just the manner in the contractors' bodies had been violated, but there was a deep revulsion of the triumphant jubilation and approval of the actions of the insurgents by the crowd itself. Any lingering belief that the Iraqi people were viewing the Coalition forces as liberators had been shattered, but the question has to be asked, "What effect did Fallujah and these other attacks have on Blackwater mercenary contractors themselves?"

The author has experienced this himself, when serving in Northern Ireland with the Royal Ulster Constabulary on 19 March, 1988. Two plainclothes soldiers, Derek Wood and David Howes, were pulled from a car by a mob, dragged to some waste ground, stripped, brutally assaulted, and executed by Provisional IRA gunmen. The reaction of one SAS man who was operating in Ulster at the time who the author spoke to in the immediate aftermath of the atrocity probably summed up what every undercover soldier operating there at the time felt: "If they are ever going to get me out of a car, they're going to have to climb over a lot of dead bodies to do it."

In the author's opinion, much the same thoughts, and perhaps even darker ones of revenge and payback, must have gone through the minds of every Blackwater mercenary contractor working in Iraq at the time. In addition, the two sustained attacks on Blackwater from both sides in the ethic divide of Sunni and Shiite in Iraq and the involvement of the local Iraqi military in the Fallujah ambush, in all probability must have convinced many Blackwater contractors that the whole population was against them, that no one could be trusted, and nowhere was safe. This may well explain, but never justify, the tragic events that were to unfold.

Over the coming months and years, Blackwater contractors would be involved in a number of controversial shooting incidents in Iraq, and they would also continue to suffer heavy casualties. Paul Bremer, who headed the Coalition Provisional Authority, stated in October 2007 that between 2005 and September 2007, Blackwater security staff were in 195 shooting incidents, and in 163 of those cases, Blackwater personnel fired first.[17] The following is a breakdown of the most significant ones that are known. In May 2005, US soldiers witnessed Blackwater contractors "shoot up a civilian vehicle," along the "Route Irish," the code name for the road to the Baghdad airport. The driver of the civilian vehicle was killed, and his wife and daughter were maimed. The US field report also accused the contractors of firing in the direction of the American soldiers during the incident.[18]

On 21 April, 2005, Blackwater suffered seven fatalities in one day. In the first incident, a helicopter carrying six Blackwater mercenary contractors—Robert Jason Gore, Stephen Matthew McGovern, Jason Obert, David Patterson, Luke Adam Petrik, Eric Smith, as well as Stoyan Anchev, Lyubomir Kostov, Georgi Naydenov, Jim Atalifo, Timoci Lalaqila, three Bulgarians and two Fijians was shot down by Iraqi insurgents using a rocket-propelled grenade, near Tarmiya, north of Baghdad.

After the attack, a video purportedly showing the attack was posted by the Iraqi insurgents responsible. In it, a lone survivor was found lying in a ditch by insurgents. He told insurgents that his leg was broken, but was forced to stand. As the video zoomed out, showing the man in the middle of the frame, the cameraman gave the order to shoot. Bullets struck him repeatedly, even after he fell to the ground. "We are applying God's law," a voice declared in Arabic.[19] Later that day, Blackwater contractor Curtis Hundley was killed by a roadside bomb near Ramadi.

In April 2006, American soldiers came upon the scene after Blackwater contract mercenaries had shot three unarmed civilians in Baghdad. Blackwater guards claimed they were engaged in a shootout with insurgents who had escaped.[20] On 23 January, 2007, American dignitaries escorted by Blackwater contractors were leaving what was then known as the "Green Zone" in eastern Baghdad where they were ambushed. What started as sniper fire soon degenerated into an all-out firefight, with light and heavy machine gun fire, small arms, and grenades.

With some of their dismounted elements cut off from the vehicles, the security teams were unable to leave the area. Two of the relief helicopters—flown by brothers Arthur Laguna and Dan Laguna—were dispatched to the scene. Arthur's was shot down, and five Blackwater contractors—Steve Gernet, Ron Johnson, Artur Laguna, Shane Stanfield and Casey Casavant—were killed. A US defence official later confirmed that four of the five killed were shot execution-style in the back of the head.[21] After a sustained gun battle, the American dignitaries and their security teams were evacuated from the area by US regular forces.

Blackwater contractors opened fire in Baghdad twice in two days on 10 May, 2007. In the first, a Blackwater-protected convoy was ambushed in downtown Baghdad when an Iraqi vehicle drove too close to a convoy. When guards tried to wave off the driver, they then shot into the car's radiator, and finally shooting into the car's windshield. In the second, Blackwater contractors shot an Iraqi civilian said to have been "driving too close" to a State Department convoy.[22]

There were, in all likelihood, given the lack of official reporting of Blackwater contractors "engagements," many more undocumented shootings and killings by them. The picture that emerged from those that are recorded is one of a brutal, no-holds-barred war of attrition by both sides. On the insurgent side, it is clear that no Blackwater contractor could expect any mercy, even if wounded and taken alive. It is also clear the majority of the population seemed to approve of these tactics. On the Blackwater side, contractors, either out of fear or in direct retaliation, were capable of gunning down everything that moved, Iraqi civilian or insurgent. In this volatile and toxic mix of fear and relation, the scene was set for what was perhaps an inevitable tragedy.

On 16 September, 2007, US and Iraqi officials were meeting near the Izdihar Compound in Baghdad when a car bomb exploded. "Raven 23," a nineteen-man Blackwater Tactical Support Team, commanded by Jimmy Watson, took up positions at a checkpoint on the south side of Nisour Square to secure a planned evacuation route for the American officials and another Blackwater team providing security for them. Watson received a stand by order and was told to not leave the Green Zone upon reaching the checkpoint but, after waiting a few minutes, he made a "tactical decision" to advance into Nisour Square.

When Watson informed the Blackwater Tactical Operations Centre of his entry into Nisour Square, he was ordered to return to the Green Zone. Watson then apparently received a second order to "lock down the traffic circle to expedite the travel of [the other] Blackwater team." Watson attempted to comply with the second order. As they took up their positions, a Kia sedan approached his team. Raven 23 began firing in response, and by the time the firing ended, seventeen Iraqis were dead and twenty were wounded. The incident would become known as The Nisour Square Massacre."

There were, as always in war, conflicting accounts of what actually happened. The Blackwater contractors maintained, in later court proceedings, that the Kia sedan kept driving toward the convoy, ignoring verbal orders, hand signals, and water bottles thrown at the car, and continued to approach even when fired upon. An Iraqi policeman went over to the car, possibly to help the passenger, but the vehicle kept moving and it looked to the Blackwater contractors as if the policeman was pushing the car towards them.

In the view of the Blackwater contractors, this confirmed that they were under attack by a vehicle bomb. In response to what they perceived as a direct threat, they fired at the car and killed both people in it as well as the Iraqi policeman. Nearby Iraqi policemen, in response to the killing of one of their own men, began to fire at the Blackwater contractors, who returned fire. There is some confirmation of this from a State Department employee who was working in the department's Baghdad operations centre on the day of the incident and heard a radio call from the convoy: "Contact, contact, contact! We are taking fire from insurgents and Iraqi police."[23]

The Blackwater account was directly contradicted by an Iraqi government account of the incident. It stated that as the convoy drew close to Nisour Square, a Kia sedan carrying a woman and her adult son drove slowly on the wrong side of the road, and that the driver ignored a policeman's warning whistle to clear a path for the convoy. The Blackwater contractors fired warning shots and then lethal fire at the Kia before setting off stun grenades to clear the scene. Iraqi police and Iraqi Army soldiers mistook the stun grenades for fragmentation grenades and opened fire at the Blackwater team, to which they responded.[24]

In the wake of Nisour Square events, Blackwater's rights to conduct work in Iraq were temporarily suspended, and Iraqi Prime Minister Nuri al-Maliki called on the US government to end its contract with Blackwater and for those involved in the shooting to be held "accountable." As a consequence, the US House of Representatives passed a bill titled the Military Extraterritorial Jurisdiction Act that would make all private contractors working in Iraq and other combat zones subject to prosecution by US courts. There were numerous government and US Federal reports into the shootings, and almost all were critical of the Blackwater contractors' actions. To highlight but one, an FBI report issued on 13 October, 2007, concluded that at least fourteen of the seventeen Iraqi casualties were killed without cause. The three otherwise "justifiable" killings were those of the two passengers in the white Kia sedan and an unidentified Iraqi nearby.[25]

After protracted legal proceedings in which charges against the Blackwater contractors were first dropped before being reinstated and sentences challenged, former Marines Dustin Heard and Evan Liberty, former army sergeant Nicholas Slatten, and army veteran Paul Slough, faced trial on 17 June, 2014. After ten weeks of testimony and twenty-eight days of jury deliberations, all four men were convicted on 22 October, 2014.

Nicholas Slatten, a trained sniper and former member of the crack 82nd Airborne unit, was found guilty of first-degree murder. Slough, Liberty, and Heard were found guilty of voluntary and attempted manslaughter charges and using a machine gun to commit a violent crime. Blackwater contractor Jeremy Ridgeway of California, struck a deal with prosecutors on 4 December, 2008, where he eventually plead guilty to a single count of attempted manslaughter and one count of voluntary manslaughter, and also agreed to testify against the other five men.

On 22 December, 2020, President Donald Trump granted full pardons to Slatten, Slough, Liberty, and Heard. A White House spokesman stated the men had a "long history of service to the nation" as veterans of the US Armed Forces, and that there remained public and official support for the pardons. The granting of pardons by the Trump administration caused international outrage. UN Human Rights Office spokeswoman Marta Hurtado noted that each pardon contributed to impunity and each had the effect of encouraging people to commit such crimes in the future.[26] The Iraqi Foreign Ministry at the time urged the United States to reconsider the decision, declaring that the pardons "did not take into account the seriousness of the crime committed."[27]

In December 2008, the US State Department recommended that Xe, previously known as Black Water Company, be dropped as the primary private security contractor for American diplomats in Iraq and on 30 January, 2009, the State Department told Blackwater Worldwide that it would not renew its contract in Iraq. Blackwater, renamed Xe Services in 2009, was known as Academi since 2011, after it was acquired by a group of private investors.

The CIA had previously hired Blackwater in a secret, unapproved deal to locate and assassinate Al-Qaeda terrorists in 2007.[28] In 2010, Blackwater was awarded a $100 million contract from the CIA to continue to operate in Iraq. Xe has always defended its actions in Iraq, and a company spokeswoman stated: "When the US government initially asked for our help to assist with an immediate need to protect Americans in Iraq, we answered the call and performed well. We are proud of our success—no one under our protection has been killed or even seriously wounded."[29]

Postscript

Comparisons could be drawn between the Nisour Square Massacre and the Bloody Sunday in Northern Ireland in 1972 when members of the British 1st Parachute Regiment shot dead fourteen rioters in Londonderry, one of the victims was later confirmed to be a member of the Provisional IRA.[30] For what it's worth, the author gives his opinion as a former soldier (not as a barrister at law). There had already been a car bombing, and secondary attacks against those responding to such incidents were a common tactic of Iraqi insurgents, so the Blackwater contractors would have been in a heightened state of fear and alert. On any objective view of the accounts given by both sides, Iraqi policemen were engaging the Blackwater mercenary contractors with automatic gunfire after they had engaged with the Kia sedan which they, in the authors opinion, genuinely believed to be an imminent deadly threat.

If you place aggressive, highly trained, heavily armed young men in a situation where they are in fear that they might be killed, it is inevitable that they will react with lethal violence to that threat. Add to that the fact that, by virtue of Order No 17, they believed that there would be no consequences if they "over reacted" and you have a situation where this type of excessive use of lethal force is all but inevitable. This of course, does not excuse the Blackwater contractors of blame, but those that put them in that situation and gave them a virtual unfettered "licence to kill" should, in the authors opinion at least, share equal responsibility.

South African Contract Mercenaries

For ex members of the South African Defence Force (SADF), who fought in South Africa's decades-long fight to maintain white rule, Iraq too was a bonanza and a gift for contract mercenary firms. Many members of Apartheid-era security groups, such as the Civil Cooperation Bureau (CCB), the 32 Battalion, the Parachute Brigade, Reaction Unit 9, the Reconnaissance Commandos, the covert intelligence unit Koevoet, and the secret police unit Vlakplaas found employment in Iraq during the insurgency. One of them was François Strydom, a former member of Koevoet, which operated in Namibia against SWAPO insurgents during the apartheid era, and was killed in Bagdad on 29 January, 2004 by a suicide bomber. He was working for SAS International at the time. Four other South African mercenary contractors were injured in the attack, one of them was Deon Gouws, a former officer of the Vlakplaas.

When the Hart Group, a British-based mercenary contract firm needed to hire 170 English-speaking guards with military experience quickly to fulfil a contract, they turned to this large pool of ex-professional, anti-insurgent experts. Simon Falkner, a retired British Army Colonel and the company's chief of operations explained why: "We had to recruit people in very, very short order. They're good soldiers, the South Africans. They're tough people, and they're well-disciplined and there are a lot of them who want to do the work. A lot of people have left the South African Defence Force since Nelson Mandela came in."[31]

One of the contract mercenaries hired as a result of the Hart Group's recruiting drive in South Africa was 55-year-old Gray Branfield, a former covert operations specialist in South African Intelligence. Branfield was killed on 6 April, 2004, during street fighting in Al-Kut. His body was mutilated and hanged for public display. Only after his death was it revealed that Branfield was part of an assassination team set up in the early 1980s, when the apartheid government decided to assassinate the top fifty African National Congress (ANC) officials who lived beyond the country's borders. Branfield was charged with finding apartheid opponents in Zimbabwe, Botswana, and Zambia. In an interview given shortly before his death, Branfield justified his actions: "We saw it as a battle in the global war to fight communism."[32]

In July 1981, Branfield led an assassination team into Harare in Zimbabwe and killed Joe Gqabi, ANC's chief representative in Zimbabwe and its militant wing's operations chief. The team, armed with Uzis, sub machine guns, and Beretta pistols, shot Gqabi nineteen times after they scaled a fence and waited until the anti-apartheid activist emerged from the house. It is estimated that anywhere between 5,000-10,000 South African contract mercenaries were employed by the US, British, and other contract mercenary firms during the Iraqi insurgency.

Chapter Eight

Nigeria
2014 - 2015

Nigeria is the most populous country in the nation of Africa and is also its largest oil producer. Boko Haram—which is one of the biggest Islamist militant groups in the nation—has conducted terrorist attacks on local police, political groups, and the military since 2011. In addition, the fanatical terrorist group has launched indiscriminate attacks on civilians. In April 2014, more than 200 young female students were kidnapped from school and drew global attention to the continual threat from Boko Haram and the government's inability to contain it. The girls were eventually released following negotiations between Boko Haram and the Nigerian government in a deal that was brokered by the International Committee for the Red Cross.

President Muhammadu Buhari was elected in 2015, ousting the former military dictator Goodluck Jonathan on a counter-terrorism platform. Despite heavy handed attempts by the Nigerian army to combat the terrorist movement, these efforts proved ineffectual and were directly undermined by economic difficulties, such as the uneven distribution of oil revenue and high levels of corruption. In addition, political challenges, including internal violence in the Middle Belt region of Nigeria, further complicated the fight against Boko Haram, which had pledged allegiance to the Islamic State in early 2015, which prompting the United States to boost its military assistance and deploy 300 troops to Nigeria to help in the fight against the movement.

Despite the increased US presence and the best efforts of the Nigerian army, Boko Haram continued its rampage. By July 2014, Nigeria was estimated to have suffered the highest number of terrorist killings in the world over the past year with 3,477 killed in 146 attacks. The Governor of Borno, Kashim Shettima, a member of the main opposition party, noted in February 2014: "Boko Haram are better armed and are better motivated than our own troops. Given the present state of affairs, it is absolutely impossible for us to defeat Boko Haram."[1]

Despite the fact that President Muhammadu Buhari condemned the move even before assuming office, and that using private contractors to deliver military services goes against the African Union's Convention for the Elimination of Mercenaries in Africa—which Nigeria ratified in 1986 but never signed—in 2014, Nigeria turned to mercenaries to combat Boko Haram. Executive Outcomes had proved its expertise in combating insurgent groups in Angola and Sierra Leone, and it was to this mercenary contractor that the Nigerian government turned to in order to combat the increasing threat from the fanatical Islamic terrorist group.

The mercenary unit that was deployed consisted of white mercenaries from South Africa led by an experienced and ruthless mercenary by the name of Eeben Barlow, a former Lieutenant Colonel in the Civil Cooperation Bureau (CCB), a specialist anti-terrorist unit of the South African Defence Force (SADF). The CCB carried out covert operations during the apartheid era bush wars, which included assassinations of government opponents. The CCB, along with all the other major anti-apartheid era specialist counter insurgency units like 32 Battalion and the Reconnaissance Commandoes, was disbanded after Nelson Mandela took power in South Africa in 1981, leaving a large pool of highly trained counter insurgency troops without employment.

Once in the country, Barlow formed and led a specialist anti-terrorist unit called the Specialised Tasks Training, Equipment and Protection (STTEP). The unit comprised about 147 South African mercenaries (mostly ex-members of 32 Battalion and the Reconnaissance Commandoes) and 163 specially trained Nigerian soldiers which formed the 72 Mobile Strike Force special unit. Their initial mission was to rescue the 273 schoolgirls kidnapped from Chibok in northeast Nigeria. However, this changed after the negotiated release of the majority of the kidnapped girls. STTEP would instead be used in a full-scale counter insurgency operation against Boko Haram.[2]

Barlow quickly realised that the British-trained Nigerian army was still using tactics modelled after the needs of colonial Britain to defend its domestic and colonial territories during the First and Second World Wars. He also realised, from his previous experience, that the Nigerian army doctrines and strategies had not been adapted to the nature of modern warfare on the African continent, where such conventional doctrines were outmoded and often redundant.[3] In addition, the Nigerian army was dispirited after its failures against Boko Haram, whilst Barlow's mercenaries were highly motivated and well paid.

Barlow's STTEP used the same tactics that had been highly successful in South Africa's bush wars and had been used to such good effect in both Angola and Sierra Leone. STTEP adopted a counter insurgency doctrine called "relentless pursuit," which consists of confusing, dispersing, and putting pressure on the enemy through small mobile attacks, forcing it to withdraw from the areas they were operating in. Thereafter, STEPP would then relentlessly pursue the enemy, giving it no time to rest, disperse or regroup, and eventually exhausting it. The pursuit phase was done at all hours, using helicopters to leap-frog troops ahead of the enemy. The disembarked troops would then take up the pursuit, letting the present pursuers rest. The ultimate result was the eventual cornering and annihilation of the enemy force.[4] Barlow has argued that this is the only method to deal with terrorist organisations on the African continent, stating "...they are thugs with guns using terror tactics and committing widespread atrocities, there is too much at stake for political correctness."[5]

STTEP's offensive against Boko Haram was highly effective, and destroyed much of the terrorist organisation while driving many survivors outside of Nigeria's borders. According to Barlow, the Muhammadu Buhari administration eventually caved to pressure from the US after he was sworn in as president in 2015 and STEPP was prevented from finishing the job it started.[6] Whilst the use of mercenaries on the continent of Africa is largely deplored by the international community, the tactics adopted by Barlow's STEPP mercenary force in Nigeria were, in the author's opinion, sound and highly effective against fanatical terrorist organisations like Boko Haram. They are, in fact, classic special forces tactics that have been developed over the decades that saw the end of colonial rule in Africa. As noted above, they were used to great effect by the South African special forces in their colonial bush wars. In turn, they have largely been adopted by special forces, especially the British and French, when they have been deployed on the African continent and other theatres of conflict.

Barlow has also argued that, in addition to relentless pursuit on the ground, terrorist sources of income and finance also have to be eroded, as he points out in his book: "Anyone fighting an insurgency or terrorist campaign ought to know that one of the primary objectives is the denial of funds to the enemy. Without finances, they are deprived of the ability to purchase weapons, ammunition, medical supplies, transport, fuel, closing, food, and other supplies to sustain themselves." (Barlow, 2010: p. 356) From the author's own experiences in counter insurgency operations, he is of the firm opinion that these tactics are a sound doctrine and may in fact be the only effective means of meeting the challenges of and combating terrorist organisations like Boko Haram on the continent of Africa and elsewhere.

Afghanistan
2002 - 2020

In the aftermath of the gruesome terrorist attacks on the United States on 11 September, 2011, American launched an invasion of Afghanistan. The resulting conflict would see America and its allies dragged into a prolonged and costly counter-insurgency war against an implacable enemy in the Taliban. It would be America's longest war, and history will probably record that the war was one of colossal failures of broken and unfulfilled promises. In the author's opinion, the American and coalition forces deployed into Afghanistan may well have defeated the Taliban, had not the effort been totally undermined by the ill-judged decision to invade Iraq, which drew much-needed forces out of the country. The American presence officially ended on 31 October, 2021, in the hurried and inglorious retreat where nearly 200 Afghans and thirteen US service members died and left the Taliban in complete control of the country.

The involvement of private mercenary companies in Afghanistan largely replicated the Iraqi experience, with private mercenary companies providing logistical support for various American and NATO bases, providing highway security for supply routes, and guarding embassies and government installations. Some would provide training for both the Afghan Army and police. As in Iraq, there was a deliberate police force on behalf of succeeding US administrations to "outsource" the war in Afghanistan, and by 2016, one in four US personnel serving in both Iraq and Afghanistan was a private mercenary contractor. By 2021, the US Defence Department had 16,832 workers employed by private contractors in Afghanistan. Of that number, 6,147 were US citizens, more than double the remaining 2,500 US troops who were in the country at the time. From 2002 to 2021, the Pentagon spent $107.9 billion on contracted services in Afghanistan.[7]

This was private mercenary contract employment on a colossal scale, turning the corporate giants that deployed the private contractors into millionaires and the contractors themselves into wealthy men. Most contractors in Afghanistan earned between $300 and $750 a day, or between $9,000 and $22,500 per month.[8] DynCorp was the largest American contractor in Afghanistan. In the eleven years between 2002 - 2013, the US State Department paid DynCorp nearly $3 billion in contracts to train and equip police and counter-narcotics forces, according to US military auditor SIGAR.[9] Whilst American mercenary contract firms obtained the vast majority of these contracts, British firms such as G4S, one of the world's largest security groups, obtained lucrative contracts to guard government buildings, including the British Embassy in Kabul.

The vast amounts of treasure spent by the US resulted in private mercenary contractors spending years in training and equipping the Afghan forces with some of the latest weaponry in the American arsenal. Despite this gigantic effort, the Afghan army, numerically superior and better armed than its main advisory, collapsed and crumbled in a matter of weeks in the face of the ragtag Taliban offensive, lacking both air cover and heavy artillery, leaving the Taliban in control of the entire country and in possession of the American weapons.

Many reasons have been cited for the swift Taliban victory. It could, and has, been argued that a Taliban victory was inevitable because, like in Vietnam, the local forces lacked both leadership and the will to fight once American forces left. The Taliban, on the other hand, had a cohesive central leadership and an ideological will to win, no matter what the cost in human lives might be. That was certainly the view of the American leadership at the time. Top Pentagon spokesman John Kirby told reporters after the collapse of the Afghan forces, "You cannot buy will, you cannot purchase leadership, and leadership was missing, as we've been saying for weeks."[10]

Others have accused the private mercenary companies of inherent corruption, and that was certainly the view of one anonymous British military source in the immediate aftermath of the collapse of the Afghan army: "When I was in Afghanistan, private military contractors numbered almost 30,000. Some were engaged in protection tasks, but many more were responsible for training and mentoring Afghans who held positions of significant influence. They advised on intelligence, war-fighting, diplomacy, policing, you name it. Some of them were doing their best. Many more didn't give a damn. Many were on six figures and had been for years. Afghanistan for them was a cash cow, a way of putting their kids through college (most were American) or paying off a mortgage. In sum, there were too many poorly qualified people working without accountability [and] getting paid far too much. If you want an answer to the question of why Afghanistan's military crumbled in weeks, take a long hard look at their so-called mentors."[11]

The accusations of corruption has some force, following accusations that some private mercenary companies were supplying weapons and equipment to local warlords. In September 2010, Afghan President Hamid Karzai issued a decree disbanding all private security firms within four months. He stated: "In order to protect Afghan life and property, avoid corruption, security irregularities, and the misuse of military weapons, ammunition, and uniforms by the private security companies which have caused tragic incidents, and after the required assessment, I approve shutting down all private security companies within four months, including both domestic and foreign."[12]

The eight mercenary companies that were banned included XE, the company formerly known as Blackwater, NCL, FHI, White Eagles and other small companies. The ban was never fully instigated, and private mercenary companies continued to operate in Afghanistan until a few weeks before the Taliban victory. Whilst both these views have some force, in the author's opinion, they are too simplistic. The author has spoken to many private mercenary contractors who have stated that whilst they were in the country, the Afghan army, properly supervised, could go toe-to-toe with the Taliban and win, especially if it had proper air support, an essential element in any counter-insurgency operation.

As for the accusations of corruption and the lack of proper qualifications of some of the mercenary contractors deployed in the country, that in itself would not explain the rapid collapse of the Afghan army. As in all mercenary deployments, due to the desire to put boots on the ground, some unqualified and unmotivated personnel were undoubtedly employed by the various mercenary contract companies. Some, like Santos Cardona, had dubious military backgrounds, including being a convicted war criminal.

Cardona joined the US Army in 1993 when he was 17 years old and became a dog handler, serving in that capacity in deployments to Kosovo and Iraq. While deployed to Iraq, Cardona was accused of using his Belgian Malinois dog "Duco," to threaten Iraqis in Abu Ghraib prison. When photos of the event were publicised, he faced trial in the US, and in May 2006, was convicted of dereliction of duty and aggravated assault. A military judge imposed a fine and reduction in rank, and he was required to serve ninety days of hard labour at Fort Bragg, North Carolina. After release, he returned to the army and on 29 September, 2007 he left with an Honourable Discharge. Cardona and his working dog, a German Shepherd named "Zomie," were killed on 28 February, 2009, in Uruzgan Province, Islamic Republic of Afghanistan, when the vehicle he was riding in struck a buried Improvised Explosive Device (IED).

Against that, from the author's research, he is of the opinion that the vast majority of those who served there were high calibre, highly motivated, ex-professional military men. Men like Ryan Lozier who, at the time of his death, was working for Global Security Systems. He had a long history of service to his country. Lozier went into the Army when he was 19 years old and served with the Army Ranger Battalion for eight years in Iraq and Afghanistan before leaving the Army to work in the private sector. He was killed in May 2010 by an IED while he was working in Afghanistan.

Retired Master Sergeant Robert Wayne Pittman, Jr. is another example of a highly trained and motivated mercenary contractor. He joined the US army in 1990 and served multiple tours of duty in Iraq and Afghanistan. He was killed on 29 July, 2010, whilst working as a combat advisor. The author could go on with further examples, both living and dead, of ex-professional soldiers doing a competent job in a difficult and dangerous environment, often at risk of being killed by the very people they were training. If neither lack of leadership, the will to fight, nor corruption was the biggest factor in the Afghan army's sudden collapse, what was?

In the author's opinion, the reason for the sudden and complete collapse of the Afghan army is actually quite straight forward. The Biden Administration's ill-fated desire to disengage from the country by a fixed date and the decision in early May 2021 that the US should begin the process of removing all contractors from Afghanistan[13] ignored the fact that in reality, the Afghan army had become totally dependent upon contract mercenary support for its very existence. The Afghan army relied on contractors for every important function, from training and gear maintenance to intelligence gathering and, even more crucially, close air support in its battles against Taliban fighters.

As David Sedney, a former deputy assistant secretary of defence for Afghanistan, pointed out in an interview shortly after the Taliban victory: "We built the Afghan army in our image to be an army that operates with air support and intelligence and whose backbone is contractors."[14] Without the structural support of private mercenary companies, the Afghan army was no match for their implacable enemy and an inglorious collapse and defeat was all but inevitable. In the author's opinion, had the Biden administration kept on funding the mercenary contractors in Afghanistan, events may well not have unfolded in the chaotic and humiliating way they did.

The disintegration of the Afghan army was so swift and complete, that it left the Talban in possession of a powerful air force and seven major air bases. Thankfully, for the stability of the region, it was unable to use them to any great effect. There were reports that the Taliban were seeking to employ Russian mercenaries to enable them to operate it.[15] Such reports have never been verified, and the author doubts whether they are accurate. Given the history of brutality and war crimes committed by Russian forces during their occupation of the country and the long memories of the Afghan people, it is highly unlikely that any Russian mercenary undertaking such a contract would live long enough to cash his pay check. In all likelihood, without proper maintenance, these powerful weapons will by now have been rendered useless.

Far more worrying for the long term stability of the region is that it has been known for decades that the Taliban has a mercenary force of around 30,000 men inside Pakistan, trained and directed by the Pakistani security service the ISI.[16] There are real fears that this external mercenary force may be deployed elsewhere, for example into the highly volatile Indian province of Kashmir.[17] What is certain is that this powerful mercenary force will continue to be used by Pakistani intelligence—both in Pakistan and elsewhere—to further the aims of the ISI, and it has the potential of dragging other regional powers, such as India and China, into the quagmire that is present day Afghanistan.

Sudan
2003 - 2018
"The Rise of the Janjaweed"

To understand how a small group of nomad raiders rose to become one of the richest and most feared mercenary groups in Northeast Africa, it is necessary to look at the recent history of the troubled country of Sudan. Omar Hassan Ahmad al-Bashir came to power in Sudan in 1989. He was a brigadier general in the Sudanese Army, and led officers in a military coup to oust the democratically elected government of Prime Minister Sadiq al-Mahdi. Ever since 1968, the central Sudanese government has tried to create separate factions of "Arabs" and "Africans" in the western area of Darfur, a difficult task, as the population is substantially of mixed race via intermarriage and could not be distinguished by skin tone.

The Black African population of Darfur resisted the attempts and rose up in open rebellion. This internal political instability was aggravated by cross-border conflicts with Chad and Libya. The rise of the predatory mercenary group known as the Rapid Support Forces (RSF) also called the "Janjaweed" has its roots in 2003, when Bashir's government mobilised Arab herders to fight against the Black African insurgents in Darfur. Camel-herding nomads from the Mahariya and Mahamid branches of the Rizeigat ethnic group of northern Darfur and adjoining areas of Chad formed the core of the Janjaweed. These two ethnic groups ranged across the desert edges of both Sudan and Chad long before any border was drawn.

During the resulting 2003 - 2005 Darfur War, the rebel Sudan People's Liberation Army (SPLA) had considerable initial success against the Sudanese government forces. In response to his army constantly losing, Bashir switched his war effort to emphasize military intelligence, the air force, and the Janjaweed. The result was a campaign of ethnic cleansing against Darfur's non-Arabs, which resulted in the deaths of hundreds of thousands of civilians at the hands of the Janjaweed. In October 2007, the US government declared the Janjaweed killings in Darfur to be genocide. It is estimated that anywhere between 200,000 - 400,000 civilians had been killed by the Janjaweed over a three year period.[18] The UN Security Council called for the Janjaweed to be disarmed.

Because of its bloody efficacy, this merciless force was formalised by Bashir into a paramilitary force called the Border Intelligence Units. The leadership of the Janjaweed at that time was never clear, but it is believed that they were led during the Darfur Massacres by Musa Hilal. Within its ranks was an ambitious and ruthless young Brigade Commander called Mohamed Dagolo, who was known as "Hemeti" due to his baby-faced looks (Hemeti was his mother's term of endearment for "Little Mohamed").[19]

Hemeti, a member of the Mahariya clan of the Rizeigat, dropped out of school at an early age and became a small trader before joining the Janjaweed. In 2007, his troops became discontented over the government's failure to pay them. Hemeti and his fighters mutinied, and vowed to fight Khartoum "until judgement day."[20] Hemeti then tried to cut a deal with the Darfur rebels, and it was at this time that Hemeti began recruiting mercenary groups from outside of his original tribal base, including former members of his old foe, the SPLA, and volunteers from Black African Fur ethnic group of Darfur, into his army to fight alongside his Arabs.

Fearing a new revolt, the Khartoum government agreed to pay his troops, granted officer rank to some of his men, and promoted Hemeti to the rank of Brigadier General. His troops were placed under command of the National Intelligence and Security Service (NISS), at that time organising a proxy war with Chad. The NISS deployed some of Hemeti's fighters as mercenaries, serving under the banner of the Chadian opposition, into Chad. Its tactics were, as always, brutal. After one Janjaweed attack in the village of Djawara, which killed 118 people in mid-April 2006, Hassan Moussa, helped bury victims after the Janjaweed massacre. He stated, "When the Janjaweed come, there are also Chadians with them. The Janjaweed are from Sudan, they don't know where the villages are, or who owns which cattle. So it's the Chadians here, certain ethnic groups who act as guides and accomplices for the Janjaweed."[21]

Survivors in Djawara said the Janjaweed wore military fatigues, while the Chadians were in civilian clothing. Abdulaye Yaya Abdulaye, who at 40 was one of the few survivors of Djawara stated, "Every man was armed. The Janjaweed carried Kalashnikovs and M14s. The Chadians also had arms, but carried machetes as well. After people were shot, if they were still alive, they were finished off with machetes."[22] Human Rights Watch's Africa head, Peter Takirambudde, stated: "Civilians in eastern Chad are trapped between the carnage in Darfur and Chad's downward spiral into chaos. It's a political problem. We've had different ethnic groups living together here for thousands of years. Why has this violence happened so suddenly? I think this Janjaweed problem is just a pretext. The Janjaweed have a relationship with the Chadian rebels. They are working for the Sudanese government; Sudan is trying to destabilise Chad."[23] During their campaign in Chad, some Janjaweed mercenary fighters fought their way as far as the Chadian capital, N'Djamena, in 2008 before being called back to Sudan.

In the Sudan, the NISS restructured the Janjaweed into the Rapid Support Forces (RSF) in August 2013 to help it fight against rebel groups in Darfur, South Kordofan, and the Blue Nile states. Hemeti was placed in command of the new unit and it was at about this time that he fell out with his original mentor, Hilal. Their dispute turned into a violent feud that was to be a feature of Darfur for the next ten years.[24] The Sudanese army chief of staff, General James Hoth Mai, disapproved of the formation of the RSF, and wanted the expenditure to go instead to the strengthening of regular forces, but was overruled by Bashir.

Bashir, too, was worried that the creation of the RSF would give too much power to the NISS, whose director he had just fired for conspiring against him. Bashir decided to take control of the RSF and gave Hemeti the nickname "Himayti," meaning "My Protector."[25] At the instigation of Bashir, training camps were set up for the newly formed RSF near Khartoum. The RSF were equipped with hundreds of Land Cruiser pick-up trucks that had been specially imported and fitted out with machine guns. Once equipped and trained, they were deployed against both the rebels in South Kordofan and Darfur, but with mixed results. In Kordofan, they proved undisciplined and ineffective, but they did better in Darfur.

Although he did not realise it at that time, the turning point in Hemeti's career came in April 2012 when a small team of wandering miners discovered gold in the Jebel Amir hills of North Darfur, Sudan. The deposits in one of the mines was so rich that it was nicknamed "Switzerland" by its owners. Perspective gold miners rushed in from all over Sudan, as well as from the Central African Republic, Chad, Niger, and Nigeria. Hemeti's former commander, Hilal, saw the immediate advantages of seizing control of this vital asset and took over the area with such force that more than 800 people from the local Beni Hussein ethnic group perished. Hilal grew rich by mining and selling the gold. This increased the already bitter rivalry and feud between the two men.

Hemeti's RSF was too heavily involved in the war in Darfur to take immediate action against Hilal. Between 2014 and 2015, his RSF forces, supported by air and ground support from the Sudanese Armed Forces, launched a systematic campaign of terror in Darfur, repeatedly attacked villages, burning and looting homes, and raping and executing villagers. The RSF executions and rapes typically took place in villages after rebels left. The attacks were systematic enough to qualify as crimes against humanity, according to Human Rights Watch.[26] One Sudanese researcher, Eric Reeves, estimated that it is "likely" that Hemeti has "... accumulated more Sudanese blood on his hands in conflict in Darfur and in the conflict in South Kordofan, as well as in Khartoum and elsewhere, than any other man in the country…" and that Hemeti's management of the war was carried out "by means of serial atrocity crimes, including genocide and crimes against humanity."[27]

In April, 2005, the Sudan government signed a ceasefire agreement with Sudan People's Liberation Army that later led to the end of the Second Sudanese Civil War. Released from the genocidal campaign in Darfur, Hemeti and his RSF began a vicious campaign against Hilal's forces, culminating in them seizing the gold fields in November 2017 and arresting Hilal as well as seizing the goldmines the RSF also took control of the borders with Chad and Libya, thereby controlling the gold trade and making Hemeti the country's biggest gold trader almost overnight. By 2019 he would become one of the richest people in Sudan.

Most of Sudan's gold, whether legal or otherwise, is trafficked through Dubai in United Arab Emirates (UAE). Hemeti, as Sudan's main gold exporter, forged strong contacts with the UAE. With the cooperation of the UAE, Hemeti set up front companies and bank accounts in both the UAE and Sudan to receive funds from the gold mines it had seized and its "taxes" on other lawful or unlawful gold exports.[28] Hemeti had now created a totally independent, self-funded, private militia ready to be deployed anywhere at his will. The RSF had grown in strength by now to some 70,000 men and had more than 10,000 armed pick-up trucks, although separately funded, to all intents and purposes it was by now Sudan's *de facto* infantry unit.[29] The UAE had good reasons for cooperating with Hemeti and the RSF's looting of Sudan's gold deposits.

Since 2015, the Sudanese government had deployed a battalion-seized force into Yemen as part of the coalition campaign in Yemen against the

Ansar Allah (Houthi) movement and its allies, composed mainly of forces that were loyal to the former Yemeni President Ali Abd-Allah Saleh. In 2007, through mutual self-interest, Hemeti struck a deal with the UAE to deploy a force of some 40,000 of his RSF into Yemen as a mercenary force.[30] Once deployed into Yemen, the RSF became the most effective unit of the Saudi coalition forces and the core ground component of coalition forces in Yemen, serving in multiple regions of the country.

Its effectiveness as combat troops has been recognised by its enemies on the ground. Majed Ghurbani, a 43-year-old Houthi Yemeni fighter told reporters in 2019 that "The Sudanese are brave fighters, and they have more experience in fighting than Saudis, Emiratis or Yemenis. We have been learning a lot from them, and we have achieved many advances thanks to them."[31] Despite their expertise on the battlefield, the RSF has suffered significant casualties: the Houthi claim that more than 4,000 Sudanese have been killed in Yemen since 2015.[32] In October 2019, 10,000 RSF mercenaries were withdrawn from Yemen.[33]

In July 2019, Hemeti again used the RSF as a mercenary force during the 2019 Western Libya offensive phase of the Second Libyan Civil War, deploying them into the oil-rich region crescent area of the country to protect Libya's oil installations. The arrival of the RSF mercenary force allowed local units loyal to Gen Khalifa Haftar's Libyan National Army (LNA) to concentrate all their power on attacking Tripoli and the internationally recognised Government of National Accord (GNA) that was based there.[34] This mercenary intervention may have been bankrolled by the UAE, but may also have been in an effort by Hemeti to curry favour with Egypt, which had also backed Gen Haftar's self-styled Libyan National Army.[35]

Hemeti's acquisition of power and wealth as a result of his control of gold fields and the sanctioned mercenary activity of the RSF made him the most powerful man in Sudan. On 11 April, 2019, Hemeti used that power and ordered the RSF to remove the man who had once called him "My Protector," Bashir from office in a *coup d'état*. As a result, he became the Deputy Head of the Transitional Military Council that replaced him. Bashir was imprisoned for corruption in Sudan and has an outstanding indictment against him by the International Criminal Court on charges of war crimes committed during the Darfur War.

Hemeti had now completed the transition from being a semi-literate, small time trader to becoming a member of the ruling body of his country with a privately funded, fiercely loyal militia army at his disposal, ready to be deployed anywhere as a mercenary force at his command. In the process, he and his immediate family became incredibly rich. His RSF mercenaries had become a formidable fighting machine that was feared throughout the region. It was a true tale of rags-to-riches and real power, with the only people suffering the wretched, blood drenched population of Sudan.

Chapter Nine

The Wagner Group

The author does not have the space in this book to outline every alleged commander, member or deployment of the Wagner Group by Russia abroad. Similarly, there is insufficient space to describe in detail every brutality, massacre, extra judicial killing and illegal act attributed to the Wagner Group as a whole and to individual members of the organisation. Such an effort would require an entire book in itself. To give the reader an overview of the Wagner Group, the author has concentrated on its origins, the organisation, training and the initial emergence of the Wagner Group in the Ukraine in 2014, followed by four examples of its use by Russia in Africa, Syria, Sudan, Central African Republic, and Mali to give the reader an understanding of this shadowy mercenary company, its operational methods, and some of the motivations behind its use by Putin's Russia. The Wagner Group's involvement in the present Ukrainian war will be dealt with in the next chapter.

Origins

A mercenary company called the Slavic Corps was organised in Russia in the autumn of 2013 by two managers from the international Moran Security Group, which specialised in providing armed vessel protection against pirates. Following training in Latakia in October 2013, the Slavic Corps fielded two companies of over 250 mercenaries to the east. Their mission was to shield oil fields of strategic importance. Unfortunately for the mission, on its way to the oil fields, it had to fight a hard battle with fanatical jihadists from the Islamic State terrorist group. During the course of several engagements in which there were reports of suicide attacks by the jihadists, the Slavic Corps suffered heavy losses which effectively ended the project. One of those company managers involved in the failed mission would go on to be one of the founders of the Wagner Group, which today is probably the largest private mercenary company in existence.

That former director was Dmitriy Valeryevich Utkin. Born in 1970, Utkin was a former commander of the 700th Special Forces Unit of the 2nd Separate Special Forces Brigade of the Russian Ministry of Defence. Utkin was a veteran of the brutal First and Second Chechen Wars, during which Chechin resistance to Russian authority was crushed with the use of almost genocidal tactics by the Russian forces. When he was transferred to the reserve with the rank of Lieutenant Colonel, he founded the Moran Security Group. Ironically the Russian state security services, the notorious FSB, arrested him as a result of his activities in Syria.

After the outbreak of the Russian aggression against Ukraine in 2014, the Kremlin needed Utkin and his mercenary contractors, so the FSB investigation was quietly dropped. This naturally led to the Wagner Group's formation at the beginning of 2014. Utkin is believed to have been the founder and leader of the Wagner Group but many, including Ukrainian intelligence, believe that Utkin is in reality only the "field commander" of Wagner and the true owner is Russian businessman Yevgeny Prigozhin, sometimes called "Putin's chef" because of his catering businesses that hosted dinners for the Russian President. Prigozhin has consistently denied having any connection with Wagner whatsoever. In reality, the origin, ownership, and ultimate control of this shadowy mercenary company will never be really known.

The symbol of the Wagner Group is a skull, and the group does not exist as an official structure in Russia, were mercenary groups are, in fact, banned by law. From studies of the group's activities, it seems to have three types: mercenary and the security, disinformation and information warfare and the exploitation of natural resources in Africa.[1] The origin of the name "Wagner" has been a subject of some debate. There are some suggestions that the name came from Utkin's call sign when he served in the Russian military, chosen because of his passion for the German composer Richard Wagner, who was in fact Adolf Hitler's favourite composer. This led to speculation that Utkin was a Neo Nazi and that he sported several Nazi tattoos.[2] Still, others believe that Utkin and the present and former leadership of the mercenary group are devotees of the Slavic Native Faith, which is a modern Pagan religious movement, and that its name is somehow linked to that faith.[3]

Many of these reports are purely speculative and, in reality, the origins of the Wagner group's name, as with its leadership remains shrouded in mystery. What is clear is that the mercenary group is a major arm of Russian military intelligence that allows Russia to deploy military force worldwide and at the same time avoid direct involvement of conventional military units, thus giving the Kremlin both "plausible deniability" while avoiding high regular Russian force casualties. There was conjecture as to whether the group is a true mercenary company or simply an unofficial arm of Russian Ministry of Defence.[4]

In the author's opinion, given the latest recruiting drive of the Wagner Group after its distortions and losses in Ukraine,[5] it is the latter. Again, in the author's opinion, who actually owns or directs the Wagner Group is of little importance. Its members are mercenaries in every sense of the word and, as the following narrative will show, perhaps the best equipped, financed, and ruthless modern mercenary group active today.

Training and Organisation

The Wagner Group has a training facility in a barracks situated near the Russian village of Molkin, Krasnodar Krai. Whilst it is a Russian Ministry of Defence (MoD) facility, it is listed in court documents as a "children's vacation camp."[6] Analysis of known Wagner Group mercenaries has revealed that the average age of a Wagner contractor is about 40 years old, and that recruits are drawn from as many as fifteen countries. However, the core majority of Wagner mercenary contactors are Russian. New recruits are immediately deprived of mobile phones and denied all access to the internet or social media platforms whilst in training. Secrecy is paramount: recruits are not allowed to tell anyone that they are a member of the group, take photographs, video recordings or make any record of their training.

In addition, every recruit has to sign a ten-year confidentiality agreement. Training is conducted by Russian military officers and recruits receive $1,100 per month whilst in training.[7] Once through training, pay is estimated to be between 80,000 and 250,000 Russian roubles a month ($667 - $2,083 USD). A "Wagner Code of Honour" was instigated in late 2019, listing ten commandments for Wagner mercenaries to follow, including "to protect the interests of Russia always and everywhere, to value the honour of a Russian soldier, to fight not for money, but from the principle of winning always and everywhere."[8]

The Wagner Group is believed to have within its ranks a Serb unit commanded, at least until early 2016, by a Bosnian Serb named Davor

Savičić. Under Bosnian law it is illegal for residents to fight in foreign wars and most of Serb mercenaries are registered as temporary workers in Russia in order to avoid prosecution at home as foreign fighters.[9] Savičić got his first battlefield nickname, Elvis, during the 1990s Bosnia conflicts given because of his enthusiasm for fighting Bosniaks.[10] Savičić was a member of various Bosnian Serb units, particularly the "Arkan Tigers," a notorious militia led by criminal Željko Ražnatović, alias Arkan, who was killed in 2000 before he could be tried for war crimes by the International Tribunal in the Hague on changes of mass murder and war crimes as a result of "ethnic cleansing operations" during the Balkan wars. The Arkan Tigers had strong links with the Serbian state security service for whom Savičić also worked.

When in 1998 the conflict in Kosovo started to escalate, Savičić joined the official Serbian state security unit known as the "Frenkijevci," meaning "Frenki's Men," led by Franko Simatović, known as Frenki. (who was later to face trial in The Hague for alleged war crimes).[11] After NATO forced the Serbian military and police units out of Kosovo in July 1999, most of the unit's members moved to the Montenegrin capital Podgorica and Belgrade. Many turned to crime to become wealthy through criminal activity. In 2001, Montenegrin prosecutors accused Savičić and three others of planting a bomb which killed six people in the house of a man called Duško Martinović in the town of Berane. It was alleged that Martinović owed them approximately 15,000 euros. Savičić was sentenced to twenty years in absentia in Montenegro, but it was eventually ruled, on appeal, that there existed insufficient evidence to prove that he was responsible for the bombing.[12]

In the same year he was cleared of the bombing, Savičić appeared in photographs on the front-line in Lugansk, along with an estimated fifty other Serb fighters assisting the pro-Russian uprising against the Ukrainian government. Serbia denied any direct involvement in the fighting and insisted all the Serbian citizens who took part in it were volunteers.[13] It was after this that Savičić joined the Wagner Group. Savičić was highly appreciated by his superiors at Wagner due to his previous extensive combat experience and was allegedly given the code name "Wolf" to reflect his strength and courage in combat, Savičić's Facebook profile is also a picture of a wolf. During the conflict in eastern Ukraine, Savičić was recognised as a rising star among the mercenaries fighting there.[14] He would eventually feature prominently in many of the mercenary group's foreign deployments in Africa and beyond.

Wagner also has a unit known as Rusich, or Task Force Rusich, which earned a reputation for its self-declared neo-Nazi ideology and brutality when it was first deployed to eastern Ukraine during the peak of fighting between Russian separatists and the Ukrainian military in mid-2014. Rusich left Ukraine in the summer of 2015, a few months after the UK, Canada, and European Union sanctioned one of the group's commanders, Alexey Milchakov, after reports of his unit's involvement in alleged war crimes in Donbas. The Rusich group was founded in 2014 as the Sabotage and Assault Reconnaissance Group Rusich in St. Petersburg by Milchakov—a former Red Army paratrooper—when he met another former paratrooper Yan Petrovsky, at a white supremacist event.

Milchakov and Petrovsky fought against Ukraine as volunteers in the Donbas in 2014 - 2015. Both proudly displayed patches awarded to them as part of the "Union of Donbas Volunteers." Officially, at the time, Russia repeatedly denied its forces were fighting in the Donbas, asserting that local forces battling Ukrainian troops were merely local partisans. In September 2014, near the Luhansk Oblast village of Shchastya, Rusich mercenaries were involved in battle with a Ukrainian paramilitary group called Aidar. Dozens of Ukrainian soldiers were killed, and afterward, images of mutilated and burned bodies circulated online, and Milchakov later openly bragged about photographing the bodies. He also gained international notoriety that same year when bloggers and reporters discovered photos and videos from two years earlier where he was shown killing a puppy, cutting off its head and allegedly eating it. Both Milchakov and Rusich were active in the Wagner deployment in Syria, where it earned a well-deserved reputation for excessive brutality, including collecting ears from its slain victims.

Ukraine

Crimea and the Donbas (2014 - 2015)

Wagner was first noticed globally during the Russian annexation of Crimea in February 2014, were it supported regular Russian troops. The annexation of the Crimean peninsula was all but bloodless, and Wagner mercenaries were reported to have been polite, often carrying unloaded weapons. Amongst the nicknames they acquired was "little green men" because they were masked, wore green unmarked uniforms, and their official status was unknown.[15]

With the annexation complete, Wagner mercenaries moved to the Donbas region of eastern Ukraine to assist pro-Russian forces in a campaign aimed at destabilizing Ukrainian government security forces in the region, immobilizing local government institutions, and eventually seizing and controlling towns. The exact number of Wagner mercenaries involved is unknown, but the best estimates are that at least 300 were deployed. Amongst them was a mercenary who would become both notorious and a hated figure for the Ukrainian people, named Vladimir Andonov. In the Donbas fighting, Andonov used the call sign "Vakha" or "The Buryat Volunteer" after the region in Russia that he came from. The Ukrainians had another name for him: "The Executioner."

Andonov was born in 1978 in the Trans-Baikal Territory in Russia's Far East, and served in the Russian regular army from 1997 to 2005, after which he moved to the city of Ulan-Ude and began studying at a college, but he dropped out of school before completing his studies. He got a job in a warehouse before being recruited into the Wagner mercenary group and was deployed into Ukraine to join the fighting in 2014. Andonov was part of a unit that "liberated" the Donbas town of Logvinovo in early 2015. Later, three Ukrainian prisoners were found executed in a shallow grave, including one who had been shot through the eye. He would later brag about the mission to Russian media, describing how his unit was instructed to "destroy all the forces of the enemy," and that no one survived the attack.

During operations in the Donbas, Wagner mercenaries were linked to the shooting down of a plane at Ukrainian Luhansk International Airport that killed forty Ukrainian paratroopers as well as a crew of nine in June 2014. They also took part in the decisive Battle of Debaltseve in early May 2015, which ended in the defeat of Ukrainian forces. Dmitry Utkin was wounded during the fighting in Ukraine, getting a splinter in his liver. The Wagner Group suffered other casualties, including fatalities, but the exact number of victims is not known. Following the end of major combat operations, Wagner mercenaries were reportedly given a much different assignment. They were ordered to kill dissident pro-Russian warlords that were acting in a rebellious manner. One of those killed was Aleksey

Mozgovoy, a leader of the pro-Russian Prizrak Brigade and commander of the self-proclaimed Luhansk People's Republic in Ukraine. Mozgovoy also served as a "judge" on the "People's Court," notorious for issuing controversial death sentences.

On 23 May, 2015, on the road between Luhansk and Alchevsk, Mozgovoy was killed in a car ambush. A roadside bomb brought his car to a halt after which the occupants were then shot to death with machine guns. The Russians officially blamed Mozgovoy and other "warlord" deaths on the Ukrainians, but in late November 2017, Ukrainian intelligence published what it claimed were intercepted audio recordings that proved there was a direct connection between Dmitry Utkin and Igor Kornet, the Interior Minister of the "Luhansk People's Republic" (LPR) the Russian puppet authority. Kornet was said to have personally led the initiative of eliminating dissident warlords and commanders. With the start of the Russian military intervention in the Syrian Civil War in autumn 2015, the Wagner Group left Ukraine and returned to Russia, ready for deployment in the Syrian conflict.

Syria

What was to become known as the "Syrian Civil War" launched in mid-March 2011 as part of the wider 2011 Arab Spring Protests when protest calling for the removal of Syrian President Bashir Al-Assad were violently suppressed, eventually leading to escalating armed conflict between the Syrian government and varying combatants. Several foreign countries, including the United States, Russia, Iran, and Turkey have either become directly involved in the conflict themselves or provided support to one or another faction involved in the conflict. Broadly speaking, Russia, Iran, and Hezbollah (a Lebanese militia group) support President Bashir Al-Assad's government forces; whilst the US has supported the Autonomous Administration of North and East Syria and its armed wing, the Syrian Democratic Forces (SDF). This support has been material, financial and logistical since 2015.

In addition, since 2014, the US has led an international coalition with the declared purpose of countering the Islamic terrorist group ISIL. During the US-led coalition offensive against ISIL, they have conducted air strikes primarily against ISIL but also against some Syrian government and pro-government targets. The US also deployed special forces and artillery units to engage ISIL on the ground. The peak of the war came around 2015 when the Syrian President made a direct appeal to Vladimir Putin for help. The Russian President had vested interests in Syria, among them a large naval base, and was only willing to assist, ordering the deployment of Russian aircraft, some ground troops, and the Wagner Group into Syria.

About a month after the Russian intervention in Syria, between three and nine members of the Wagner Group were killed in a rebel mortar attack on their base in Latakia province in late October 2015.[16] This was the first indication that mercenary group was operating in the country. Wagner mercenaries would later become involved in the two offensives to retake the strategic city of Palmyra in 2016 and 2017. In the first attack on Palmyra, an ex-Wagner mercenary stated that they had been used as "cannon fodder," and as a result they suffered thirty-two killed and about eighty wounded. After the attack, the Wagner group was withdrawn from Syria between April and May 2016, to regroup and recruit replacements.

They returned for the Second Palmyra offensive to capture ISIL-held oil fields at the beginning of 2017. According to reports, they suffered more significant casualties of between forty and sixty killed and between eighty and 180 wounded, as a result of equipment problems and the poor quality of the new recruits. As one former Wagner mercenary explained later, "The Wagner fighters who showed up in Syria were mostly unlucky in life. As a rule they were former cops, convicts and soldiers. About 40 per cent of them had been in prison for serious crimes, murder, robbery, etc."[17]

As with most mercenary groups, Wagner was also involved in training local units. In Syria, they trained a unit called the ISIS Hunters. During the Syrian attack in late April 2017 on the ISIS forces controlling the Al-Shaer gas fields, the ISIS Hunters were one of the leading units. The gas fields and the areas of the phosphate mines were only fully captured by Wagner mercenaries in July 2016, and by mid-September, started to get back into production. Thereafter, the Wagner Group took over responsibility for guarding them. ISIS made several attempts to retake the gas fields, all of which were repulsed; however, in one attack, a Wagner mercenary was reported to have been captured and tortured to death by ISIL insurgents.

In 2017, Wagner mercenaries were involved in one of the most disturbing incidents in the Syrian Civil War, the torture and killing of Muhammad Abdullah al-Ismail at the al-Shaer oil field near Homs. Ismail fled Syria earlier during the war for Lebanon, but returned in 2017, after which he was arrested and forcibly conscripted into the Syrian military. Wagner mercenaries accused him of being a deserter and a jihadist for wanting to desert. A video was taken during the killing and later went viral. What it showed was truly horrific: four Russian-speaking men in military fatigues were pictured surrounding a man lying on the ground and continued to record as they broke his legs with a sledgehammer and then crushed his chest before cutting off his hands, his head, and finally setting his corpse aflame. In the aftermath, they kicked al-Ismail's head around like a football.[18]

At that time, Russia still had an independent media, and reported that one of those involved in the killing was Stanislav Yevgenyevich Dychko—a confirmed member of the Wagner Group—who previously worked for the Russian Interior Ministry. A second was identified only as Ruslan from Bryansk, a former soldier who was at that time employed as a "patriotic educator" in local schools. In December 2019, further investigation by Russian media identified the remaining perpetrators as Vladimir B., Dzhakhongyr M. ("Pamir"), Ruslan ("Chichi") and Vladislav Apostol, who was killed in Syria in February 2018. Despite all the known information being passed to the office of the Prosecutor General of Russia, no criminal charges were ever filed. In December 2021, the Council of the European Union sanctioned Utkin for the killing, stating in a resolution that "According to a former member of the Wagner Group, Dimitriy Utkin personally ordered the torturing to death of the deserter as well as the filming of the act."[19]

From mid-September 2017, Wagner mercenaries assisted Syrian forces in the capture of Uqayribat from ISIL in the central Hama province. During an ISIL counter-offensive later in the same month in the Deir ez-Zor Governorate, two Wagner mercenaries were captured and later executed by ISIL after the ISIS Hunters killed a leading member of the group.[20] By late November, Russia announced plans to withdraw some troops from Syria by year's end. To avoid potential security losses, it was reported that Russia would fill the open spots with private military companies, including Wagner. On 11 December, 2017, Russian President Vladimir Putin announced victory against "terrorists" when he visited Russia's Khmeimim air base located in Syria.

Ruslan Pukhov, director of the Moscow-based *Centre for Analysis of Strategies and Technologies* think tank, noted that using PMCs was one of the decisive factors that contributed to Russia's victory in Syria. "Russia has managed to obviate the need for deploying large numbers of troops on the ground by bringing in private military companies. These companies consist of well-paid mercenaries, most of whom are retired Russian servicemen. The difference from the similar practice in the United States is that the Russian private military companies are not relegated to supporting roles. They are used as highly capable assault forces, and their personnel are often embedded with Syrian units to augment those units' fighting ability. This approach has proved very useful both militarily and politically, as it minimizes the political cost of direct military intervention. The Russian public has proved completely indifferent to reports of the losses suffered by the mercenary companies, rightly believing that 'these people are highly paid, and knew what they were getting into.' As a result—and contrary to Western expectations—Russian losses in Syria have not led to any negative domestic repercussions for the Putin administration."[21]

With the withdrawal of regular Russian forces, the Wagner Group continued to assist the Syrian army in mopping up operations against ISIL. This would eventually lead to a major confrontation between the Wagner Group and the American troops on the ground. From the start of the Russian intervention in Syria, the risks of Russian military forces and American troops colliding on the battlefield has long been of great concern to both the American authorities and troops on the ground. Many feared that such a clash might plunge both countries into bloody conflict and perhaps even all-out war. As a result, commanders of both sides had long avoided confrontation by speaking through various unofficial and official channels to prevent such a situation from occurring. This was of particular concern in the days leading up to what would become known as the Battle of Khasham, as both Russia and the United States were backing separate offensives against the ISIL on opposite sides of the Euphrates River in Syria's oil-rich Deir al-Zour Province, which borders Iraq.

As a component of the US-led coalition operations against ISIL, on 7 February, 2018, a combined team of about thirty US Delta Force special forces and Rangers from Joint Special Operations Command worked alongside Kurdish and Arab forces at a small, dusty outpost next to a

Conoco gas plant near Deir al-Zour in Syria. About 20 miles from the Conoco gas plant, at a base known as a mission support site, Green Berets and a platoon of infantry Marines monitored their computer screens as drone feeds showed a massive build-up of forces on the opposite side of the river and passed the information on to the Americans at the gas plant.

The Russian commanders were contacted through the usual channels. Despite the fact that American surveillance equipment monitoring radio transmissions had revealed the ground force was speaking in Russian, Russian command informed them that they had no control over the fighters assembling near the river. Speaking to the US Senate later in April 2018, Defence Secretary Jim Mattis told the assembled senators: "The Russian high command in Syria assured us it was not their people," so he directed General Joseph F. Dunford Jr., who was chairman of the Joint Chiefs of Staff, "for the force, then, to be annihilated, and it was."[22]

For the American troops on the ground, it was not quite that simple. At about 3:00 p.m. that day, the Syrian force began edging toward the Conoco plant. By early evening, more than 500 troops and twenty-seven vehicles—including tanks and armoured personnel carriers—had assembled in preparation for an assault on the American base. In the American air operations centre at Al-Udeid Air Base in Qatar and at the Pentagon, stunned military officers and intelligence analysts watched as the battle began to unfold and they immediately put American aircraft on standby to support their troops on the ground if needed.

At the mission support site, the Green Berets and Marines prepared a small reaction force of about sixteen troops in four mine-resistant vehicles, ready to support the American troops at the Conoco plant if needed. By 8:30 p.m. the same evening, three Russian-made T-72 tanks, each armed with 125-millimetre guns, advanced to within a mile of the Conoco plant. In view of the impending threat, the Green Berets and Marines prepared to launch the reaction force to assist their heavily outgunned comrades.

By 10:00 p.m. at the Conoco plant, the amazed American troops observed an armoured column of tanks and other armoured vehicles emerging from a neighbourhood of houses where they tried to gather undetected, before turning and driving straight towards them. During the first fifteen minutes of the Russian assault, American military officials desperately called on their Russian counterparts to stop the attack. When those efforts failed, American troops fired warning shots at the group of approaching armoured vehicles. Almost immediately, the Conoco outpost was hit with a withering barrage of heavy fire from tanks, artillery and mortar rounds. Most of the rounds fired by the advancing Russian forces were anti-personnel rounds which forced the beleaguered American special force defenders to take cover. Very quickly, the well-trained, disciplined American forces began to return fire on the advancing column of armoured vehicles with anti-tank missiles and machine guns.

Despite the American resistance, the Russian advance continued. At the American command centre, it was decided only airpower could stop the attack. American warplanes arrived in several waves involving a whole inventory of American aircraft, including Reaper drones, F-22 stealth fighter jets, F-15E Strike Fighters, B-52 bombers, AC-130 gunships and AH-64 Apache helicopters and, for the next three hours, scores of strikes were called in on the advancing Russian armoured column. On the ground, Marine rocket artillery was fired at selected targets. Still, the Russian forces advanced.

The Green Beret and Marine reaction team arrived at the Conoco plant at 1:00 a.m. and immediately began to engage the Russian forces. By then, some of the American warplanes had returned to base, low on either fuel or ammunition. The American troops now numbered about forty and braced themselves for close combat as the advancing Russian forces disembarked from their armoured vehicles and began to fire and manoeuvre towards them. The American troops engaged them with everything they had, including machine guns and Javelin missiles, in a close quarter battle. After an hour of desperate fighting, the enemy fighters started to retreat and the American troops stopped firing. From their outpost, the American troops watched the Russian and Syrian troops returned to collect their dead. The small team of American special forces suffered no casualties, although one allied Syrian fighter was wounded.

Casualties suffered by the attacking forces remain in some dispute. In initial Russian communiqués issued in the immediate aftermath, Russian officials said only four Russian citizens, but perhaps dozens more were killed. A Syrian officer later stated that around 100 Syrian soldiers had died. Later estimates revealed that between 200 to 300 of the "pro-regime force" were killed. An investigative Russian journalist, Maksim Borodin, interviewed relatives and commanders of Wagner Group mercenaries involved in the battle and attended their funerals in the town of Asbest.

He later wrote a number of articles as a result of his research. In the early hours of 12 April, 2018, he rang a friend to say that there were masked men in camouflage uniforms outside his balcony, and rang the same friend an hour later to say that they were just on exercise. Later the same day, he was found badly injured at the foot of his building and died of his injuries three days later on 15 April. No suicide note was ever found, and there was no criminal investigation into his death.

It was quickly established that the Russian force was a mixture of Wagner Group mercenaries and Syrian fighters. American intelligence officials later revealed that one of the main aims of the Wagner Group in Syria was to seize oil and gas fields and protect them on behalf of the Assad government. In return, the mercenaries would earn a share of the production proceeds from the oil fields they reclaimed.

The persistence of the attack in the face of both heavy airpower and concentrated modern weaponry on the ground testifies to the tenacity of Wagner mercenaries. It also showed a complete lack of battlefield awareness, conducting what was in effect a Second World War mass infantry assault against a modern army capable of calling in coordinated modern air strikes for assistance and was probably doomed to end in failure from the start. The only real surprise was that the entire force was not completely destroyed, given the amount and variety of aircraft used to repulse the assault.

Following the Battle of Khasham, Wagner Group mercenaries supported the Syrian forces in operations to secure Damascus from rebel hands. With their assistance, by 14 April, 2018, the last stronghold of resistance in the Eastern Ghouta region was captured by government forces, effectively ending the near seven-year rebellion in and around Damascus. As late as December 2021, Wagner mercenaries were still assisting the Assad regime forces in a large-scale military operation against ISIL cells in the Syrian desert.

Exact casualty figures of Wagner Group in Syria are unknown, but in the author's opinion are likely to be much higher than any official figure released or acknowledged by the Russian authorities. Whatever casualties the Wagner Group suffered as a result of operations in Ukraine and Syria, it is clear that the Russian government viewed the deployment of the Wagner Group in these conflicts as a major success and a useful tool for optimization elsewhere to project Russian power and influence, which is exactly what President Putin and the Kremlin did.

Sudan

There were reports of Wagner mercenaries in Sudan from as early as mid-December 2017, when a video surfaced showing Wagner mercenaries training members of the Sudanese military. Reportedly, about 300 Wagner mercenaries were in the country working under the cover of "M Invest," a company linked to Yevgeny Prigozhin. Their role in the country was to protect Russian interests in gold, uranium, and diamond mines.[23] Later, Wagner mercenaries were allegedly used by the Sudanese government to help suppress popular protest in late January 2019 in which two Wagner mercenaries were killed. Ukrainian intelligence identified them as Elizarov Oleg Vladimirovich, DOB 18.04.1967, citizen of the Republic of Kazakhstan, native of Taldykorgan, Wagner ID M-2701; and Marchenko Viktor Nikolaevich, DOB 02.02.1968, citizen of the Russian Federation, native of Smolensk, stating "The Security Service of Ukraine does not rule out that these mercenaries were killed in Sudan, since we have confirmation that several members of the last year's "Prigozhin's offensive" under Deir al-Zur (Syria) took part in the suppression of popular protests in that African country in December 2018 - January 2019."[24]

In 2018, 500 PMCs were reportedly sent to Sudan's Darfur region to train the military. With the ousting Omar al-Bashir on 11 April, 2019, and the rise to power of Mohamed Hamdan Dagalo (see chapter 8) Wagner mercenaries began to work closely with the RSF. As a result, in May 2019, Russia signed a military agreement with Sudan. One of the main features of the agreement allowed the entry of Russian warships to Sudanese ports. This led in November 2020 to a draft agreement that led to the establishment of a Russian naval logistic centre and repair yard on Sudan's Red Sea coast that would host up to 300 people. The agreement is expected to stand for twenty-five years unless either party objects to its renewal.

In late October, 2021, the Sudanese military, led by General Abdel Fattah al-Burhan, took control of the Sudanese government in a military coup. Russia was one of several countries not to condemn the coup. As a result, the Wagner Group obtained lucrative mining concessions in Sudan's gold-rich north eastern region. A Russian-operated gold mine was set up in the area that was thought to be an outpost of the Wagner Group.[25] The Wagner Group is still active in Sudan at the present time, and supports Russia's attempts to construct a naval base located on the

Red Sea and using western Sudan's Darfur area as a staging point for operations in other neighbouring countries such as the Central African Republic, Libya, and parts of Chad.

The Central African Republic

The Central African Republic (CAR) is a landlocked country in Central Africa bordered in the north by Chad, in the northeast by Sudan, in the southeast by South Sudan, in the south by the DR Congo, in the southwest by the Republic of the Congo, and Cameroon to the west. Despite significant mineral deposits and other resources, including uranium, crude oil, gold, diamonds, cobalt, lumber, and hydropower, the CAR is among the ten poorest countries in the world.

The country has suffered from ongoing conflict since it gained independence in 1960. In 2013, rebels, consisting mainly of Muslims, seized control of the mostly Christian country. Self-defence militias were formed and fought back, which led to widespread massacres along religious lines. As a result, the former colonial power, France, sent an intervention force that was withdrawn in October 2016. With the country in a state of near anarchy, Russia successfully lobbied the UN Security Council to allow it to ship weapons and ammunition to the country. Russia also dispatched Wagner mercenaries to the CAR, ostensibly to fill the security vacuum left by the withdrawal of French military forces.

Wagner mercenaries set up a base camp about 60km from the capital, Bangui, at the Berengo estate that had at one time been used by CAR's dictatorial former ruler and "emperor" Jean-Bédel Bokassa. Once in the country, they quickly established themselves in the country's major mining centres, including many that were in rebel held territory.[26] By late May 2018, the number of Wagner mercenaries in the country had risen to 1,400.[27] After Utkin was blacklisted by the Americans, Colonel Konstantin Aleksandrovich Pikalov, also known as "Mazay," was put in charge of Wagner's African operations.

Pikalov previously served as an officer at Military Unit 99795, located in the village of Storozhevo, near St. Petersburg. This experimental unit was part of the Russian Ministry of Defence and was tasked, among other duties, with "determining the effects of radioactive rays on living organisms." After retirement, Pikalov continued to live at the base until at least 2012 and ran a private investigation agency before joining the Wagner

Group.[28] In early July, 2018, Pikalov arrived in the CAR. Thereafter he would intermittently return the country to oversee Wagner operations there. On 30 July, 2018, three Russian journalists filming a documentary investigating reports of Wagner's involvement in the country were shot dead, and those behind the killing have never been found.[29]

In August, 2018, Russia signed a military cooperation agreement with the CAR and also helped broker a tentative peace agreement between the warring groups in the country. The Wagner Group continued to expand its operations within the country. Five days before the 2020 - 2021 Central African general election, rebels attacked and captured the CAR's fourth-largest city, Bambari. The Government of CAR called on both Russia and the neighbouring country of Rwanda for assistance in dealing with the rebellion. Rwanda sent in troops under the umbrella of a UN deployment. The combined force of CAR, Rwandan and Wagner Group mercenaries quickly recaptured Bambari. On 25 January, 2021, CAR forces, backed by Wagner Group mercenaries and Rwandan troops went on the offensive, attacking the town of Boyali and killing forty-four rebels who were plotting an assault on the capital. The combined force then went on to seize a number of strategic towns throughout February 2021, including Bossembele, Bouar, Beloko and Bossangoa.

During the fighting, the rebel Coalition of Patriots for Change (CPC) claimed its fighters killed several Wagner mercenaries and captured one when they destroyed their truck near Bambari on 10 February, 2021. At the end of February, a Gazelle helicopter, reportedly belonging to the Wagner Group, crashed due to technical problems while on a mission to retrieve Wagner mercenaries who were wounded while engaging rebels that had ambushed a CAR military convoy. The helicopter crew survived the crash.

Wagner Group mercenaries played an important role in the CAR Government advances that continued during March, April and May 2021, including the capture of the strategic towns of Bria and Kaga-Bandoro and the Bakouma sub-prefecture. Some of these towns were retaken by Wagner mercenaries alone. It was during this period that reports first emerged that the Wagner Group was deploying Syrian mercenaries in CAR.[30] In late May 2021 a combined group of Russian and Syrian mercenaries attacked a rebel checkpoint at the entrance of a village 28km from Bria, killing three rebel fighters.[31]

By the end of May, 2021, government forces and Wagner Group mercenaries pursued CAR rebels across the border into Chad. The incursion resulted in six Chadian soldiers being killed. The Chadian government accused the invading forces of attacking a Chadian military border post, killing the soldiers, five of whom, the Chadian government said, had been abducted alive and taken back over the border before being killed.[32] By the end of July, 2021, the CAR military were leaving the front line fighting against the CPC to the Wagner Group mercenaries and were concentrating occupying the captured positions after they had been secured by the mercenaries.

A recurring theme in every Wagner Group mercenary deployment, is allegations of gross human rights violations against the civilian population, including mass killings, summary executions of captured prisoners, torture, rape, and extreme brutality. The Wagner Group's activities in CAR is no exception. This book does not give the author sufficient space to outline them all. Human Rights Watch, in an interim report, stated that it had collected compelling evidence that Russian fighters linked to the Wagner Group have committed grave abuses against civilians in CAR with complete impunity since 2019.[33]

A description of the "Aïgbado Massacre" highlights Wagner's activities in CAR. Shortly before noon on 16 January, 2022, heavily armed Wagner Group mercenaries arrived in Aïgbado village located 75km from Bria. Their arrival panicked the local residents who began running, and as a result, the Wagner mercenaries almost immediately started shooting indiscriminately into the crowd before burning at least a dozen homes. Rebels from Union for Peace in the Central African Republic who were present in nearby areas counter-attacked the Russian mercenaries and wounded four of them, with two later succumbing to their injuries.

Next, Wagner Group mercenaries moved towards Yanga village, about 70km from Aïgbado and established a base there, preventing access to Aïgbado village. After the event, the mercenaries laid down landmines to prevent peacekeepers from reaching the village. According to recent estimates, at least sixty-five people were killed in the atrocity.[34] These events, if true, show a barbarism toward innocent civilians that is quite simply beyond words to condemn, but they pale in comparison to the accusations against Wagner Group mercenaries in the West African country of Mali.

Mali

Since late May, 2021, Mali was and is ruled by a military junta that came into power following a *coup d'état*. In mid-September 2021, the military junta began to enter into an agreement that would allow the Wagner Group to operate in Mali. Despite the protests of France, the former colonial power, the United Kingdom, European Union, and Ivory Coast, by 30 September, 2021, as part of a contract with Russia agreed in December 2020, Mali received four Mil Mi-17 helicopters, as well as arms and ammunition. The contract also provided for the deployment of Wagner Group mercenaries into the country.

By mid-January 2022, Wagner PMCs were deployed at a former French military base in Timbuktu. On 19 April, 2022, a military patrol was hit by a roadside bomb near the town of Hombori, killing a Russian "advisor." An anonymous hospital official in Sevare confirmed the death and said the Russian was in his 30s. An elected official in central Mali, who also requested anonymity, said that he had "learned of the death of a Wagner agent."[35] From the first entry into the country by the Wagner Group, there was an explosion of reports of massacres and torture attributed to them.

Human Rights Watch published a report on 5 April, 2022. In it, they accused Malian soldiers and Wagner mercenaries of allegedly executing around 300 civilians between 27 and 31 March, 2022, during a military operation in Moura, in the Mopti region, which is known as a hotspot of Islamic militants. On 17 July, 2022, the British paper the *Sunday Telegraph* published a graphic description of the slaughter given by a survivor.[36] That survivor described how a Wagner Group mercenary went through a group of prisoners, and "If a man's beard was too long or his clothes too Islamic, he would get a tap on the head. 'He's a jihadist. Kill him'." At least 180 bodies were later recovered, but it is estimated that over the three days of sporadic executions, anywhere between 200 - 600 men and boys were killed in the village, and a child of 10 years old was said to have been amongst the victims.[37]

The jihadist Al-Qaeda-linked JNIM terrorist group claimed on 25 April, 2022, that it captured several Wagner Group members early in the month in the central Ségou Region, although this could not be verified from any official source. By late June, 2022, more accusations surfaced against the Wagner Group mercenaries in Mali, that they, in conjunction with the Malian military, were looting towns and indiscriminately arresting people in the northern Tombouctou Region and forcing civilians to flee into neighbouring Mauritania. Random killings were also reported to have taken place.[38]

The use of the Wagner Group by Russia, and the tactics used by them mirrors, to a large extent, the original "grab for Africa" of the former colonial powers of Britain, France, Portugal, and Germany. Using the African continent to extend their power and influence whilst at the same time raping the natural resources of their colonies, Russia is using what it considers a tried and tested tactic to carve out and extend a sphere of influence for Putin's expansionist Russia in unstable countries on the continent of Africa, and thereby challenging western goals in the region and at the same time securing vital natural resources. By using the Wagner Group, Russia also has plausible deniability. Mvemba Phezo Dizolele, director of the African program at the Centre for Strategic and International Studies in Washington D.C., explains the rationale of Russia in Mali in these terms: "The Russians are resetting the region's dynamics. For the last six decades, the French have convinced the US—and themselves—that they are indispensable in Francophone Africa. The Malians and the Russians are testing that indispensability."[39]

Unlike western interventions in peacekeeping roles in Africa—which are governed by strict rules of engagement and international law—the Wagner Group's use of extreme violence in its operations is very attractive to military dictatorships like the one in Mali and other similar dictatorships in Africa and beyond. These dictatorships are no strangers to violations of human rights and see in the Wagner Group a kindred spirit. Andrew Lebovich, a Sahel expert at the European Council of Foreign Relations puts it succinctly, "Russia can offer something much narrower and more purely security focused (than France) which suits the perceptions and interests of certain Mali officials who think that extreme violence is needed to solve the problem in the centre of the country."[40]

Putin's Russia has used the Wagner Group extensively in interventions in the African countries of Libya, Madagascar, Mozambique, and in South America in Venezuela. All of these interventions are almost always characterised by an initial arms sale by Russia, followed by the insertion of the Wagner Group, ostensibly as "trainers." Once in the country, they seize and hold vital assets like gold mines, oil fields, and other natural recourses. This is quickly followed by a brutal, no-holds-barred attempt to eliminate any armed or unarmed opposition to the ruling elite in power. In many cases, this is followed up by shadow Russian "shell companies," which are often linked directly to the Wagner Group, and that seek to exploit the assets secured by the Wagner Group.

Without condoning in any way the breaches of international law committed by western mercenary companies in Iraq and possibly Afghanistan—with the notable exception of the debacle of western mercenary involvement in Angola—they pale into insignificance compared to the systematic brutality of the Wagner Group in its various military campaigns in Africa and beyond. This is not due, in the author's opinion, to the fact that they are mercenaries lacking sufficient oversight, as was certainly the case of British mercenaries in Angola. Nor can it be put down to the calibre of the recruits that enter into service with the Wagner Group, although this may be a contributing factor.

In the author's opinion, there is deep-seated savagery in the Russian military psyche, a systematic pattern of barbarity in warfare which, even the briefest look at recent modern Russian history quickly establishes. During the Russian Civil War fought from 1917 onwards between "White" Russians and the communist Bolsheviks, massacres and summary executions were prevalent on both sides. Many forget that during the invasion of Poland in 1939—which resulted in Britain declaring war on Nazi Germany—Russia also invaded eastern Poland. What became known as the "Katyn Massacre" occurred on 5 March, 1940, during which, after a decision from the highest level of the Soviet authorities, the NKVD murdered nearly 22,000 Polish citizens. Those murdered represented the Polish elite: its defensive, intellectual, and creative potential. Killing them was an attack on "Polishness" and the entire Polish nation, aimed at preventing a sovereign Polish state from being rebuilt.

During Russia's final assault on Berlin in 1945, Russian soldiers systematically raped most of the female population. In more recent times, Russia's occupation of Afghanistan was brutal, with well documented cases of gross violations of even the most basic of human rights. The complete disregard for the rules of warfare in the First and Second Chechen wars, where whole cities were almost obliterated, is also well documented. Similar tactics were used by Russians in their assault on the Syrian city of Aleppo. Russia's present war in Ukraine, with the indiscriminate use of artillery and air strikes against civilian targets, is just the latest example of Russian armed forces ignoring even the most basic rules of international law.

The world, and any right-thinking human being may recoil in horror at the descriptions of the excesses of the Wagner Group in Africa, Ukraine, and beyond, but, whether it be in fact an actual true mercenary company or an arm of Russian intelligence, its activities are merely a modern variation on the type of warfare that has always been conducted by Russian forces in almost every conflict it has been involved in during modern times. It is precisely for that reason that Wagner Group mercenaries do not need the protection of something like Order No. 17, that protected western mercenary companies in Iraq. Their conduct is not only condoned by Russian authorities but actually encouraged as part of Russian military doctrine and under Russian law: no Russian can be extradited to a foreign country to face prosecution.

Victims of every atrocity committed cry out for justice, whether perpetuated by mercenaries or regular troops of any nation. The International Criminal Court has brought that justice for many of the victims of both the Balkan wars and African outrages. Although at the moment, the Wagner Group acts with total impunity, perhaps one day there will be a reckoning. That reckoning will depend on whether the present Western World Order can eventually triumph over the expansionist ambitions of Putin's Russia and that question remains, at this time, very much in the balance.

Academi

As evidenced in previous chapters, the US private mercenary company Blackwater re-branded as Xe Services LLC in 2010. Then in 2011, after private investors took over, the company rebranded again as Academi. In 2006, whilst still called "Blackwater," Cofer Black, then the Vice Chairman of Blackwater USA, allegedly proposed at an international conference in Amman, Jordan, that the company was ready to move towards providing security professionals up to brigade size (3,000 - 5,000) for humanitarian efforts and low-intensity conflicts, but the company denied making this claim. Given its size and client base, Academi is probably the closet western equivalent of the Wagner Group. Obviously, unlike the Wagner Group, Academi operates with the oversight of Western governments, particularly the United States. This oversight means that if Academi, or other western mercenary companies do transgress, then at least some effort is made to make them accountable under international and/or national law.

As a result of the vast amounts of money ploughed into private mercenary companies both before and after the Iraqi and Afghanistan wars, there has been an explosion of western mercenary companies. Academi now operates in an ever-crowded, competitive, and competing market place. The next chapter will explore the roles of both mercenaries and western mercenary companies today, which are expanding into fields never envisaged by their original founders.

Chapter Ten

Mercenaries Today

Columbian Mercenaries

At 01:00 local time on 7 July, 2021, a group of twenty-eight men in all-black clothing pulled up outside the home of Haitian President Jovenel Moïse in the Pelerin 5 neighbourhood in the hills above Port-au-Prince ostensibly to serve a search warrant. A security guard at the gates of the residency was forced to lie face down in the street while another man began to shout in English over a loudspeaker, "DEA." Having gained entry, the attackers tied up staff. However, this was no drug search, this was carefully planned and calculated political assassination. The Haitian President died at the scene and was found lying on the floor on his back, his shirt soaked in blood. Martine Moïse, the first lady, was also shot, but survived, and one of the couple's three children survived by hiding in a bedroom.

Later investigations revealed that Moïse, 53, had been shot twelve times, with bullet wounds to his forehead and several to his torso. He had also been tortured: his left eye was gouged out and bones in his arm and in his ankle were broken. The assassination shocked the world and destabilised the already fragile country of Haiti. In the immediate aftermath of the outrage, the assassins were traced to a house, which was surrounded by Haitian police. After a gun battle that left four of the assassins dead, Haitian police arrested the surviving assassins.

During the follow-up investigation, led by the Haitian police, it was established that a group of mainly foreign mercenaries—twenty-six Colombians and two Haitian-Americans—made up the group that carried out the killing. Most of the Colombians arrested were later identified as being former soldiers, including a Lieutenant Colonel who was said to have led the group. The two Haitian-Americans arrested later told interrogators they had been hired as interpreters on the internet and that they did not know there was a plan to kill the president, but believed they were to act as interpreters in an arrest operation.

Who actually hired the Columbian mercenaries to assassinate a sitting president is still a matter of investigation in Haiti, but the use of Colombian mercenaries was no isolated incident. Colombia has been the go-to country in the global market in which US, British, French, Belgian or Danish private mercenary companies recruit. The reasons are easy to understand: the regular armed forces of Colombia numbers some 220,000 men, thousands of which retire each year for various reasons. Jorge Mantilla is a criminal phenomenon researcher at the University of Illinois in Chicago, and explains that there's terrific experience in "terms of irregular war...the Colombian soldier is trained, has combat experience, and on top of that, is cheap labour."[1]

In addition, the country is awash with ex-paramilitary guerrillas, both right and left wing, just as well trained and even more ruthless than Columbia's former soldiers. This results in Colombia having an almost inexhaustible pool of trained soldiers for private mercenary companies to call on. They are cheaper to employ than their western mercenary counterparts in the US, Britain and France. In addition, they are battle-hardened and conditioned to withstand extreme violence after more than half a century of conflict in their native land. Sean McFate is a professor at Georgetown and the National Defence as well as a senior fellow at the Atlantic Council, and explains in detail the advantages to hiring Columbian mercenaries: "Mercenaries change warfare in profound ways, they commercialise it, and Colombians are in demand because they are good value. They are ex-special forces Colombians who are often trained by the US. They have field experience fighting the Colombian guerrilla group the Revolutionary Armed Forces of Colombia (FARC) and narcos. They're also good warriors, they respect the chain of command, they're tactically proficient and they cost about half to a quarter [lower] of the price."[2]

This mix of both ex-soldiers and paramilitaries means that Columbian mercenaries are only too willing to undertake "missions" that western mercenaries might balk at, such as the assassination of the President of Haiti. Two similar assassination attempts allegedly occurred in Venezuela: the first occurred in 2004 when Venezuelan authorities detained 153 Colombian paramilitaries who were accused of taking part in a plan to assassinate then-President Hugo Chavez.[3] The second occurred in 2013, when the Venezuelan government announced that it had arrested nine

Colombian right-wing paramilitaries who were plotting to assassinate Hugo Chavez's successor, President Nicolas Maduro.[4]

In May, 2011, an airplane carrying dozens of Colombians hired by the US mercenary firm Blackwater (now Academi), landed in Abu Dhabi. The Colombian mercenaries, were all ex-soldiers and entered the UAE posing as construction workers. Once there, the Columbians and other mercenaries were given further training at an Emirate base—Zayed Military City—by former American, German, British, and French Foreign Legion special forces mercenaries. After this specialised training, they joined a force that was intended to conduct special operations missions worldwide, defend oil pipelines and skyscrapers from terrorist attacks and put down internal revolts.[5]

In 2015, six Colombian Academi-employed mercenaries were reportedly killed in Yemen whilst conducting combat operations as part of a UAE and Saudi coalition force advancing towards the al-Amri area in the heavily contested Taiz province in southwest Yemen. The mercenaries were allegedly led by an Australian commander who was also said to have been directly hired by the UAE to fight the Houthi insurgency.[6] The Columbian mercenaries proved to be a valuable source of manpower that by late 2015, the UAE directly hired hundreds of Colombian mercenaries to fight the Houthi rebels in Yemen.[7]

Other Mercenaries and Mercenary Operations in Yemen

As the reader will have grasped from the previous chapters, the unfortunate country of Yemen is facing yet another bloody chapter in its already tragic history. The present conflict is known by several names: the Houthi insurgency, the Houthi rebellion, the Sa'dah War, and the Sa'dah conflict. It has origins in the 2004 attempt by the government to arrest Hussein Badreddin al-Houthi, a former parliamentarian and a Zaidi religious leader of the Houthis. Iran backed the Houthis from the onset of the insurgency. In the first stage of the conflict, most of the fighting took place in Sa'dah Governorate in northwest Yemen.

However, this soon spread to neighbouring governorates Hajjah, 'Amran, al-Jawf and the Saudi province of Jizan. With the backing of Iran, the Houthi were able to take over the capital city of Sanaa in late 2014. It was at this stage that the insurgency became a full-blown civil war with a major Saudi-led intervention in Yemen, beginning in March 2015. The

UAE was a major part of the Saudi coalition forces that intervened in the conflict.

Mercenaries from Sudan, Columbia, and other nations hired by the UAE have been used operationally in the ground fighting in Yemen as "shock troops" by the Saudi-led coalition forces in Yemen. Their entry into the conflict has enabled the Saudi-led coalition to both contain and push back the Houthi rebellion in many areas, but it has come at a heavy cost to the mercenaries involved. Official casualty figures are difficult to obtain, but on 6 January, 2016, the Houthis claimed that a Tochka missile strike on a Saudi-led command canter in Ma'rib resulted in the death of over 120 mercenaries, including fifty-five Saudi (nine officers), eleven UAE and eleven foreign commanders of Blackwater.[8] On 31 January, 2016, the Houthis also claimed that two hundred Sudanese mercenaries employed by Blackwater and their commander, US Colonel Nicolas Petras, were killed when another Tochka missile strike hit a gathering of the Saudi forces at Al-Anad military base in Lahij province.[9] Given the intensity of the fighting on the ground, the death toll amongst the mercenaries fighting in Yemen is likely to be considerably more than those that have so far been disclosed.

However, the UAE has found another, more sinister, role for the mercenaries it employs. At 9:57 on 29 December, 2015, a heavily armed mercenary team, made up of former American special forces, including ex-Navy SEALs, Green Berets and at least one ex-CIA operative, made its way through the dimly lit streets of Aden, a key Yemeni port city, in an armoured SUV. Their mission that night was not a combat or a reconnaissance patrol, but one of assassination. Their intended target was Anssaf Ali Mayo, the local leader of the Islamist political party Al-Islah.

The UAE put Ali Mayo on its target list for assassination because it considered his party, Al-Islah, as the Yemeni branch of the global Muslim Brotherhood, which the UAE branded a terrorist organization. Many independent experts do not share this view, believing that Al-Islah, who counts amongst its members a Nobel Peace Prize recipient, is no terror group, but rather a legitimate political party that just so happens to threaten the UAE not through violence, but by politically opposing and speaking out publicly against its military activities and political ambitions in Yemen.

The American ex-Special force mercenaries' plan was to attach a shrapnel bomb to the door of the Al-Islah's headquarters—located near a soccer stadium in the centre of the city—and kill everybody in that office.

The assassination plan was aborted when a member of team prematurely opened fire before the bomb could be attached to the door. The mercenary team was led by Abraham Golan, a Hungarian Israeli mercenary, who founded the private mercenary company Spear Operations Group, which employed the assassination team.

Reports of the attempted assassination were first broken by the American news outlet BuzzFeed.[10] Abraham Golan gave an interview to the news outlet where he is quoted as saying "There was a targeted assassination program in Yemen. I was running it. We did it. It was sanctioned by the UAE within the coalition." In the article, *BuzzFeed* reported that attempts to verify Golan's story were met with silence from both the UAE and Saudi Arabia, adding that "the CIA said it had no information about the mercenary assassination program, and the Navy's Special Warfare Command declined to comment."[11]

BuzzFeed then contacted a former CIA official who worked in the UAE, who initially told them that "There was no way that Americans would be allowed to participate in such a program."[12] Later, the unnamed former CIA source—after checking with contacts inside the UAE—rang the news organisation back and reportedly said: "There were guys that were basically doing what you said. What vetting procedures are there to make sure the guy you just smoked is really a bad guy?" The mercenaries, the former CIA contact said, were "almost like a murder squad."[13]

Although the first operation failed, the team stayed in Yemen for several months. Golan confirmed that the team he headed was responsible for several major assassinations, but refused to specify the victims' identities. He also noted that America needed an assassinations program similar to the one he has been running for months in Yemen."[14] When the reports of a mercenary assassination team in Yemen first surfaced, the author was, despite BuzzFeed's statement that it had verified the existence of the assassination programme, sceptical about the reliability of the report.

However, as the report spread, more confirmations came to light, leading US Senators Elizabeth Warren and Bob Menendez to write letters to the State Department demanding answers about Spear Operations Group, and questioning whether the US Federal Government knew about its involvement in the war in Yemen. Additionally, Warren sent a letter to the Justice Department calling for an investigation into the group.

In December 2020, the International Institute for Rights and Development as well as the Rights Radar Foundation issued a statement on the now confirmed assassination programme in Yemen at the 45th Session of the Human Rights Council in Geneva, Switzerland: "The UAE hired American mercenaries to carry out high-profile assassinations in Yemen. They conducted several operations in Aden and several cities, resulting in the assassinations of dozens of politicians and public figures during the past five years of conflict in Yemen."[15]

The assassination programme conducted in Yemen is not an isolated incident, and seems to be part of worrisome modern new pheromones of using mercenaries not as soldiers, but as paid killers. According to an ongoing UN investigation, UAE-based mercenary companies Lancaster 6 DMCC and Opus Capital Asset Limited deployed American, Australian, and European mercenaries to assist the warlord General Khalifa Haftar in his efforts to overthrow the UN-recognised government in Tripoli. On 27 June, 2019, twenty mercenaries—each paid $80,000 for a three-month contract—arrived in Benghazi to fulfil their commitments ahead of an $80 million contract that the companies signed with the Libyan warlord.

The mercenaries were hired to operate as Haftar's Special Forces, with a specific goal of identifying, hunting down and killing members of the Libyan government in Tripoli. However, when the mercenaries arrived without the attack helicopters that had been promised as part of the overall contract, Haftar was furious and threatened to kill them. Fearing summary execution, the mercenaries fled to Malta where they were arrested and detained for 24 hours before being released without any charges being filed against them.[16] The legality of such mercenary operations will be discussed in the next chapter.

Mercenaries in the War in Ukraine

The Wagner Group

The first component of Vladimir Putin's "Special Operation" in Ukraine in early February 2022 envisaged the decapitation by assassination of the heads of government, including President Volodymyr Zelensky followed by a lightning strike against Kyiv, the Ukrainian capital, and the installation of a puppet government. Initially, the Russians decided to use Chechen Special Forces for the mission, but their first attempt failed because Ukrainian intelligence was tipped off by anti-war members within Russia's own Federal Security Service (FSB). After the Ukrainians ambushed and destroyed a Chechen Special Forces column composed of around fifty-six tanks near Kyiv, and inflicting heavy casualties and killing top Chechen general Magomed Tushayev, head of the 141 Motorized Regiment of Chechnya, the Russians turned to the Wagner Group to complete the mission.[17]

The Wagner Group mercenaries were reportedly given a twenty-four-person "kill list," including Ukraine's Prime Minister, the entire cabinet, Mayor of Kyiv Vitali Klitschko and his brother Wladimir, both of whom had become the official faces of the resistance to the Russian invasion. Wagner mercenaries made two serious attempts to assassinate President Zelensky, again reportedly foiled by information supplied by anti-war sympathisers within the FSB. On 5 March, 2022, and as a result of the supplied intelligence, Kyiv Mayor Vitali Klitschko declared a 36-hour "hard" curfew, ordering everyone indoors so that soldiers could sweep the streets for Russian infiltrators.[18]

As a direct result of the heroic and determined Ukrainian resistance to the Russian invasion, according to the *Institute for the Study of War* (ISW) by 14 March, 2022: "Russia continues to face difficulties replacing combat losses and increasingly seeks to leverage irregular forces including Russian PMCs and Syrian." There were also reports by the Ukrainian General Staff that Russia had "recruited over a thousand Syrian fighters in 'recent days' and that approximately 400 Syrian fighters have arrived in Russia." Training camps near Rostov (in Russia, directly east of Donbas) and Gomel (in Belarus, north of Kyiv) had been set up for the Syrian mercenaries. The report also confirmed the death of the first Wagner Group mercenary in the war, Senior Lieutenant Sergey Zavadsky was confirmed killed on 13 March, 2022.[19]

From the start of the present war in Ukraine, Russian President Putin had actively encouraged foreign fighters to join in on the war against what he termed "neo-Nazism." In the Middle East, the only country to answer Putin's call was Syria, primarily because of Putin's intervention in that country on behalf of the government forces. To promote and encourage recruitment, the Syrian government offered potential recruits a contract from the Military Intelligence Division, which included perks of $3,000 for volunteer fighters, $7,000 for wounded fighters, food rations for the families of volunteers, and a $15,000 insurance pay out if the volunteer died while fighting. Those Syrians who entered into the contract would fight in Ukraine under the direction and control of the Wagner Group.

Despite the attempts by the Syrian government to energise a recruitment drive and produce an avalanche of Syrian mercenary volunteers, the effort seems to have failed dismally. This is certainly the view in an assessment by US Marine Corps General McKenzie, who confirmed that "There has not been a flow of Syrian fighters up to this point. Those who have volunteered are not producing the desired effect, as the military skills of the volunteers are generally weak, and they are mostly motivated by money. Armed groups with solid experience and specific knowledge, including those with snipers and training in explosives handling, have stayed away from the conflict. They are decidedly hostile to the Syrian regime and its Russian ally."[20]

Interestingly, the deployment of Syrian mercenary volunteers proved to be more of a hindrance than an asset to the invading Russian forces. According to an assessment conducted by the Institute for the Study of War (ISW), the Russian army's inherent weakness in junior non-commissioned officers (NCOs), coupled with inexperience in commanding Syrian troops under fire, has resulted in an inability to properly utilise the Syrian mercenary volunteers in Ukraine, resulting in them being relegated to "menial tasks such as guarding, handling, and cleaning at a lower cost to the Russian army."[21] The ISW also assessed that because of mounting casualties, the Russian army was increasingly turning to the use of Wagner Group mercenaries to maintain the Russian Special Operation.

The ISW assessment of heavy Russian casualties and the use of Wagner Group mercenaries to replace them was further confirmed by a UK Defence Ministry report issued on 28 March, 2022, emphasising that the regular Russian military had sustained "heavy losses" during their invasion of Ukraine, and that Wagner Group mercenaries were being deployed into the eastern part of the country to make up the shortfall in manpower.[22]

As with every Wagner Group deployment, reports of atrocities against civilians quickly follow, and the present war in Ukraine is no exception. According to Germany's Federal Intelligence Service, which intercepted battlefield radio transmissions, Wagner Group mercenaries played a leading role in the Bucha massacre of civilians in early April 2022. The massacres were orchestrated by the invading Russian forces to instil fear in the population, thus reducing the will to resist.[23] Given the documented history of the Wagner Group's previous activities, their direct involvement in the Bucha massacre should come as no surprise. There should be no question that when future historians come to chronicle the present war in Ukraine, it will be littered with similar accounts of atrocities committed by Wagner Group mercenaries during the war.

The author is confident that this point does not need emphasising, but the mindset of Wagner Group mercenaries in Ukraine is clearly illustrated by the aftermath of a major battle in Bakhmut in the Donetsk region of Ukraine in August 2022. Following the battle, Ukrainian soldiers reported that they found dozens of bodies of Wagner Group mercenaries on the battlefield. They were identified by their uniforms that bore a "Grim Reaper" patch and the legends "Death is our business and business is good" and "I don't believe in anything, I'm here for the violence."[24]

Ukrainian Intelligence was kept well informed of the build-up of the Wagner Group in the eastern area of the conflict by residents in the occupied region. The information provided by these brave, informal intelligence agents pinpointed with extreme accuracy the exact location of the Wagner Group's mercenary base. Not surprisingly, the Ukrainians did not wait to be attacked but launched a pre-emptive strike with artillery on 9 June, 2022 that is reported to have killed anywhere between 50 - 200 Wagner Group mercenaries, and at the same time destroyed their weapons depot.[25]

On 5 June, 2022, in what might be described as poetic justice for his victims, Wagner Group mercenary Vladimir Andonov—"The Executioner"—was shot dead by a sniper near Kharkiv during a night-time mission. He was 44 years old at the time of his death. Another unnamed Wagner mercenary was also killed alongside him. The two deaths were confirmed to a Russian newspaper by Zhambal-Zhamso Zhanaev, head of the region where Andonov lived.[26] It has not been conclusively established whether or not Andonov's elimination was a targeted killing or just another battlefield casualty of war. In the author's opinion, given the Ukrainian forces penetration of Russian radio and telephone communications, it was the former.

Another blow to the Wagner Group's morale came when another of its "stars," Battalion Commander Sergei Kononov, was killed in Ukraine in early August, 2022. Kononov served in Donbas in 2014 and in the Donetsk People's Republic in 2015. He was part of the Wagner Group deployment in Syria and fought in the battles to retake Palmyra, Latakia, Aleppo, and Daraa; and received the highest award of the Syrian Arab Republic from Syrian President Bashar al-Assad. He was known for his love of mortars and was "…able to shoot even without a coaster, from under his elbow." For example, in 2014, he shot down an enemy *Bucephalus* (a Polish armoured personnel carrier)."[27]

If the Russian forces hoped the deployment of the Wagner Group into Ukraine would have the same impact as in Syria and other war zones, those hopes were soon dashed. Russia has refused to acknowledge either its regular or Wagner Group losses in the Ukraine war. However, in a briefing given to British MPs of the Commons Foreign Affairs Select Committee on 21 April, 2022, an estimated 3,000 of the 8,000 members of the Wagner Group were said to have been killed in Ukraine.[28] A subsequent US estimate on 8 August, 2022, put the number of Wagner Group mercenaries killed in the invasion at 5,000.[29]

The reasons for the staggering losses sustained by the Wagner Group in Ukraine are the same as the colossal losses suffered by regular Russian forces. The Ukrainian army that they are now facing is not the badly organised and ill-equipped force they encountered in 2014. In the intervening years, the Ukrainian Army has been highly trained, mostly by British troops and has, unlike the Russian army, a cadre of high-calibre junior and senior NCOs, who are the backbone of any fighting army. Add to this the influx of modern weaponry, mainly supplied by Britain and the United States, and it is easy to understand the true cost to both Russia's regular and irregular forces in its "Special Operation."

Faced with such extreme losses, the Wagner Group has turned to some desperate measures to re-fill its ranks, first by lowering its recruiting standards and launching a glitzy recruiting drive in Russia, promising "adventure abroad."[30] Despite this major recruiting campaign, Wagner was still struggling to find recruits. As a result, Putin's chef, Yevgeny Prigozhin, reportedly the true owner of the Wagner Group (see previous chapter) undertook a tour of seventeen Russian prisons and persuaded 1,000 inmates to join the Wagner Group and fight in Ukraine.

During this unusual recruiting drive, Prigozhin showed a particular interest in inmates convicted of murder and robbery, while those convicted of sex offences were not normally selected. The new recruits were offered an initial salary of 200,000 roubles (£2,700), a presidential pardon, and a so-called "coffin payment" to their families in the event of death.[31] It is apparent that these new Wagner recruits will be thrown into the conflict with a bare minimum of training. When they meet the battle-hardened Ukrainian troops on the ground, it will inevitably result in even heavier casualties for this nefarious mercenary company. Equally, given the calibre of the new recruits, more atrocities like the Bucha massacre are equally inevitable.

In early August, 2022, a pro-Russian journalist visited the top secret headquarters of the Wagner Group in Popasna in eastern Ukraine, and he was greeted warmly as he took many photographs to commemorate his visit. The journalist then wrote on his social media "I arrived in Popasna. Went to Wagner's HQ. They greeted me like family, told me a few funny stories." As if disclosing the location of Wagner's HQ was not bad enough, the journalist then posted a number of his photographs on the internet. In one of them, Wagner mercenaries could be seen posing next to a building with shattered windows. On a plaque on the building, located in the left corner of the photo, was the exact address of the Wagner Group's HQ. In another photo, Yevgeny Prigozhin was seen shaking hands with a man in uniform. The Ukrainian forces did not take long to act on this colossal intelligence blunder. On 15 August, 2022, they used their newly acquired, US-supplied HIMLAR rockets to attack the building. Over 100 Wagner mercenaries were reported to have been killed in the Prigozhin attack. Perhaps more importantly, Prigozhin himself was reported as "missing" after the attack and believed to have been killed. At the time of writing, Prigozhin's death has not been confirmed, but the elimination of the man believed to be the actual head of the Wagner Group would not only be a devastating blow to the moral and operational effectiveness of the Wagner Group, but a deeply personal loss to Vladimir Putin himself.

Western Mercenaries In Ukraine

Two days after the beginning of the Russian invasion, President Zelensky made an appeal for foreign volunteers to enlist in a newly formed International Legion. His call was quickly supported by Denmark's Prime Minister, Mette Fredericksen, and by the then-UK foreign secretary, Liz Truss (although she later retracted the comment). They and many other leaders who did not openly voice their support for foreign enlistment saw the Ukraine struggle as a battle for freedom for the whole of Europe.

Thousands of western mercenary volunteers answered President Zelensky's call and formed an "International Brigade" within the Ukrainian forces. Most of the western volunteers are from Britain and the United States, but exact numbers are unknown. The first British mercenary volunteer to die in the conflict was Scott Ridley, a former five-year veteran who had served with the British Commando Logistic Support Squadron. He was killed by mortar fire whilst on active service on 28 April, 2022. A second, Jordan Gatley, was killed on 12 June, 2022, in the battle in Severo Donetsk region of Ukraine. Gatley was part of a special unit of the International Brigade and was shot whilst covering the retreat of his unit after it came under heavy fire during a Russian counter attack. His sacrifice undoubtedly saved many of his comrade's lives.

There have been, at the time of writing, unconfirmed reports of up to twenty more British deaths during the fighting, amidst accusations the British mercenary volunteers were "being used as cannon fodder" by the Ukrainian army.[32] From the author's own research, it is clear that many western mercenary volunteers do not find the reality of the Ukrainian experience in the International Brigade lives up to their preconceived and perhaps romanticised misconceptions. There seem to be well-founded reports that some of the International Brigade have been sent on what they describe as "suicide missions" without the proper weaponry or logistical support. Many complain about not being able to even get to the front lines because of red tape.[33]

Despite the difficulties facing western mercenary volunteers in Ukraine war, hundreds, perhaps even thousands, do remain and fight. In the author's opinion, the complaints made by many who have volunteered and become disillusioned, stems from the fact that this is an all-out war, unlike anything these volunteers will have faced in the past, even in Iraq or Afghanistan. All-out war is a brutal affair that consumes men and material like a wolf eats rabbits. The Ukrainian War is even more acute because it is a struggle for the very survival of a free nation, and in such a struggle, it is inevitable that some will be sacrificed. That is the reality of war. The attitude of those who do stay and fight is best summed up by Daniel Brady, an ex-member of the British Parachute Regiment, fighting with the Ukraine International Brigade: "Unless you're willing to fight and die here, don't come."[34]

The perils of combat are not the only menace facing western mercenary volunteers in Ukraine. Summary execution or torture after capture are real possibilities, if not even guaranteed ends. As mercenaries, the perils do not end there. If taken prisoner, they face the very real prospect of "show trails," followed by a conviction and a death sentence. At the time of writing three Britons, Aiden Aslin, Shaun Pinner, and Andrew Hill have been sentenced to death in the pro-Russian, so-called "Donetsk Peoples Republic." Whether or not such trials and sentences are legal will be dealt with by the author in the next chapter.

The Modern Mercenary

Modern mercenary companies in both Russia and the West are big business. Western mercenary companies have well-funded private armies of thousands of men. The size and reach of the giant mercenary company Academi and the ravenous accruement of natural resources by the Wagner Group in Africa has already been covered, but there are other western giants in the ever-expanding private security industry, and here are just a few examples:

Northbridge Services Group is registered in the Dominican Republic, but with offices in Kentucky, Ukraine, and the UK, and run by ex-US Army Lieutenant Colonel and Vietnam veteran Robert Kovacic, its promotional literature describes it as providing "highly confidential and effective security-related services designed to address the needs of governments, multinational corporations, non-governmental organizations, the corporate sector, and prominent individuals." It is also heavily involved with law enforcement agencies in the theatres of terrorism, narcotics, organized crime, poaching, smuggling, maritime defence, and the protection of natural resources. In April 2003, the company was criticised by Baroness Symons of Vernham Dean for its operations in Côte d'Ivoire that were seen as seriously undermining the peace process. In May 2003, Northbridge commandos rescued many oil workers who had been held hostage on an oil rig. The last financial records, published in 2012, showed that Northbridge's revenue totalled $50.5 million.

Triple Canopy is another giant. Based in Reston Virginia, it was established by former US Special Forces soldiers, including former Delta Force operators, in Chicago in 2003. According to its official website, the company "provides mission support, security, and training services to government agencies and multinational corporations worldwide." The company has a registered employment of some 5,500 staff and includes amongst its national and international clients telecommunication companies, oil and gas businesses, mining firms, and financial organizations. As with many western mercenary companies, Triple Canopy benefited from the Iraqi War boom, with just one of its Iraq defence contracts valued at $1.5 billion.

Western mercenary companies often find niche areas. ICTS International was set up by former Israel Security Agency and El Al-Israel Airlines security agents who formed this Israeli private security company in 1982. The firm's head offices are in Amstelveen in the Netherlands. The company advertises itself as "providing advanced, comprehensive security solutions for the aviation and homeland security sectors, with an emphasis on transportation security in general, and railroad and mass transport security in particular." In 2005, the company set up "I-SEC International Security BV," specialising in airport and airline security. Towards the end of the 1990s, ICTS International set up a computer technology wing called "Advanced Passenger Screening." The new wing created a computer algorithm which, based on passenger information, calculates the likelihood of passengers posing some kind of threat. The algorithm is now used by the majority of major US airlines. In 2008 ICTS International's revenue totalled $98.8 million.

Growth Areas

Cyberspace

The above is but a small sample of the present, ever-expanding private security industry. The industry is expanding into areas never before envisaged for mercenaries. Cyberspace is a prime example. Yevgeny Prigozhin, in addition to allegedly heading the Wagner Group, is also believed to have been at least partially responsible for the activities of the IRA, better known within the United States as the Russian Troll Factory. The US government has both sanctioned and indicted Prigozhin and associated companies in connection with IRA for its cyber support of the 2014 invasion of Ukraine and its attempts to influence the 2016 US presidential election. In the IRA and other private mercenary "Troll" companies, Russia has an offensive cyberattack capability, whilst at the same time having plausible deniability for its activities.[35]

These types of agencies, and individual computer hackers, attack government and corporate computer networks. The most vicious of these attacks are ransomware attacks, which are one of the fastest-growing malware hazards of the 21st century. They threaten businesses and public institutions around the world, and are a particularly virulent and fast-evolving species of malicious software. Attacks infect computers and mobile devices, often spreading across networks to other devices. Once an attack compromises a system, it silently encrypts every data file that it locates, then displays a "ransom note" to the user that demands an online payment of hundreds or thousands of pounds, often to be paid in untraceable cryptocurrency like Bitcoin, in return for the decryption keys needed to restore the user's locked files.

A devastating example of a ransomware attack is the WannaCry ransomware attack in May 2017 which infected more than 230,000 computers in over 150 countries. Victims included the United Kingdom's National Health Service, Spain's Telefónica, Germany's Deutsche Bahn, and US companies including Federal Express. Both the British and US government have proven unable to protect private companies from such attacks. For help, the private sector is turning increasingly to the private cybersecurity industry, many staffed by former National Security Agency (NSA) employees. These companies offer what is called an "active defence."

In reality they are, unofficially, "hack back companies," which attack the original hackers—i.e. "hack back," doing to the hackers exactly what they have done to their intended targets. Whilst they cannot undo the damage of a network breach, their employment is a potential deterrent to would-be hackers, intended to persuade them to choose unguarded targets. In the United States, any form of hacking is a federal crime, including "hack back." However, given the failure of national governments in preventing ransomware attacks, many of the larger firms in the US and elsewhere are now hiring these cyberspace mercenaries who often disguise their true function from everyone but the would-be hackers themselves.

Humanitarian Relief

Humanitarian relief is another growth area for private mercenary companies. In the immediate aftermath of the Hurricane Katrina disaster in the US, Blackwater provided security, airlift, logistics, and transportation services as well as humanitarian support, which cost the US taxpayers

$240,000 per day.[36] This clearly set a pattern, as traditionally, relief efforts relied upon state military capacities for logistics, air transport and protection provided either independently, through the UN, or other multilateral arrangements. The primary reason the growth of private military security companies involvements in humanitarian relief operations can be explained in what is called the "Mogadishu Syndrome."

As a result of a UN Security Council Resolution adopted to authorize use of "all means necessary" to establish safe, secure environments for humanitarian relief operations in Somalia, in 1993, the United States led "Operation Restore Hope" to the country. The US abandoned the mission after public outrage when a firefight erupted and led to the deaths of eighteen American soldiers and more than 300 Somali locals. As a direct result, many Americans called into question the need to get involved in humanitarian conflicts, especially when US interests were not directly at stake. This was where the concept of the so-called "Mogadishu Syndrome" was born. It refers to the unwillingness of governments to intervene in conflicts for humanitarian reasons other than for their own national interests.

The growing dominance of private military companies offers humanitarian organisations an enhancement to their capacities and reach without turning to traditional state military units for help. This option is increasingly being chosen by international humanitarian agencies, such as CARE, Save the Children, CARITAS, and World Vision. It has raised concerns in many sectors, including the United Nations. Jelena Aparac, Chairperson-Rapporteur of the United Nations Working Group on using mercenaries as a means of violating human rights and impeding the right of peoples to self-determination, presented a report of her working group, stating: "...an increasing number of private military and security companies were operating in the humanitarian space, which exacerbated the risk of violations of human rights and international humanitarian law and undermined humanitarian principles. The growing reliance on private military and security companies by humanitarian actors had come with significant challenges with regards to the protection of civilians and the guarantee and respect of human rights and international humanitarian law. Most importantly, the role of these private companies in humanitarian action and the commercialisation of humanitarian aid, raised concerns over their impacts on the humanitarian principles of impartiality, neutrality, and operational independence."[37]

The reluctance of many major states to deploy armed troops to protect relief workers in disaster zones involved in an armed conflict, stems primarily because of the inherent fear of being drawn into another war. Coupled with the inherent intuitional slowness of the UN to deploy blue helmet peacekeepers means that, despite the reservations of organisations like the UN itself, the need for urgent action to protect the vulnerable victims will almost certainly compel international humanitarian agencies to continue to employ the private security sector in their relief efforts around the globe.

The Future of Mercenaries

Where will mercenaries go next? Perhaps into space: the growth of private companies sending satellites into orbit raises the prospect of mercenaries being hired to disrupt or even destroy a rival's satellites. Major corporations could turn to mercenaries to promote and expand their global interests, leading up privately funded wars over natural resources like oil, mining, water or new gas fields. These may seem like flights of fancy or works of fiction, but the reality is that the modern mercenary, whether called a contactor or not, is now more powerfully imbedded in the everyday workings of most nations than ever before. Two things are certain, they will not go away, and, without control, will continue to expand their activities into any area were a profit can be made. In the next chapter, the author will look at mercenaries and the law and what controls are presently in place.

Chapter Eleven

Mercenaries and the Law

The Legality of Mercenaries

The question many people ask is, are mercenaries legal? International Law actually prohibits the use of mercenaries in armed conflict and certain peaceful situations. As a result, various international instruments have sought both to define what a mercenary is and limit their use in armed conflicts the first of these being:

Hague Convention V respecting the Rights and Duties of Neutral Powers and Persons in Case of War on Land **(1907), article 4**

Article 4 of the Hague Convention V, which is considered to represent customary law, stipulates that "…corps of combatants cannot be formed nor recruiting agencies opened on the territory of a neutral Power to assist the belligerents." The effect of this provision is that a neutral country, for example Switzerland, has an obligation to prevent such activities from occurring on its territory. It cannot be held responsible for citizens or inhabitants who decided to cross the border of their own accord to offer mercenary services to the countries involved in conflict. **Article 4** creates an obligation on neutral states to prevent the recruitment and organising of mercenary groups on their territory for the purpose of a mercenary intervention in an armed conflict to which they have chosen to remain neutral. Failure to comply would be violation of their obligations under international law.

The next major international instrument concerning mercenaries was:

Charter of the United Nations **(1945), article 2, paragraph 4**

Article 2, paragraph 4 of the UN Charter stipulates that: "All Members shall refrain in their international relations from the threat or use of force against the territorial integrity or political independence of any state, or in any other manner inconsistent with the Purposes of the United Nations." This provision outlaws the use of force by one state against another, except in very specific circumstances spelled out elsewhere in the Charter. In simple terms, this restricts the use of military force by countries to acts of self-defence or enforcement measures sanctioned by the UN Security Council. This cannot be circumvented by employing mercenaries, and their use would come within the scope of this prohibition.

Moving forward in time:

Common Article 3 of the *Geneva Conventions* (1949)

Article 3 explicitly states that in any conflict, whether of international or non-international character, "persons taking no active part in the hostilities, including members of armed forces who have laid down their arms and those placed hors de combat by sickness, wounds, detention, or any other cause, shall in all circumstances be treated humanely, without any adverse distinction founded on race, colour, religion or faith, sex, birth or wealth, or any other similar criteria." Under the Geneva Convention, mercenaries are not recognized as legitimate combatants, and therefore do not have to be granted the same legal protections as captured service personnel of the armed forces. As will be explained below, this has important ramifications in the present war in Ukraine.

The first attempt to properly define what a 'mercenary' was contained in:

***Protocol I Additional to the Geneva Conventions relating to the Protection of Victims of International Armed Conflict* (1977), Article 47**

Article 47 of Additional Protocol I According to **Article 47,** a mercenary is any person who:

1. Is specially recruited locally or abroad in order to fight in an armed conflict;
2. Does, in fact, take a direct part in hostilities;
3. Is motivated to take part in the hostilities by the desire for private gain and is promised, by or on behalf of a Party to the conflict, material compensation substantially in excess of that promised or paid to combatants of similar ranks and functions in the armed forces of that Party;

4. Is neither a national of a Party to the conflict nor a resident of territory controlled by a Party to the conflict;
5. Is not a member of the armed forces of a Party to the conflict; and
6. Has not been sent by a State which is not a Party to the conflict on official duty as a member of its armed forces.

These requirements are cumulative, which means that they must all be applicable for an individual to be categorized as a mercenary. The intended purpose of international humanitarian law is to extend rather than restrict the protection afforded to armed combatants in conflict zones. This definition of a mercenary is specifically narrow in order to ensure that the loss of special protection, such as prisoner of war status, occurs only in very limited circumstances. Again, as will be explained below, this has important ramifications in the present war in Ukraine.

The first real attempt both to restrict and impose sanctions for the use of mercenaries was outlined in the:

International Convention against the Recruitment, Use, Financing and Training of Mercenaries **(1989)**

The Convention established a range of offences that may be committed by individual mercenaries, persons recruiting, using, financing or training mercenaries, by states or individual parties. It also imposes on states and parties a number of related obligations:

Article 1 of the convention keeps the definition of a mercenary contained in article 47 of the Protocol Additional I to the Geneva Conventions (see above), but expands it to cover situations other than wars or similar armed conflicts, to include circumstance were mercenaries are recruited for the purpose of participating the armed overthrow a government or otherwise undermining a constitutionally elected state or threatening its territorial integrity.

In such a situation, "a mercenary" is a person who:

1. Is motivated to take part essentially by the desire for significant private gain, and is prompted by the promise or payment of material compensation;
2. Is neither a national nor a resident of the State against which such an act is directed;

3. Has not been sent by a State on official duty; and
4. Is not a member of the armed forces of the State on whose territory the act is undertaken.

To commit an offence under the Convention, a mercenary must not only fall within the definition contained in **article 1**, but also participate directly in armed combat or in an act of armed violence, or have attempted to do so. An offence is also committed by any person who recruits, uses, finances or trains mercenaries, attempts to do so, or is the accomplice of a person who commits or attempts to commit an offence set forth in the Convention. This indirect offence is judged to have been committed even where the mercenaries in question have not yet taken part in hostilities. The purpose of the direct combat requirement is to distinguish a mercenary from a military adviser who takes no direct role in combat.

The Convention also sets out a framework to facilitate the prosecution of offenders at the national level. It requires states to ensure that their legislation makes such a prosecution possible. Any alleged mercenary present on their territory should be taken into custody and a preliminary inquiry opened. If the person concerned is not extradited to another state for trial, the case should be submitted to the competent national authorities. Throughout the proceedings, the alleged mercenary should benefit from fair treatment and judicial guarantees. It is intended that states should cooperate with one another in both the prevention and prosecution of offences, including through the exchange of information. Lastly, the Convention establishes a procedure for the settlement of disputes between states parties concerning the interpretation or application of the instrument.

Apart from the international attempts to restrict the use of mercenaries there have been regional instruments the most important of which is:

Convention for the Elimination of Mercenaryism in Africa **(1977)**

The Africa Union's Convention prohibits both mercenaries and mercenaryism, which is characterized as a crime against peace and security in Africa, whether committed by an individual, a group, an association, a state or a state representative.

Article 1 of the Africa Union's Convention defines a mercenary as any person who:

1. Is specially recruited locally or abroad in order to fight in an armed conflict;
2. Does in fact take a direct part in the hostilities;
3. Is motivated to take part in the hostilities essentially by the desire for private gain and in fact is promised by or on behalf of a party to the conflict material compensation;
4. Is neither a national of a party to the conflict nor a resident of territory controlled by a party to the conflict;
5. Is not a member of the armed forces of a party to the conflict; and
6. Is not sent by a State other than a party to the conflict on official mission as a member of the armed forces of the said State."

The framework of this Convention criminalizes the sheltering, assisting, training, equipping, promoting, supporting, employing, or enlisting mercenaries. The regime also criminalizes the allowing of such activities as "to be carried out in any territory under its jurisdiction or any place under its control or afford facilities for transit, transport or other operations" of mercenary forces. **(Article 2) The International Convention against the Recruitment, Use, Financing and Training of Mercenaries 2001** was ratified by thirty-five countries, including Germany, Italy, Canada, New Zealand, Belgium, and Poland. However, the major powers, including the United Kingdom, the US, France, Russia, and China refused to sign it and are not covered by the international prohibition on the use of mercenaries. This is hardly surprising, given the dependence these countries have on private mercenary companies. The position of these countries on the use of mercenaries is outlined below.[1]

The United States Position on Mercenaries

The US position is that being a mercenary is not illegal under international law. The *Department of Defence Law of War Manual* (¶ 4.21) says:

"The act of being a mercenary is not a crime in customary international law nor in any treaty to which the United States is a Party. Under the customary law of war and the GPW, 'mercenaries' receive the rights, duties, and liabilities of combatant status on the same basis as other persons."

The US does recognize that there are a "number of treaty provisions that are intended to repress mercenary activities" but points out that the "United States has not accepted any such provision because these efforts are not consistent with fundamental principles of the law of war." (¶ 4.21.1).

The US does however hold that mercenaries must be accountable in law for any violations of basic human rights: "Mercenaries must comply with the law of war and may be tried and punished for violations of the law of war on the same basis as other persons. States that employ mercenaries are responsible for their conduct, including their compliance with the law of war." (¶ 4.21)[2]

The British Position on Mercenaries

The British position on mercenaries can best be explained by a question tabled by Baroness Tonge on 24 February in the British House of Lords regarding mercenaries.

Question:

"To ask Her Majesty's Government whether UK citizens are permitted (1) to act as mercenaries, and (2) to train with foreign militaries; and if so, (a) under what legislative or other framework such activity is permitted, and (b) in what countries they permit such activity."

Answer:

Given by Lord Ahmad of Wimbledon on behalf of the Foreign, Commonwealth, and Development office:

"The UK government notes Article 47 of Additional Protocol I to the Geneva Conventions, of which the UK is a party, which sets out the definition of a mercenary. There is no licensing system or permission process in UK law for a UK citizen who intends to act as a mercenary to follow. UK law focuses on the activities of UK citizens abroad, which may be prosecuted in the UK where UK law makes such provision. For example, under the International Criminal Courts Acts of 2001, UK courts have jurisdiction to prosecute acts of genocide, war crimes and crimes against humanity committed by UK nationals either inside or outside of the United Kingdom, and offences of murder committed outside the jurisdiction may be prosecuted in the UK Additionally, the direct or indirect provision of armed personnel, where it enables or facilitates the conduct of armed hostilities, may constitute an offence under UK sanctions regimes. This legislation enables the UK to prosecute a UK citizen accused of committing such crimes overseas as a mercenary or whilst working for a private security company.

We draw a clear distinction between mercenaries and private security companies (PSCs). We promote high standards for PSCs internationally through voluntary regulation of the sector and played a leading role in the drafting of the International Code of Conduct for Private Security Service Providers (2010), which sets out principles for security providers, and related standards, governance, and oversight mechanisms, and the launch of its oversight mechanism to monitor compliance with the Code, the International Code of Conduct Association (ICoCA) (2013).

Members of UK Armed Forces regularly undertake training and engage in exercises with a wide range of international partners in that professional capacity, where this best supports the development of UK military capability, contributes to the development of international defence relationships and supports wider government objectives."[3]

So are mercenaries legal or not? The answer to this question depends entirely on the country in question. The use of mercenaries is legal in countries that did not sign the UN treaty, including Britain, the United States, and Russia. This allows the formation of private mercenary companies in those countries. In addition, if a mercenary is hired by a sovereign nation to fight for them in another country that is not a signatory of the UN Treaty, then they are legal to that country as well. If mercenary is deployed to and captured by any other country that's a party to the UN Treaty, then they would be considered illegal in that country and could face prosecution. Where mercenaries, or private military contracts (PMCs) as they now preferred to be called in the West, are legal, what controls and constraints are placed upon them? In simple terms, not much. As indicated in the replay from Lord Ahmad in the British House of Lords, the first real attempt to set standards and penalties in private military sector was by self-regulation.

Self-Regulation: International Code of Conduct for Private Security Service Providers (ICoC)

The ICoC is a set of principles for the private security industry. The code reinforces and articulates the obligations of private security providers particularly with regard to international humanitarian law and human rights law.

The ICoC also sets the foundation for developing an institutional framework to provide oversight of—and accountability to—the ICoC. Those private security companies or states that sign up to it agreed on "Articles of Association" setting up an oversight mechanism, the International Code of Conduct Association (ICoCA). It now includes over 100 private military and security company members, including Academi, formerly known as Blackwater.[4]

Whilst it has to be applauded that this has been a real attempt both to regulate and set standards for the western private security industry, for those that have signed up to the ICoC, the main criticism is that it has no real teeth. It is a voluntary code and the main penalty for those violating the code is expulsion from the ICoCA. This may harm the public relations efforts of major western private security companies eager to clean up their acts, but is no real deterrent to those more concerned with profit than morality. In addition, mercenary groups like Wagner and the Spear Operations Group, which carried out an assassination programme in Yemen, do not sign up to a public registry and the ICoC and therefore it has no impact on their activities.

Alternatives to Self-Regulation

More Rigorous Regulation?

There have been repeated calls for a more rigorous regulatory regime to be introduced both by the British and American authorities, such as the introduction of formal legislation into law dealing specifically with the private security industry and the setting up of a formal regulatory system to administer the implementation of the legislation. The legislation would include the registering and licensing of individuals and private military companies wishing to supply military services abroad and establish corporate responsibility for the actions of those it employed. The regulatory authority would have the power to remove licences and seize the assets of an offending private military company. Both the UK and American governments have so far resisted any such moves.

Accountability

If self-regulation is not the answer to controlling the private security industry and with no real prospect in sight of formal legislation being introduced, accountability has been proposed as a possible solution to the growing power of the private security industry. The question is, how to make them more accountable? One idea that has been considered is bringing mercenaries employed by a state under their country's Code of Military Conduct to control their activities. However, that solution has been rejected by all nations that have considered it as being impractical. Given the multinational configuration of most private mercenary companies, the question inevitably arises as to where a potential transgressor would be tried? Would it be in the country he was serving in, his country of origin, or by the state who hired him? As a lawyer, the author can state that this would be a legal nightmare that would be all but impossible to resolve.

Whilst bringing mercenaries under a nation's governing Code of Military Conduct is not an option, in the author's opinion, making private mercenary companies more accountable for their actions must ultimately be the solution. The tools already exist under both British and American law to prosecute those that violate basic human rights in combat zones. Although the process was eventually undermined by the pardons issued by then-President Trump, the successful prosecution of Blackwater mercenaries in the United States is ample testimony of that. To its credit, the British government did investigate possible human rights violations by Keenie Meenie in Sri Lanka, but as far as the author can determine at this time, there was insufficient evidence to pursue a successful prosecution. More rigorous application of existing domestic law, both in the US and Britain, should curtail the worst excesses of the established western private security industry. However, that still leaves rogue actors on the international stage who take no notice of either domestic or international law.

International Prosecution of Rogue Mercenary Groups

On any view, the activities of these types of mercenary groups are heinous and a clear violation of both humanitarian and international law. Whilst the activities of the Wagner Group can be explained but never condoned, the fact that they are carrying out activities on behalf of a rogue nation with no regard to human rights and dignity, and the failure to curb the accesses of some western mercenary groups is worrying.

The Spear Operations Group's activities in Yemen are a classic example. The so-called "War on Terror" has resulted in western nations conducting targeted assassinations of persons deemed to be terrorists and a threat to that state. The most recent example being on 31 July, 2022, when Al-Qaeda leader Ayman al-Zawahiri was killed on his balcony in a downtown Kabul compound by two American Hellfire missiles. Israel, of course routinely assassinates any person deemed a "terrorist" and a threat to its national survival. The author himself, when part of the South African Special Forces, attempted the assassination of Robert Mugabe, the then-leader of the main insurgency group in Rhodesia, in Mozambique in the late 1970s.

If states can summarily execute "terrorists," why can this not be outsourced to the private security industry? The answer, of course, is blindingly simple: who selects the target list? Are those chosen for summary execution really a threat or political opponents to be disposed of, which, in the author's opinion was exactly the situation in Yemen in the extra judicial murder campaign against Al-Islah. In the author's opinion, mercenaries conducting such "operations" are not soldiers but contract killers who should be brought before the International Criminal Court as war criminals.

However there are problems in pursuing such prosecutions. The 1986 International Court of Justice decision in *Nicaragua v. United States of America ("Nicaragua"). **Nicaragua*** created an exceptionally high attribution threshold for holding paramilitary of mercenary groups accountable for a state's actions. Under ***Nicaragua***, a paramilitary or mercenary unit can only be found a *de facto* state organ were:

(1) the state paid, financed, and coordinated/supervised the group's actions, and
(2) the state "specifically 'directed or enforced' the perpetuation" of IHL violations by the group "with respect to the specific operation in the course of which IHL breaches may have been committed."

In simple terms under **Nicaragua**, the unit's action could be attributed to the state only if it was completely dependent on the state. The answer to this problem may be found in the **International Criminal Tribunal for the Former Yugoslavia (ICTY)** case of the *Prosecutor v. Tadić*.[5] This landmark legal decision provides a possible solution as to how a prosecution of rouge mercenary groups like Wagner and Spear might be framed. The test applied by the court was one of "overall control" by the country that engaged, paid, and directed the mercenary group in question. Such prosecutions would result in not only holding the individual mercenary group to account but would also establish liability for both Russia and the UAE for the actions of both of these rogue mercenary groups.

One thing is clear: unless international action is taken against such groups, the failure of western liberal democracies—particularly the United States and Britain—to both condemn and take action against such activities leaves the door wide open to a further expansion of the use of mercenaries for privately funded murder. If that happens, where will it end? No head of state would be safe from an opponent with enough money to hire a mercenary group to assassinate him. Huge multinational corporations—or for that matter, any wealthy person or private organisation—could, in theory, hire mercenaries to assassinate any who oppose their commercial interests. In an already fragile and dangerous world, that would be a world where no one was really ever safe.

The Prosecution by Russia of Western Volunteers in Ukraine

The classification and treatment of persons taking part in any armed conflict depends in large part on the classification of that armed conflict. It cannot be in doubt that there is an ongoing international armed conflict with partial occupation in Ukraine by Russian forces. Therefore, both the Geneva Conventions and the Additional Protocol I thereto, which have been ratified by both Russia and Ukraine, applies to this armed conflict.

As outlined above, the definition of what constitutes a mercenary is a narrow one and does not apply where foreign volunteers are part of a volunteer corps, as long as that incorporated unit is part of a professional fighting force, fulfilling the criteria spelled out in Article 4A(2) and be subordinate to the regular army command of the country in question. The fact that an individual is a national of a third state and not a national of the armed forces in which he is serving is widely considered to *not* be a deciding factor in determining either combatant or POW status.

The Ukrainian authorities have regularized its volunteer corps in domestic law and placed them under responsible command. On 17 March 2015, *Law No. 2389* amended certain legislative acts to allow foreigners to join the Armed Forces of Ukraine (AFU) on a contract basis, at the same level of remuneration as citizens of Ukraine of equal rank. In 2016, *Presidential Decree No. 248* affirmed that "Foreigners, legally present on the territory of Ukraine, can be accepted for military service on contract with the Armed Forces of Ukraine on a voluntary basis." The Decree stipulates that foreigners who pass medical, psychological, and professional competencies assessment become members of the AFU.[6]

Ukraine has therefore fulfilled all the requirements under international law to protect the foreign fighters within its armed forces, and they are therefore combatants who should be entitled to POW status upon capture by Russia. The prosecution and punishment that British and other foreign volunteers have endured, in what many consider to be show trials conducted by Russia's puppet state in eastern Ukraine on charges of directly participating in the armed conflict, or for the crime of mercenaryism. This is contrary to Articles 43 and 44 of the Geneva Convention are therefore unlawful and, in the author's opinion, amount to war crime.

Notes

Chapter One

1. '*The Civil War Was Won by Immigrant Soldiers.*' Time.
2. Malet, David, cited in '*Framing to Win: The Transnational Recruitment of Foreign Insurgents*', In Nonstate Actors in Intrastate Conflict.

Chapter Two

1. Smiley, D and Kemp, P, '*Arabian Adventure*'.
2. Smiley, D and Kemp, P. '*Arabian Adventure*'.
3. Hoare, M. '*Congo Mercenary*'.
4. Hoare, M. '*Congo Mercenary*'.
5. Hoare, M. '*Congo Mercenary*'.
6. Personal recollections of the author.
7. '*Biafra: The Mercenaries.*' Time, 25 October 1968.
8. Steiner, Rolf, *The Last Adventurer* Boston, Little, Brown & Co., 1978.
9. Martell, Peter '*First Raise a Flag: How South Sudan Won the Longest War but Lost the Peace*', Oxford University Press, 2009.
10. O'Ballance, Edgar, *Sudan, Civil War and Terrorism, 1956-99*, New York, Springer 2003.
11. Poggo, Scopas, *The First Sudanese Civil War: Africans, Arabs, and Israelis in the Southern Sudan, 1955-1972*, New York, Springer, 2008.
12. Poggo, Scopas, *The First Sudanese Civil War: Africans, Arabs, and Israelis in the Southern Sudan, 1955-1972*, New York, Springer, 2008.
13. Baxter, Peter, *Biafra: The Nigerian Civil War 1967-1970*. London, Helion and Company, 2004.
14. Poggo, Scopas, *The First Sudanese Civil War: Africans, Arabs, and Israelis in the Southern Sudan, 1955-1972*, New York, Springer, 2008.
15. Martell, Peter, '*First Raise a Flag: How South Sudan Won the Longest War but Lost the Peace*', Oxford University Press, 2009.

16. Martell, Peter, '*First Raise a Flag: How South Sudan Won the Longest War but Lost the Peace*', Oxford University Press, 2009.
17. O'Ballance, Edgar, *Sudan, Civil War and Terrorism, 1956-99*, New York, Springer 2003.
18. Steiner, Rolf, *The Last Adventurer.* Boston, Little, Brown & Co., 1978.

Chapter Three

1. Hoover, Mike J., '*The Laws of War and the Angolan Trial of Mercenaries: Death to the Dogs of War*'. Case Western Reserve Journal of International Law, 1997.
2. Time Magazine, 23 February, 1975.
3. *No Mean Soldier*, Peter McAleese.
4. Dempster, Chris, *Fire Power*, London, St Martin's Press, 1980.
5. United Nations Report on the question of the use of mercenaries as a means of violating human rights and impeding the exercise of the right of peoples to self-determination, submitted by Mr. Enrique Bernales Ballesteros, Special Rapporteur, pursuant to Commission resolution 1995/5 and Economic and Council resolution 1995/254.
6. Weinberg, Samantha, *Last of the pirates; in search of Bob Denard.* London, 1994.
7. UPI Archives, 8 February, 1981.
8. The Guardian, Friday, 28 December, 2007.
9. TRC, pp. 163-164.
10. Hansard.
11. Tamil Guardian report, 2001.
12. Tamil Guardian report, 2001.
13. Rajasingham, K. T., *Sri Lanka: The Untold Story*, Asia Times, 9 March, 2002.
14. BBC News Report, 30 November, 2020.
15. Pech, Khareen, '*Executive Outcomes – A Corporate* Conquest', in Jakkie Mason, Cilliers and Peggy (eds.) '*Peace, Profit or Plunder?: Privatisation of Security in War-Torn African Societies*', 1999.
16. Howe, Herbert M., '*Private Security Forces and African Stability: The Case of Executive Outcomes*', The Journal of Modern African Studies, Vol. 36, N0. 2, 1998.
17. The Today Programme, BBC Radio 4, 16 April, 2002.
18. The Daily Telegraph, 29 March, 2013.

Chapter Four

1. '*A Fighter with Castro*' New York Times, 15 August, 1959.
2. Dalle, Robert, *'The Untold Story of the Bay of Pigs*'.
3. Dalle, Robert, '*The Untold Story of the Bay of Pigs*'.
4. Dalle, Robert, '*The Untold Story of the Bay of Pigs*'.
5. Dommen, Arthur J. *Conflict in Laos: The Policy of Neutralization*, revised edition, New York, Praeger, 1971, and Stevenson, Charles A., *The End of Nowhere: American Policy Toward Laos Since 1954*, Boston, Beacon Press, 1973.
6. Cockburn, Alexander and St Clair, Jeffrey, '*Whiteout: the CIA, drugs and the press*', 1998.
7. For example, see conflicting views of historians William M. Leary*: 'Air America was not involved in the drug trade*,' and Alfred W. McCoy *who noted that mostly, the CIA's role involved different forms of complicity, tolerance, and even studied ignorance about the drug trade.*
8. *Cates, Allen, 'Air America: A Historical Synopsis from the Beginning to End'*, 5 November, 2021.
9. Dommen, Arthur J. *Conflict in Laos: The Policy of Neutralization*, revised edition, New York, Praeger, 1971, and Stevenson, Charles A., *The End of Nowhere: American Policy Toward Laos Since 1954* Boston, Beacon Press, 1973.
10. Drudge, Michael W., 'An American mercenary who left his wife and daughter…' UPI Archives, 25 January, 1984.
11. Bradley, Graham, '*Public Honours for secret Combat*' Washington Post, 6 May, 1996.
12. Sub Committee on Western Hemisphere Affairs, US Congress, 13 May, 1987.
13. Druge, Michael, UPI Archives, January 1984.
14. Little, Micahael '*The War on Information*'.
15. McCartney, Robert J. '*Soldiers of Fortune Lend a Hand in El Salvador*', Washington Post 29 August, 1983.
16. McCartney, Robert J. '*Soldiers of Fortune Lend a Hand in El Salvador*', Washington Post 29 August, 1983.
17. McCartney, Robert J. '*Revolution and Counterrevolution in Nicaragua*', 1991.
18. Pallmeyer, Jack Nelson, '*War Against the Poor: Low-Intensity Conflict and the Christian Faith*'.

19. Gill, 1989, p. 329.
20. UPI, 25 April, 1995.
21. '*National Security Decision Directive Reagan Administration*', Fas.org., 30 May, 2008.
22. United Press International (UPI), 6 April, 1984, '*CIA Reported Directing Mine Laying in Nicaraguan Waters*'.
23. *The Assassination Business*, The Scotsman 26 July, 1988.
24. Riesenfeld, Stefan '*The Powers of Congress and the President in International Relations: Revisited*', California Law Review, January 1987.
25. "*The Contras, cocaine, and covert operations: Documentation of official U.S. knowledge of drug trafficking and the Contras*", The National Security Archive / George Washington University, c1990.
26. *Hansard References*, 1 December, 1987.

Chapter Five

1. BBC Documentary '*Killing Escobar*', 4 May, 2021.
2. Znak, '*Bałkański dżihad*', September 2016, p. 208.
3. Darko Trifunović, Ioannis Michaletos, '*Nexus between terrorism and organized criminal group from Balkan as threats to EU Security*', in: Asymetryczne Bałkany: działania asymetryczne, militarne i polityka bezpieczeństwa na Półwyspie Bałkańskim w XX i XXI wieku: materiały i studia, ed. Danuta Gibas-Krzak (Częstochowa: Wydawnictwo im. Stanisława Podobińskiego Akademii im. Jana Długosza, 2015), p. 277-279; Vladimira Janková, Wahhabism in the Balkans, p. 19.
4. The International Criminal Tribunal for the Former Yugoslavia case no: it-01-47, The Prosecutor of The Tribunal against Enver Hadzihasanovic, Mehmed Alagic and Amir Kubura.
5. The Independent, Tuesday 9 February, 1993.
6. The Independent, Tuesday 9 February, 1993.
7. ITN News Report, 9 February, 1993.
8. BBC News Report, 2 July, 2012.
9. '*The Bosnian Jihad: An interview with Abu Abdel Aziz Barbaros*', Sunday Times, 27 July, 1993.
10. International Criminal Tribunal for the Former Yugoslavia, (IT-04-83) p. 238.
11. PBS Newshour with Jim Lehrer, 14 December, 2010.
12. Independent, 10 February, 1993.

13. BBC broadcast, '*Inside Story*', 20 May, 1992.
14. Amazon Book Reviews, '*War Dogs*'.
15. Times, 26 September, 2000.
16. The Guardian, 30 September, 2000.
17. *Krott, Rob 'Save the Last Bullet for Yourself: A Soldier of Fortune in the Balkans and Somalia'*.
18. Sandelin, Magus, '*The Black Nazi* (*Den Svarte Nazisten*).
19. Williams, Carol J, *Los Angeles Time,* 12 April, 1993.
20. Williams, Carol J, *Los Angeles Time,* 12 April, 1993.
21. Gros-Verheyde, Nicolas, Newspaper Article, 24 June, 1993.
22. Williams, Carol J, *Los Angeles Time,* 12 April, 1993.
23. Michael Innes estimated in April 1994 the VRS was 100,000 members strong. Of that number, 1,000 - 1,500 were mercenaries from Russia, Ukraine and Bulgaria. Mikhail Polikarpov, a participant in the war and now a historian, noted the probable number of Russian soldiers in the hundreds, with about 40 dying and 20 injured.
24. Konstantinidis, Petros, Published in '*AthensLive*', 8 December, 2017.
25. Konstantinidis, Petros, Published in '*AthensLive*', 8 December, 2017.
26. Konstantinidis, Petros, Published in '*AthensLive*', 8 December, 2017.
27. Konstantinidis, Petros, Published in '*AthensLive*', 8 December, 2017.
28. Konstantinidis, Petros, Published in '*AthensLive*', 8 December, 2017.
29. Konstantinidis, Petros, Published in '*AthensLive*', 8 December, 2017.
30. Takebe, Masaki, *Yohei-no-Hokori* (The pride of a mercenary) Shogakukan Inc, 24 March, 2002.
31. Avant, Deborah, '*The Market for Force: The Consequences of Privatizing Security*'.
32. Vaknin, Sam, *CorpWatch*, 16 March 2005.
33. Silverman, Ken, '*Private Warriors*'.
34. Quoted in: Kemp, John S., '*Private Military Firms and Responses to Their Accountability Gap*' Washington University School of Law, 10 January, 2010.
35. Chossudovsky, Michel, '*Washington Finances Ethnic Warfare in the Balkans*', April 2001.
36. Burns, Robert, *Pentagon: Russians Fought for Serbs*, AP Military Writer 23 June, 1999.
37. Burns, Robert, *Pentagon: Russians Fought for Serbs*, AP Military Writer 23 June, 1999.

38. Burns, Robert, *Pentagon: Russians Fought for Serbs*, AP Military Writer 23 June, 1999.

Chapter Six

1. Santa Cruz Sentinel, 5 July, 1979.
2. UPI Archives, 13 April, 1990.
3. Scully, William, '*Always a Pilgrim*'.
4. Scully, William, '*Always a Pilgrim*'.
5. BBC News Report, 10 January, 2021.
6. Stephen, Ellis, *Prince paid thousands into wildlife sting*, The Independent, 8 January, 1991.
7. Stephen, Ellis, *Prince paid thousands into wildlife sting*, The Independent, 8 January, 1991.
8. Brown, Paul, *WEB OF AFRICAN INTRIGUE FOILS IVORY PLOT*, The Guardian, 2 March, 1992.
9. Brown, Paul, *WEB OF AFRICAN INTRIGUE FOILS IVORY PLOT*, The Guardian, 2 March, 1992.
10. Kemp, Anthony, *The SAS: Savage Wars of Peace, 1947 to the Present*, John Murray (publishers) Ltd, 1994, pp. 203-204.
11. Kemp, Anthony, *The SAS: Savage Wars of Peace, 1947 to the Present*, John Murray (publishers) Ltd, 1994, p. 204.
12. Stephen, Ellis, *Prince paid thousands into wildlife sting*, The Independent, 8 January, 1991.
13. '*Pirates Hijack Two Tankers Within 24 hours off Somali Shore*' Fox News Channel. 26 March, 2009.
14. Eager, Charlotte, '*To catch a pirate: The British ex-servicemen battling to protect international shipping from the clutches of Somali pirates*', Daily Mail, 20 December, 2011.
15. Bloomberg Reports, 2012.
16. Campion, Phil, '*Born Fearless*'.
17. '*Official US sea captain faced imminent danger.*' Associated Press. 12 April, 2009.
18. Yanofsky, David, '*Somali piracy was reduced to zero this year*': US Office of Naval Intelligence report, 27 December, 2013.
19. Eager, Charlotte, '*To catch a pirate: The British ex-servicemen battling to protect international shipping from the clutches of Somali pirates*'. Daily Mail, 20 December, 2011.
20. Firma, Rusty, (*The Regiment*).

Chapter Seven

1. '*Tug-of-war over PNG arms*', The Sydney Morning Herald, Saturday, 29 March, 1997.
2. Gibson, Jano, '*Russian-built Mil Mi-24 attack helicopters buried in Darwin dump*', ABC News 29 October, 2019.
3. Leigh, David '*Pentagon link to Guinea coup plot*'. The Guardian, 27 September, 2004.
4. The Guardian, 23 June, 1999.
5. The Guardian, 17 February, 2009.
6. '*The Business of War*', Vanity Fair, April, 2007.
7. '*The Baghdad boom*', The Economist 25 March, 2004.
8. '*The Business of War*', Vanity Fair, April, 2007.
9. '*The Business of War*', Vanity Fair, April, 2007.
10. Phinney, David, '*From Mercenaries to Peacemakers? Scandals Confront Military Security Industry*', CorpWatch, 29 November, 2005.
11. The Guardian, 18 November, 2016.
12. Washington Post, September, 2005.
13. '*Blackwater's rich contracts*'. The New York Times, 3 October, 2007.
14. Gettleman, Jeffrey, New York Times report, 31 March, 2004.
15. '*Report: Blackwater 'impeded' probe into contractor deaths*', CNN, 27 September, 2007.
16. Deignham, Tom, '*Navy SEALS tragedy in Afghanistan chronicled in new film,' "Lone Survivors*', IrishCentral, 22 December, 2013.
17. '*Blackwater boss grilled over Iraq*'. BBC News, 2 October, 2007.
18. WikiLeaks disclosure of 391,832 United States Army field reports, of the Iraq War from 2004 to 2009 and published on the Internet on 22 October, 2010.
19. '*Militants' video shows apparent execution of survivor*', CNN News report, 22 April, 2005.
20. WikiLeaks disclosure of 391,832 United States Army field reports, of the Iraq War from 2004 to 2009 and published on the Internet on 22 October, 2010.
21. Pelton, Robert Young '*Licensed to kill, hired guns in the war on terror,*' Crown, 29 August, 2006.
22. '*Contractors accused of firing on civilians, GIs*'. Associated Press. 11 August, 2007.
23. '*US Lawyers for Blackwater Guards: 2007 Baghdad Shooting was Self-Defense*'. Voice of America News, 18 June, 2014.

24. Johnston, David and Broder, John M, '*F.B.I. Says Guards Killed 14 Iraqis Without Cause*', The New York Times, 14 November, 2007.
25. Glanz, James and Rubin, Alissa J., '*From Errand to Fatal Shot to Hail of Fire to 17 Deaths*', The New York Times. 3 October, 2007.
26. '*UN criticises Trump's pardons for Blackwater guards jailed over Iraq killings*', BBC News. 23 December, 2020.
27. Tucker, Eric and Knickmeyer, Ellen '*Pardons in killings of Iraqi civilians stir angry response*', AP News, 23 December, 2020.
28. '*Blackwater 'hired for CIA plan*'. BBC News, 20 August, 2009.
29. '*Profile: Blackwater Worldwide*', BBC News, 8 October, 2007.
30. See '*Tirghra*' page 35.
31. Yeoman, Barry, '*IRAQ: Dirty Warriors*', 'CorpWatch' 1 November, 2004.
32. Yeoman, Barry, '*IRAQ: Dirty Warriors*', 'CorpWatch' 1 November, 2004.

Chapter Eight

1. '*Nigeria Islamists better armed, motivated than army: governor*', Reuters, 17 February, 2014.
2. Barlow, Eden, '*Inside the world of private military contractors*', Talk to Al Jazeera 4 January, 2020.
3. Private session with Eeben Barlow at the Danish Defence College, Denmark, 28/04/2015.
4. Murphy, Jack, '*Eeben Barlow Speaks Out South African Contractors Withdrawal from Nigeria*', 17 April, 2015.
5. Lecture by Eeben Barlow at the Danish Defence College, Denmark, 30/04/2015.
6. Barlow, Eeben, '*Inside the world of private military contractors*', Talk to Al Jazeera 4 January, 2020.
7. Tiron, Roxana and Murphy, Paul, '*Bloomberg Government*', 23 April, 2021.
8. '*Private Military Contractors v Military Pay*' DBA: Attorney Blog.
9. Sopko, John F., Special Inspector General for Afghanistan Reconstruction, High Risk List 2021.
10. Detsch, Jack, '*Departure of Private Contractors Was a Turning Point in Afghan Military's Collapse*', Foreign Policy, 16 August, 2021.

11. '*Anonymous*', The Guardian, 27 August, 2021.
12. '*CNN News Report*', 17 August, 2010.
13. '*CNN News Report*', 16 August, 2021.
14. Detsch, Jack, '*Departure of Private Contractors Was a Turning Point in Afghan Military's Collapse*', Foreign Policy, 16 August, 2021.
15. '*Thanks To The US, Taliban Now Has A Powerful Air Force And 'Russian Mercenaries' May Help It Take Off*', The Eur Asian Time 30 July, 2022.
16. '*The Hindu*', 16 August, 2021.
17. '*The Hindu*', 16 August, 2021.
18. *Sudan Genocide Declaration Stirs World*, NewsHour Extra, 15 September, 2004.
19. de Waa, Alex, '*Meet the Janjaweed*', 20 July, 2019.
20. de Waa, Alex, '*Meet the Janjaweed*', 20 July, 2019.
21. Hancock, Stephanie, '*Chadian civilians help Janjaweed attack countrymen*', 22 June, 2006.
22. Hancock, Stephanie, '*Chadian civilians help Janjaweed attack countrymen*', 22 June, 2006.
23. Hancock, Stephanie, '*Chadian civilians help Janjaweed attack countrymen*', 22 June, 2006.
24. Shuaib, Salah, '*What about the leaked Sudanese regime documents?*', 1 October, 2014.
25. de Waa, Alex, '*Meet the Janjaweed*' 20 July, 2019.
26. Leob, Jonathan, '*Men With No Mercy – Rapid Support Forces Attacks against Civilians in Darfur, Sudan*'. Human Rights Watch, 9 September, 2015.
27. Reeves, Eric, '*Peace in Sudan*?', 8 September, 2019.
28. '*Exposing the RSF's secret financial network*' Global Witness 9 December, 2019.
29. '*Meet the Janjaweed*' by Alex de Waa 20 July, 2019.
30. Heras, Nicholas A., '*Sudan's Controversial Rapid Support Forces Bolster Saudi Efforts in Yemen*', Jamestown Foundation, 27 October, 2017.
31. '*Huge Sudanese losses in Yemen highlight fighters' role in the conflict*' Middle East Eye, 10 November, 2019.
32. '*Huge Sudanese losses in Yemen highlight fighters' role in the conflict*' Middle East Eye, 10 November, 2019.
33. '*Sudan withdraws 10,000 troops from Yemen*', Sudan Tribune, 30 October, 2019.

34. '*1,000 Sudanese militiamen arrive in Libya*', Al Jazeera, 25 July, 2019.
35. de Waa, Alex, '*Meet the Janjaweed*', 20 July, 2019.

Chapter Nine

1. '*An ex-member of one of the world's most dangerous mercenary groups has gone public*', NPR, 6 June, 2022.
2. '*What is the Wagner Group, Russia's mercenary organisation?*', The Economist.
3. '*Radio Free Europe/Radio Liberty*', 7 March, 2018.
4. Higgins, Andrew Higgins and Nechepurenko, Ivan, '*In Africa, Mystery Murders Put Spotlight on Kremlin's Reach*', The New York Times, 7 August, 2018.
5. '*Russian mercenary group promises 'adventure' in recruiting drive*' The Daily Telegraph, 18 June, 2022.
6. '*Exclusive: Kids' camp on a defence base? How Russian firms masked secret military work*', Reuters, 4 April, 2019.
7. '*За Башара Асада – без флага, без Родины*' by Denis Korotkov: 22 October, 2015.
8. '*Russian News Accidentally Reveals Evidence of PMC Wagner in CAR*', POLYGRAPH.IFO.
9. Ristic, Marija, '*Serb Fighters' Mercenary Path from Ukraine to Syria;* Balkan Transitional Justice, 22 April, 2016.
10. Ristic, Marija, '*Serb Fighters' Mercenary Path from Ukraine to Syria;* Balkan Transitional Justice, 22 April, 2016.
11. Ristic, Marija, '*Serb Fighters' Mercenary Path from Ukraine to Syria;* Balkan Transitional Justice, 22 April, 2016.
12. Ristic, Marija, '*Serb Fighters' Mercenary Path from Ukraine to Syria;* Balkan Transitional Justice, 22 April, 2016.
13. Ristic, Marija, '*Serb Fighters' Mercenary Path from Ukraine to Syria;* Balkan Transitional Justice, 22 April, 2016.
14. Ristic, Marija, '*Serb Fighters' Mercenary Path from Ukraine to Syria;* Balkan Transitional Justice, 22 April, 2016.
15. '*Little green men' or 'Russian invaders?*' by Vitaly Shevchenko: 11 March, 2014.
16. Gove, Thomas, '*Up to Nine Russian Contractors Die in Syria, Experts Say*', The Wall Street Journal, 18 December, 2018.
17. *Self-Identified Wagner Mercenary Sovershenno Seketro Interview*, 19 December, 2017.

18. UCL News, 28 February, 2022.
19. Regulation (EU) No 2021/2195 of 13 December, 2021 implementing Regulation (EU) 2020/1998 concerning restrictive measures against serious human rights violations and abuses.
20. '*Russian-Trained Syrian Unit Eliminates Scores Of ISIS In Black Operation*', 4 December, 2017.
21. Pukhov, Ruslan, '*Russia's unexpected military victory in Syria*' DefenceNews Weekly, 11 December, 2017.
22. '*How a 4-Hour Battle Between Russian Mercenaries and U.S. Commandos Unfolded in Syria*' by Thomas Gibbons-Neff: New York Times 24 May, 2018.
23. Hrytsak, SBU Head Vasyl, *Russian military intelligence units break up democratic protests in Sudan.*
24. Security Service of Ukraine Official Web-Site, 8 February, 2019.
25. Walsh, Declan, '*From Russia With Love: A Putin Ally Mines Gold and Plays Favourites in Sudan*', New York Times, 4 June, 2022.
26. '*How Russia Is Displacing the French in the Struggle for Influence in the Central African Republic*', Jamestown Foundation.
27. Walsh, Declan, '*Russian Mercenaries Are Driving War Crimes in Africa, U.N. Says*', New York Times: 27 June, 2021.
28. '*Democracy Centre for Transparency*'.
29. Higgins, Andrew and Nechepurenko, Ivan, '*In Africa, Mystery Murders Put Spotlight on Kremlin's Reach*', The New York Times, 7 August, 2018.
30. Higgins, Andrew and Nechepurenko, Ivan, '*In Africa, Mystery Murders Put Spotlight on Kremlin's Reach*', The New York Times, 7 August, 2018.
31. '*RCA: les mercenaires russes et syriens ont repris la ville de Yalinga sans affrontement – Corbeau News Centrafrique ou si b il LPP Corbeau News Centrafrique ou si b il LPP*'. entrafrique, Corbeaunews, 23 April, 2021.
32. '*Russian Mercenaries Recapture Nzako Town In Central African Republic*', 28 April, 2021.
33. '*Russian mercenaries behind Central African Republic atrocities – HRW*', BBC News, 2 May, 2022.
34. '*UN probing alleged killings by CAR forces, Russia paramilitaries*', Yahoo News, 21 January, 2022.
35. '*First Russian 'adviser' killed in Mali blast, report*', www.aljazeera.com.
36. Millard, Matteo, '*We collected 180 bodies. We only recognised our friends by their clothes*', Sunday Telegraph, 17 July, 2022.

37. Millard, Matteo, '*We collected 180 bodies. We only recognised our friends by their clothes'*, Sunday Telegraph, 17 July, 2022.
38. Millard, Matteo, '*We collected 180 bodies. We only recognised our friends by their clothes'*, Sunday Telegraph, 17 July, 2022.
39. Millard, Matteo, '*We collected 180 bodies. We only recognised our friends by their clothes'*, Sunday Telegraph, 17 July, 2022.
40. Millard, Matteo, '*We collected 180 bodies. We only recognised our friends by their clothes'*, Sunday Telegraph, 17 July, 2022.

Chapter Ten

1. '*Mercenaries: the sinister export from Colombia's conflict*', France 24, 10 February, 2021.
2. '*Venezuela arrests Colombians over Maduro assassination plot*', BBC News, 10 June, 2013.
3. '*Mercenaries: the sinister export from Colombia's conflict*', France 24, 10 February, 2021.
4. '*From Haiti to Yemen: Why Colombian mercenaries are fighting foreign wars'*, New Arab News, 4 August, 2021.
5. *Secret Desert Force Set Up by Blackwater's Founder,* New York Times, 14 May, 2011.
6. '*Australian mercenary reportedly killed in Yemen clashes*', The Guardian, 8 December, 2015.
7. '*Emirates Secretly Sends Colombian Mercenaries to Yemen*', New York Times, 25 November, 2015.
8. '*Blackwater's US Colonel Killed, Saudi Apache Helicopters Destroyed in Yemen's Tochka Missile Attacks in Lahij*', Fars News, 31 January, 2016.
9. '*Blackwater's US Colonel Killed, Saudi Apache Helicopters Destroyed in Yemen's Tochka Missile Attacks in Lahij*', Fars News, 31 January, 2016.
10. Roston, Aram, '*American Ex-Soldiers To Kill Its Political Enemies, This Could Be The Future Of War*', BuzzFeed, 16 October, 2018.
11. Roston, Aram, '*American Ex-Soldiers To Kill Its Political Enemies, This Could Be The Future Of War*', BuzzFeed, 16 October, 2018.
12. Roston, Aram, '*American Ex-Soldiers To Kill Its Political Enemies, This Could Be The Future Of War*', BuzzFeed, 16 October, 2018.
13. Roston, Aram, '*American Ex-Soldiers To Kill Its Political Enemies, This Could Be The Future Of War*', BuzzFeed, 16 October, 2018.

14. Roston, Aram, '*American Ex-Soldiers To Kill Its Political Enemies, This Could Be The Future Of War*', BuzzFeed, 16 October, 2018.
15. '*The UAE's Alarming reliance on Mercenaries*', TRT World, 24 September, 2020.
16. '*Four Corners*', Australian TV, 14 September, 2020.
17. Sofrep, '*Putin's Private Army, the Wagner Group Out to Assassinate Zelensky, Faces Sanctions*', 25 March, 2022.
18. '*Ukraine: Kyiv's mayor imposes 36-hour curfew in city*', Punch, March, 2022.
19. '*Russian Offensive Campaign Assessment, March* 14', Press ISW, 14 March, 2022.
20. Boussel, Pierre, '*Syrian Mercenaries in Ukraine: Delusion or Reality*?', Carnegie Endowment for International Peace, 22 June, 2022.
21. Boussel, Pierre, '*Syrian Mercenaries in Ukraine: Delusion or Reality*?', Carnegie Endowment for International Peace, 22 June, 2022.
22. '*Latest Defence Intelligence update on the situation in Ukraine - 14 March,' 2022*, Yahoo, 14 March, 2022.
23. Mc Fate, Sean, '*The Mercenaries Behind the Bucha Massacre*', Wall Street Journal, 12 April, 2022.
24. Krechko, Yaroslav, '*Bodies of Russian Mercenaries Litter Field After Donetsk Battle with Ukrainian A*rmy', Radio Free Europe, 12 August, 2022.
25. Khrebet, Alexander, '*Inside Ukraine's covert operation to take out elite Wagner Group mercenaries in Donbas*', Kev Independent, 20 July, 2022.
26. '*Russian Wagner mercenary known as 'The Executioner' for butchering prisoners of war is shot dead by a Ukrainian sniper in latest blow to Putin's invasion*', The Daily Mail, 7 June, 2022.
27. '*Putin's top mercenary KILLED: Wagner thug who 'adored mortars' wiped out by Ukraine forces*', Daily Express, 3 August, 2022.
28. *BBC News Русская Служба* (in Russian), 21 April, 2022.
29. '*Heavy Losses Leave Russia Short of Its Goal, U.S. Officials Say*', The New York Times, 11 August, 2022.
30. Kiler, James, '*Russian mercenary group promises 'adventure' in recruiting* drive', Daily Telegraph, 18 June, 2022.
31. Kilner, James, '*Putin's chef' hired mercenaries from jail*', Daily Telegraph, 8 August, 2022.
32. '*Britons fight and die like cannon-fodder in Ukraine*', The Times, 1 June, 2022.

33. Freeman, Colin, '*An ex-Para, his 'Dark Angel's' and a mission to kill a Russian tank'* by Colin Freeman: Sunday Telegraph: 10 July, 2022.
34. Freeman, Colin, '*An ex-Para, his 'Dark Angel's' and a mission to kill a Russian tank'* by Colin Freeman: Sunday Telegraph: 10 July, 2022.
35. '*Hackers, Hoodies, and Helmets: Technology and the changing face of Russian private military contractors*', Atlantic Council, 25 July, 2022.
36. '*Blackwater Blues for Dead Contractors' Families*', Inter Press Service, 29 June, 2007.
37. UN Working Group on Use of Mercenaries, 21 September, 2021.

Chapter Eleven

1. '*Working Group on the use of mercenaries*', United Nations: International standard.
2. Dunlop, Charlie, '*Wagner Group Atrocities – Holding Russia Accountable Under Prosecutor v. Tadic?*', JD Lawfire, 13 August, 2022.
3. Hansard, 6 March, 2012.
4. Geneva Academy, Academy Briefing No 4, August, 2013.
5. Dunlop, Charlie, '*Wagner Group Atrocities – Holding Russia Accountable Under Prosecutor v. Tadic?*', JD Lawfire, 13 August, 2022.
6. EJIL, Talk: Blog of the European Journal of International Law, 8 March, 2022.

Index